D0559422

FOUNDING RIVALS

Madison vs. *Monroe*

The Bill of Rights and the Election That Saved a Nation

CHRIS DeROSE

MJF BOOKS
NEW YORK

Published by MJF Books
Fine Communications
322 Eighth Avenue
New York, NY 10001

Founding Rivals
LC Control Number: 2015937053
ISBN 978-1-60671-296-2

This edition is published by MJF Books in arrangement with Regnery Publishing, a division of Salem Media Group.

Printed in the United States of America.

MJF Books and the MJF colophon are trademarks of Fine Creative Media, Inc.

QF 10 9 8 7 6 5 4 3 2 1

For Anna DeRose, my mother, who taught me to love unconditionally, to forgive quickly, and to bear life's inevitable disappointments with incredible grace

Contents

Prologue

OPENING DAYS

"No people can be bound to acknowledge and adore the invisible hand, which conducts the affairs of men, more than the people of the United States. Every step, by which they have advanced to the character of an independent nation, seems to have been distinguished by some token of providential agency."

—George Washington,
First Presidential Address to Congress

On April 30, 1789, a sea of people spilled into the streets of the city of New York, standing shoulder to shoulder, crowding on rooftops, hanging out of open windows, vying for a view. Their focus was the second-story balcony of Federal Hall, the "large and elegant Bible" placed atop a crimson-draped table, and the closed door that would open at any minute.[1] But as the hours went by, nothing happened.

The First Congress of the United States of America under the new Constitution had gathered that morning to receive General George Washington as the new president, but the ceremony was delayed by fights about how that president should be received. One senator pointed out that the House of Lords is seated when the king addresses Parliament, but the House of Commons stands. Another explained that the Commons stood because they had no chairs to sit in. A third dismissed outright the idea of using or even consulting British protocol. The dispute among the legislators dragged on. It was a portrait in miniature of the essential differences still dividing the young nation, and a reminder of just how precarious the very existence of the United States of America was.

It seems inevitable to us today—the steady march of history from the colonial era to independence, a revolution against the greatest empire in the world, ending in the establishment of republican government, rather than in anarchy or despotism. In truth, the path to this place was narrow and threatened by peril at every turn. It could all have turned out very differently.

When the door finally opened and Washington stepped out onto the balcony with members of Congress, the crowd erupted in cheers. The triumph of this momentous day had been achieved by a narrow margin; one man staring out at the sea of revelers knew just how narrow. Congressman James Madison was witnessing the birth of a creation that bore his stamp more than anyone else's. But his own presence on that balcony had been decided by a swing of only 169 votes.

Nobody was there to see *him*, of course, and at 5'4"anyone who tried would likely have failed to find him. But fame did not motivate Madison. His best-known writings were anonymous. He would ask others to propose his ideas if he thought that they were less likely to succeed coming from him. Madison was motivated by the desire to create a government that worked for a union of states. This day was a product of his success.

But Madison was consumed by what he had yet to do. The United States had a crippling national debt, no credit, no revenue system, and no means of honoring obligations or meeting even the government's most basic responsibilities. As of March 4, Rhode Island and North Carolina had officially become independent states, "as independent as any other nation," in the words of one newspaper.[2] Rhode Island sea captains had lowered the flag of the United States and raised their state's flag.[3] Rhode Island had rejected the Constitution outright, and North Carolina was refusing to ratify until a bill of rights was passed. Meanwhile, New York and Virginia had called for a new constitutional convention. If two-thirds of the states agreed, the Constitution would be scrapped and entirely rewritten. Madison had guided the United States to this moment, but the moment was fraught with peril.

The country did not yet have a Supreme Court, so the oath of office was administered to George Washington by Chancellor Robert Livingston, the chief judicial officer of New York. The first Secretary of Foreign Affairs under the Articles of Confederation, Livingston had also been on the five-man committee that drafted the Declaration of Independence—a favor the British repaid by burning his house to the ground.

Chancellor Livingston read the presidential oath from Article II, Section 1, Clause 8 of the new Constitution, and Washington—clad in a deep brown suit of clothes with metal buttons, white stockings, and a sword—repeated, his left hand resting on the Bible, "I, George Washington, do solemnly swear, that I will faithfully execute the office of President of the United States, and will to the best of my ability, preserve, protect, and defend the Constitution of the United States."

Livingston announced, "Long live George Washington, President of the United States."[4] Washington then kissed the Bible raised to his lips by the Secretary of the Senate.* A flag was raised over Federal Hall, artillery was fired, and every bell in the city rang out in response.

The ceremony then moved into the Senate chamber, where Washington would deliver the first inaugural address. He spoke quietly from prepared remarks, reading nervously. According to one senator, Washington was "agitated and embarrassed more than ever he was by the leveled cannon or pointed musket."[5]

Madison had to act interested and surprised while listening to a speech he himself had written. He had Washington's confidence—an honor many men aspired to, but few had secured.

---

* The Washington Bible, as it is known today, was used at the inaugurations of Presidents Harding, Eisenhower, Carter, and George H. W. Bush, and at the funerals of Presidents Lincoln, Taylor, Jackson, and Washington himself, as well as on other important occasions, including the laying of the cornerstone for the United States Capitol and the dedication of the Washington Monument.

Ironically, Madison was later asked by Congress to prepare a response to the president's address. Washington, in turn, asked him to draft his reply to the response. Madison's understated sense of humor was on full display in that reply, which included the line: "Your very affectionate address produces emotions which I know not how to express."[6] The first formal communications between the president and Congress were essentially Madison talking to himself.

Washington's address focused on the extraordinary circumstances that had led both him and the new Congress to this place: "In the important revolution just accomplished...the tranquil deliberations and voluntary consent of so many distinct communities, from which the event has resulted, cannot be compared with the means by which most governments have been established, without some return of pious gratitude along with an humble anticipation of the future blessings which the past seem to presage."[7]

Washington had no legislative agenda; he proposed no specific policies. But Madison had made certain that Washington would set the stage for the most important task of the First Congress—and possibly the most difficult achievement of Madison's own political career: amending the Constitution with a bill of rights. Washington told the Congress that he was certain they would "carefully avoid every alteration which might endanger the benefits of an united and effective government" while expressing their "reverence for the characteristic rights of freemen."

A bill of rights was absolutely necessary to appease the doubters who were keeping Rhode Island and North Carolina out of the Union. And only a bill of rights could defuse the agitation for a new constitutional convention, led by an Anti-Federalist movement that was strong and growing daily throughout the continent. Madison had become convinced that a bill of rights was necessary to bind the United States together, that it needed to be passed in the first session of Congress, and that he needed to be the bill's leading, if unlikely, champion.

It had become clear as Congress neared a quorum at the end of March that the Anti-Federalists, who opposed the Constitution, had gained only two or three seats in the Senate, and "a very small minority" in the House.[8] That was good news for Madison, leader of the Federalists—but good news that presented a challenge. Most Federalists did not believe the Constitution needed amending. It established a limited federal government, after all, which could act only within the confines of specific enumerated powers. The Federalists believed that it was pointless to guarantee freedom of religion when the Constitution gave the government no power to regulate religion in the first place. Indeed it was not only useless, but potentially dangerous. If you began listing things the government could not do, you might assign it powers it was never meant to have. Potentially even worse, if you listed protections for some rights but omitted others, the omission might be taken to imply the abolition of those unenumerated rights. Besides, the Federalists argued, this business of amendments could wait until Congress resolved other more pressing issues—creating a revenue system, addressing the massive national debt, designing executive departments, and building a federal judiciary. Since the government was brand new, what would be the harm in waiting to see how it worked before amending it? In any case, historically such guarantees of rights had amounted to little more than "parchment barriers" that offered little real defense against a tyrannical government.[9]

Madison knew those arguments. As a Federalist, he had made them himself. But he knew that many people disagreed—he had the battle scars to prove it—and he was determined to satisfy the doubters. Madison wrote his friend Thomas Jefferson, then serving as Minister to France, "Notwithstanding this [Federalist] character of the body, I hope and expect that some conciliatory sacrifices will be made, in order to extinguish opposition to the system, or at least break the force of it, by detaching the deluded opponents from their designing leaders."[10]

Madison understood the strength of the opposition to the Constitution very well. He had only narrowly won election to the new Congress against a leading Anti-Federalist, a Revolutionary War hero who had played a key role in the opposition that nearly derailed ratification in the Virginia Convention—a former ally and close friend of Madison's turned political opponent by their differences over the new Constitution. The two candidates running to represent Virginia's 5th District in the First Congress of the United States of America were united in patriotism and distinguished service to their country, but divided over the new form of government for the United States.

On the Federalist side stood James Madison, determined to defend the Constitution and the new government he had worked so hard to create. Against him stood James Monroe, Anti-Federalist, opponent of the Constitution as written, and erstwhile ally of Madison. Both men had served in the Virginia House of Delegates and Council of State, the Congress of the Confederation, and the Virginia Ratification Convention, with distinction in every capacity. Madison, thirty-seven, was the primary author of the Constitution and one of the greatest political thinkers of his day. Monroe, thirty, was an established attorney with a record in combat that could hardly be equaled anywhere on the continent.

It was the perfect election—at least, from the voters' point of view. No other congressional race in the history of our nation ever offered a better selection of candidates. Two future presidents of the United States of America were running against each other for a seat in Congress for the first and last time in American history. The high-stakes battle between two Founding Fathers would forever alter the trajectory of the young nation.

America's long love affair with the presidency has relegated to footnotes the stories of individual races for Congress. With the exception of the Lincoln-Douglas Senate race in 1858, congressional elections are never looked at individually; 1894 and 1932 were reactions to financial panics; 1974, 1994, 2006, and 2010 were rebukes to unpopular administrations. But the battle between James Madison and James Monroe had a significance beyond these general trends: it was the most pivotal race for Congress in American history. Few presidential elections can rival it in importance. The election of President Jefferson in 1800 signaled the first peaceful transfer of power between parties; 1860 ushered in the Civil War; 1864 hastened that war's conclusion. But what other election could rival the House race that saved America?

"The present crisis is the most important that will probably ever happen in this country ... on the choice of these persons depends our future well-being and prosperity."[11] So observed the *Virginia Centinel*, contemplating the race. As the fledgling United States struggled to define itself as a unified nation, that single closely fought race for the House of Representatives resulted in the creation of the Bill of Rights, the ratification of the Constitution by every remaining state, and the effective end of the powerful counter-movement that aimed to do away with the Constitution.

Monroe and the Anti-Federalists were seeking constitutional amendments to guarantee personal liberties—or else an entirely new Constitution. Madison, Washington, and the other Federalists knew what a second constitutional convention would look like. The strongest zealots from each faction would be elected, some with the express intention of derailing the union. The conciliation that characterized Philadelphia would be gone. The essential powers of the new national government, such as trade regulation and a rational revenue policy, would likely be stripped, leaving the new government as impotent as the old.

But for the result of one election, the United States of America might well have died in infancy. Monroe was a vigorous proponent of adding a bill of rights to the Constitution. But Monroe, a young Anti-Federalist, was at odds with the overwhelming Federalist majority in Congress. He would never have persuaded them to approve constitutional amendments. And without the Bill of Rights, the Union would ultimately have failed. Madison was the leader of the Federalists. He arrived in Congress with the reputation and political skills necessary for getting the Constitution amended—and with the will to apply his prestige and all his political capital to the task.

As the 1789 election between Madison and Monroe began, Madison was in New York, far removed from the theater of action. Because Anti-Federalists in the Virginia legislature had drawn the district's boundaries to his disadvantage, Madison began the race far behind. As each day came and went, he fell even further behind Monroe.

The election of the man who would represent Virginia's 5th District in the First Congress of the United States under the new Constitution would determine whether the union under that document would stand or fall—in an election that was won by a mere 336 votes.

Chapter One

THE LAST DAYS OF THE COLONY OF VIRGINIA

"Then and there, the child independence was born."

—JOHN ADAMS

One hundred miles north of where the English first settled in the New World, James Madison and James Monroe were born within a decade and twenty miles of each other. In 1751 Madison arrived in the calm before the storm. In 1758, Monroe was born into a world at war. The French and Indian War, which began in 1754 and ended in 1763, saw the English expel their rivals from the continent. And it would set in motion the great events that would dominate the lives of these two sons of Virginia.

On the day of his baptism, the infant James Madison was attended by his five godparents. Thus the requirement was met: "not fewer than three godparents" with at least two "of the same sex as the child" and at least one "of the opposite sex."[1] The rite would be performed according to the 1662 *Book of Common Prayer*, used in the Church of England the world over—including in this far-flung outpost of the British Empire in the Hanover Parish Church on the river Rappahannock in the County of King George, Virginia.

Those gathered that morning for the baptism of James Madison were there in the belief that the infant could become a new creation. Aside from the monarchy, no institution was more enduring or revered in Virginia than the Church of England. Yet as time passed the cultural, religious, and political ties between England and her colonies would be strained. The central question of the day would soon be whether Virginia, created as a colony, could be reborn as something else.

At the time of Madison's birth, momentous events that would put that question to the test were already in play. British victory in the French and Indian War would come at a catastrophic financial cost. And French diplomat Charles Gravier, Comte de Vergennes, would predict with great prescience, "I am persuaded England will ere long repent of having removed the only check that could keep her colonies in awe. They stand no longer in need of her protection; she will call on them to contribute toward supporting the burdens they have helped to bring on her; and they will answer by striking off all dependence."[2] Indeed, the British Parliament would attempt to pass some of the costs of the war on to her colonies. What followed was a vicious cycle of rising colonial resistance and British retaliation.

Madison and Monroe were both descendants of seventeenth-century Virginia colonists. Isack Maddison (or Maddeson) had arrived in Virginia in 1611, four years after Jamestown became the first permanent English settlement in America and nine years before the arrival of the Mayflower.[3] Maddison flourished in the New World. He also established a reputation as an Indian fighter. In March of 1622 he accepted the charge of the governor of the Virginia Colony to lead a force to rescue colonists seized by Indians in a raid.[4] Isack's success as a planter grew, and he gained exclusive trading rights with the Indians in the Chesapeake Bay. Fourteen years after settling in Virginia, he died and was buried in the land where he had found wealth, adventure, prestige, and love, but far from his original home.

James Madison, future political colossus, was no rugged pioneer in the mold of his ancestor. By the time James was born in 1751, Virginia was a thriving colony. James Madison was born while his mother was visiting the home of her mother in the King George County. When mother and child were strong enough, they departed for Orange County and the estate that would one day be known as Montpelier. It would be Madison's home for his entire life.

Madison was a dedicated student. He began his formal studies in 1762 under Donald Robertson, who had been educated at the University of Aberdeen. Then he became the pupil of Thomas Martin—a brief association that would change the course of Madison's life. Martin had attended school at the College of New Jersey, located on the road between Philadelphia and New York at Princeton and today known as Princeton University. The college at Princeton had an excellent reputation, in contrast with the College of William and Mary, which at the time no longer had a well-regarded and rigorous program of study. Princeton had the additional benefit of geography; Madison's parents felt that the climate farther north, as opposed to the hot and sticky weather in Williamsburg, would be better for the sickly Madison.

Madison passed the College of New Jersey's entrance exam, which required grammatical Latin, Greek translation, and "vulgar arithmetic." The author of the First Amendment would be educated at a school with a remarkable degree of religious diversity for its time, founded as it was for "the equal and general advantage of every religious denomination of Protestants."[5] Madison had roughly 150 fellow students in the entire school. For perhaps the first time in his life, the curious and scholarly young man was in his element.

Far from Orange County, Madison was meeting brilliant peers from places and backgrounds he previously had only read about. The school was a tight-knit community, as all the pupils and their tutors would eat together, sometimes joined by the college president. Madison wrote to his mentor Martin from school in August of 1769, "I am perfectly pleased with my present situation; and the prospect before me of three years confinement, however terrible it may sound, has nothing in it, but will be greatly alleviated by the advantages I hope to derive from it."[6]

Madison plunged into his academic work, studying to the point of physical exhaustion and illness. At Princeton he had access to a library exceeding twelve hundred volumes. Madison studied science, geography, rhetoric, logic, math, "natural and moral philosophy, metaphysics, chronology,"[7] read Latin and Greek, and pored over classical texts. The college day began with prayer and ended in the evening with another devotional service. Madison was a model student. College president John Witherspoon never knew him "to say or do an indiscreet thing."[8]

He joined a fraternal organization, the Whigs, who playfully jousted in public debates with their rivals, the Cliosophians.[9] The College put an emphasis on oratory; students were required to engage one another in front of large audiences. For the quiet and introverted Madison, this aspect of his education was invaluable. Even as trouble was brewing back home in Virginia—political tensions were increasing between crown and colony—Madison was debating academic issues on a stage next to a giant portrait of King George III. After three years of study, Madison was examined by trustees, college officers, and "other gentlemen of learning" and received his degree. He had finished a four-year program in three. Madison returned to Orange County in 1772.

In Orange, Madison was isolated. He kept himself busy tutoring his younger siblings in literature. Correspondence with his former classmate William Bradford in Philadelphia was his only connection to the outside world he had left behind—and also a source of news about the historic events brewing in the colonies. Bradford was concerned about his friend's well-being. He believed that Madison had injured himself by excessive study, and he urged him to be attentive to his health. Even naturally sickly people can outlive healthy ones by working at it, Bradford wrote to the man who would live to be the "last of the Founders."

Prophetically, Bradford wrote to Madison that "you seem designed by Providence for extensive usefulness." At the time the observation must have seemed like so much fluff to Madison. He was bored, lonely, doing nothing with his life, and without prospects for a change. Bradford kept Madison abreast of the lives of their friends and acquaintances, their career advancements, successes, and marriages. The world, it seemed, was passing Madison by. He was confined in the cash-poor agricultural economy of the Virginia colony, where his father was a planter just as his ancestors had been, back to the days of Isack.

His time away from home had caused Madison to see Virginia in a new light. Madison was concerned about the lack of religious liberty in his home colony, and he asked Bradford to send him a copy of Pennsylvania's religious tolerance laws. "Is an Ecclesiastical Establishment absolutely necessary to support civil society . . . ?" he asked. Madison was increasingly concerned with the treatment of religious dissenters in neighboring counties; some were in prison on account of their faith.

Soon Bradford's letters to Madison were full of dramatic events. In December of 1773 Bradford sent Madison an account "of the destruction of the tea at Boston." To prop up the British East India Company, Parliament had licensed it to sell tea directly to the colonies. For the most part tea would be cheaper for colonists, even cheaper than in England. But the colonists maintained that Parliament had no right to levy the tax on the tea. The taxed tea was prevented from landing anywhere in the colonies. In New York and Philadelphia, it was sent back; in Charleston, it was placed in a cellar. Boston customs officials, however, refused to send the tea back and kept it in ships docked in the Harbor. On December 16, 1773, a group of fifty or sixty men dressed as Indians boarded the ships and dumped the tea in the harbor.[10]

Madison congratulated Bradford on the "heroic proceedings" in Philadelphia. He approved of that city's refusal to accept the tea. But the cautious Madison was ambivalent about the Boston Tea Party, as it later became known, wishing the patriots in Massachusetts would "conduct matters with as much discretion as they seem to do with boldness."

The British responded predictably, ratcheting up the pressure—this time past the point of no return. In 1774, Parliament adopted a series of "Coercive," or "Intolerable" Acts. The Port of Boston was closed to commerce until the tossed tea should be paid for.[11] Massachusetts public officials would henceforth be appointed at the discretion of the Crown.[12]

Public meetings were prohibited without prior permission. British soldiers sent to get Boston under control were lodged in private residences, against the will of their owners.[13]

The "Sentiments of Virginia are strongly with Massachusetts," Madison wrote to Bradford in July of 1774. An attack on one colony was perceived as falling upon them all.

The two young men sensed the increasing consequence of the moment. Bradford wrote, "Indeed my friend the world wears a strange aspect at the present day; to use Shakespeare's expression, 'the times seem to be out of joint...' our liberties invaded by a corrupt, ambitious, and determined ministry is bringing things to a crisis here in America and seems to foretell some great event."

Virginia would take the lead in resistance to the Intolerable Acts. A young member of the House of Burgesses named Thomas Jefferson successfully introduced resolutions to set aside "a day of fasting, humiliation, and prayer; devoutly to implore the Divine interposition" to avoid war and to guide the Burgesses' hands in opposing "every injury to American rights."[14]

On September 22, 1774, Madison bought two hundred acres of land from his parents at a cost of thirty pounds. He seemed resigned to the life of a country farmer. But that same month, the First Continental Congress met in Philadelphia. The Virginia delegation included George Washington and Patrick Henry.[15] Tremendous events were preparing on the political stage where Madison's talents would one day shine so brightly.

Madison was eager for information on the workings of Congress. Bradford had little to share about the secret proceedings but obliged as best he could, sending copies of the numerous political pamphlets circulating through Philadelphia. Congress adjourned October 26, having resolved that all exports to Great Britain would cease.[16] Colonies not represented at the meeting—Quebec, St. John's, Nova Scotia, East and West Florida, and Georgia—were invited to join the next Congress, and a declaration of rights enumerating the British offenses against her American colonies was adopted.[17]

To enforce the embargo with Britain, the Continental Congress created the grandly named Continental Association to boycott all British imports beginning December 1, 1774, and all exports to Britain and her territories on September 10 of the next year.[18] A committee would be created in every county and in every town to publish in local newspapers the names of any who continued to trade with the British and to take other steps as necessary to enforce the trade ban.[19] Congress concluded by agreeing to meet again in Philadelphia on May 10, 1775, if Parliament or the king failed to respond.[20] The actions of the colonies were greeted with silence on the other side of the Atlantic. The boycott's most immediate effect on Madison was the delay of the arrival of a treatise on government that he had ordered from London. More significantly, he was caught up in the patriotic fervor sweeping the colonies. "A spirit of liberty and patriotism animates all degrees and denominations of men," he wrote to Bradford. "Many publicly declare themselves ready to join the Bostonians as soon as violence is offered them or resistance thought expedient." Madison noted that independent militias were forming in many counties, drilling, and preparing for what might come.

As Virginians readied themselves for war, Madison considered the colony's many vulnerabilities. In addition to deploying their armed forces, the British might successfully incite a slave revolt. (This possibility probably held more terror for the Madisons than for the average Virginia family. Ambrose Madison, James Madison's grandfather, had been poisoned by his own slaves.) The British might also activate their alliances among the Indians as they had during the French and Indian war. Recent clashes between Indians and colonists along the frontier increased the fear of this danger.

On December 22, 1774, the Orange County Committee of Safety was organized and chaired by Madison's father, James Madison Sr.[21] As a large landowner and one of the first men of Orange County, he was a logical choice for the role. Madison gave his father and the committee his assistance. "We are very busy at present in raising men and procuring the necessaries for defending ourselves and our friends in case of a sudden invasion," he wrote to Bradford. Though Madison was still in Orange, the world had come to him. British actions, he warned, "require a preparation for extreme events."

In March of 1775, the leaders of Virginia met in St. John's Church, Richmond. In attendance were Patrick Henry, Thomas Jefferson, and George Washington. On March 23, Henry moved "that this colony be immediately put into a posture of defense," calling for the recruitment and training of more militia.[22] Reconciliation was impossible, Henry argued. "If we wish to be free, we must fight! I repeat it, Sir, we must fight! An appeal to arms and to the God of Hosts is all that is left us."[23] Henry is said to have concluded his stirring call to arms with the most famous words attributed to him: "Is life so dear, or peace so sweet, as to be purchased at the price of chains and slavery? Forbid it, almighty God! I know not what course others may take, but as for me, give me liberty or give me death."[24] The motion to mobilize passed.

As the delegates to the Second Continental Congress prepared to convene in May of 1775, the situation in Massachusetts deteriorated. Eight hundred British troops were dispatched to Lexington, Massachusetts, to destroy a stockpile of weaponry belonging to the militia. Captain John Parker and sixty or seventy militiamen were waiting for them on the village green.[25] The previous night Paul Revere and William Dawes had warned the militia of the troop movement.

Both British and Americans who stood on the Lexington green swore to their final days that their side was not the first to fire what ended up being the first shot of the American Revolution. But who fired first scarcely mattered to the men standing on that little patch of green. Great events—events that would soon engulf the entire continent—had led these men to this moment. Eight militiamen were killed and ten more were injured. The Revolutionary War had begun. From Lexington, the British marched to Concord, where they again engaged the militia in armed combat. By now, the militia had gathered in sufficient strength to drive the British back toward Boston.

The day after Lexington and Concord, Governor Dunmore of Virginia ordered British troops to seize powder and ammunition from a local militia storehouse. No one believed his stated purpose—to prevent a slave revolt. Patrick Henry, as the head of the Hanover County militia, marched on Williamsburg with three hundred men to demand retribution. A Lexington-style shoot-out was avoided only because the governor made a financial arrangement to pay 330 pounds for the lost munitions.[26]

In response to the governor's weapons-grab, college students at William and Mary began daily drills on the Williamsburg village green, antagonizing British redcoats by openly preparing for combat. Latin and history could not hold the attention of these young men who were unwittingly stationed at the front lines of a rapidly escalating conflict. Among the students preparing for war was the young James Monroe, who had turned seventeen just five days after Lexington and Concord.

Madison and Monroe's college years were thus excellent preparation for their respective roles in the Revolution: Madison, the statesman, and Monroe, the soldier.

Two turning points in the lives of the Monroes had involved rebellion against the King of England. The loyalty of Andrew Monroe, a cavalier in service to King Charles I, had led him to sever ties with England when Oliver Cromwell severed the head of his sovereign. But Andrew's most famous descendant, James Monroe, born on April 28, 1758, in Westmoreland County, Virginia, on the same land that Andrew had first farmed in the new world, would join a Revolution against the British monarch.

Monroe remembered his own father, Spence Monroe, as "a very worthy and respectable citizen of good landed and other property." He described his mother, the former Elizabeth Jones, as "a very amiable and respectable woman, possessing the best domestic qualities, a good wife and good parent."[27] When James Monroe was eleven years old, his father joined one hundred other Westmoreland planters in a boycott of British goods, consistent with the Continental Association.

Giving up British goods to advance a matter of principle was a critical early lesson in Monroe's political education, shaping his character and adult reputation for putting duty before his self-interest. That same year he began his formal studies under Archibald Campbell. The eponymous Campbelltown Academy was renowned throughout Virginia; in Monroe's words, "so high was its character that youths were sent to it from the more distant parts of the colony."[28] Monroe lived within walking distance, but those who came from farther away boarded with Campbell during the twelve-week school year between fall harvest and spring planting. Among Monroe's two dozen classmates was John Marshall, future Chief Justice of the United States Supreme Court, with whom he would form a life-long friendship. The early years of these Campbelltown Academy boys, who would grow up to fight in a war for colonial independence, were colored by the hostility between colony and crown as Vergennes' prophecy began to play itself out almost immediately.

Even setting aside the brewing American Revolution, James Monroe's teenage years were hard ones that saw him lose both of his parents. Monroe, now the head of his family, was forced to leave his studies. With little education, a modest inheritance, and responsibilities to fulfill, Monroe seemed headed for an unremarkable life. But the intervention of his mother's brother, Joseph Jones, would send the boy in a direction he never imagined.

Monroe would describe his uncle as "a distinguished revolutionary patriot, honored by his country with the highest offices and at the most difficult period.... Few men possessed in higher degree the confidence and esteem of his fellow citizens, or merited it more, for soundness of intellect, perfect integrity, and devotion to his country."[29] Jones, educated as an attorney at London's Inns of Court, was a deputy king's attorney representing the Crown in court and an important member of the House of Burgesses from King George's County.

Joseph Jones had no heirs, but he served as executor of Monroe's father's estate. It seems that he and his nephew James each found in the other what they were searching for. Monroe was an impressionable sixteen-year-old orphan in need of a strong adult interested in him, dedicated to his success, and possessed of the resources to make it possible. Jones was a wealthy man of the world looking for a protégé and a legacy, and for the kind of familial relationship that outshines all the honors the world can give. Jones enrolled his nephew in the College of William and Mary, which had revived its reputation since the time Madison was choosing schools. William and Mary, founded in 1693 by the king and queen the college is named for, was the second institution of higher learning in the New World. Monroe's classmates included the sons of the most elite Virginia families. Spence Monroe, if he had lived, probably could not have afforded to provide such an education for his son, and it is an open question whether he would have permitted his brother-in-law to foot the bill.

James Monroe arrived in Williamsburg to begin his classes at William and Mary in the run-up to the Revolution. Two weeks before Monroe arrived, the royal governor had dissolved the House of Burgesses after their public stand in support of the people of Boston. After the dissolution in May of 1774, the burgesses met unofficially at the Raleigh Tavern on Duke of Gloucester Street. They had called for a meeting of representatives from every colony—it would become the First Continental Congress—and for a convention in Virginia with representatives from every county.[30] This "Virginia Convention" would become the successor to the House of Burgesses and would itself eventually be superseded by the House of Delegates of the independent state of Virginia.

The next spring, Lexington and Concord—and the Gunpowder Affair, with the appearance of Patrick Henry and the Hanover County militia in Williamsburg itself—inspired Monroe and the other William and Mary students to train for war. Drilling with muskets, not parsing Latin sentences, was the order of the day. Monroe entered enthusiastically into military preparations.

The situation must have looked grim to Governor Dunmore. He was far from England, and as the city filled with angry mobs, the Governor's Palace became a splendid prison. Dunmore's life was in danger, and his wife was living on a ship for her own safety. When he had originally accepted the post as governor of the most populous and prosperous colony in the Americas, Dunmore could not have imagined he would see college students openly training for war in the middle of the city.

Meanwhile, in Orange County, the Committee of Safety adopted a strongly worded resolution on May 9 praising Henry's response and condemning Governor Dunmore. James Madison accompanied other members of the committee to present their resolution in person to Henry, who was by this time in Port Royal, Virginia, on his way to the Second Continental Congress.

It is likely that the party from Orange found Henry in a tavern surrounded by admirers hanging on his every word. Not yet thirty-nine, Henry had become a celebrity by taking on the British in what became known as the Parson's Cause.[31] His fame had only grown with his electrifying call to arms. Now he had marched at the head of a body of armed men, confronted the symbol of royal authority in Virginia, and forced the governor to back down without firing a shot. Next he would represent Virginia in Philadelphia, among the other great men of the colonies.

Patrick Henry probably barely noticed or acknowledged the diminutive twenty-four-year-old boy standing in front of him. We can imagine Madison sheepishly asking the man of the hour to carry a letter to Bradford in Philadelphia for him, to the merriment of Henry's hangers-on. Henry, however, graciously agreed to take Madison's letter to his friend. So went the first meeting between James Madison and Patrick Henry. That this young man would soon become his colleague, Henry would have found improbable. That the delicate, awkward boy would some day become his formidable political adversary, he would have found unthinkable.

The letter Henry carried for Madison was filled with the latest events in Virginia, but Bradford had little to contribute in response. The Second Continental Congress met in absolute secrecy. Everyone was anxious for information. The men in Congress were making life-and-death decisions. Things were tense inside the Pennsylvania State House. Any man in the room could have been arrested and hanged for treason. One attendee was suspected of being a spy—Benjamin Franklin, who had only recently returned from London where he had been serving as the colonial representative.

Boston, meanwhile, was enduring a famine. Milk and meat were scarce, and the British soldiers did not distinguish between what belonged to the people and what was theirs. No one could leave the city except on certain days, and then only with the permission of a military officer. And the hostilities that had begun on the Lexington green were spreading. On May 10 came the fall of Fort Ticonderoga in upstate New York.[32] Ethan Allen—later known as the founder of Vermont—and Benedict Arnold, entirely on their own initiative, took over the British fortress and the weaponry inside.

On June 14, 1775, the Second Continental Congress declared the Coercive Acts a violation of Americans' rights, resolved to withhold all taxes from Great Britain, and voted to raise twenty thousand troops in support of Boston. The next day a general was chosen to command these forces. The unanimous choice of Congress was George Washington of Virginia.[33] Washington was an experienced military leader, popular in the Congress, and willing to forego a salary—a definite advantage for a government with no money and no means of procuring any. Washington also hailed from the largest colony, and from the South. His selection telegraphed that the struggles of Boston were a continental concern.

Now that it would have an army, the Continental Congress needed a way to pay the soldiers. Congress resolved to print two million bills of credit, which each of the twelve colonies present (Georgia was not represented) would redeem.[34] New York's request via its delegates in Congress summed up the mood in the colonies: "Send us money, send us arms, send us ammunition!"[35] Committees of Safety throughout the colonies, like the one Madison and his father were serving on in Orange County, were preparing for war.

In Philadelphia, late in the evening of Saturday, June 24, rumors of war were confirmed by Congress. A week earlier, in what became known as the Battle of Bunker Hill, the militia had occupied and fortified the heights around Boston. The British dislodged them at the cost of a thousand men, killing fewer than half that number of American patriots. "I wish we could sell them another hill for that price," observed one militia leader.[36]

On July 6, 1775, Congress adopted the "Declaration on the Causes and Necessity of Taking Up Arms."[37] It began with an appeal to God and a history of the British belligerence that had set the colonies on their present path. Madison read it and thought it "amazing."[38]

As the situation in Williamsburg threatened to boil over, Governor Dunmore joined his wife on the frigate—just in time. On June 24, 1775, Monroe was the youngest of twenty-five armed militiamen who stormed the Governor's Palace, seizing two hundred muskets and three hundred swords. Monroe later had his musket engraved "JM. W-M 1776." It was a souvenir he treasured for the rest of his life.

A few months later, on October 2, 1775, Madison was commissioned as a colonel in the Orange County militia in recognition of his "patriotism, fidelity, courage, and good conduct.... And we do hereby require" your men "to obey you as their Colonel." His appointment was made by the Virginia Convention meeting in Williamsburg and now functioning as the government of the colony since the dissolution of the Burgesses. James Madison's commission was signed by Edmund Pendleton as Chairman of the Virginia Committee of Safety.

Madison was the number two officer in his county's militia, second to his father. But at a slight 5'4" and prey to continual bouts of debilitating illness, he was not cut out for a military career. Madison's organizational strengths meant a well-trained militia for Orange, but his infirmity made him unfit for a wartime command. He never saw action.

In November of 1775, Governor Dunmore offered slaves and indentured servants emancipation if they would enlist in the royal forces for

the pacification of the colony. The following month, a group of Virginia militiamen including Monroe's former schoolmate John Marshall marched on Norfolk to take possession of that chief commercial town. The militia engaged Dunmore's troops at the Great Bridge, killing sixty-one and losing not a single man.[39] On New Year's Day of the year 1776, Dunmore responded. The British navy shelled Norfolk for three days and three nights, until the town of nine thousand souls was "laid in ashes."[40]

And in those fateful first days of 1776, James Monroe—his destiny on the battlefield, not in the classroom—was commissioned as a lieutenant in the Third Virginia Infantry. Throughout the spring and summer, the Third trained with other regiments under General Andrew Lewis, and prepared for war.

On April 25, 1776, James Madison was elected one of two delegates to serve in the upcoming Virginia Convention. This was the fifth such convention since the dissolution of the House of Burgesses by the royal governor; anyone who had previously wanted to serve had likely already done so. Some conventions had dragged on and accomplished little, and the time away from home was a sacrifice for those with active plantations. It was a perfect opportunity for someone like Madison, who had just turned twenty-five. The rudderless, restless four years since he left Princeton were at an end.

And so was the colony of Virginia.

Chapter Two

THE SOLDIER AND THE STATESMAN

"The student is converted to the warrior."

—The Reverend James Madison
(James Madison's cousin)

America was on the verge of independence, and the spectators and delegates in the old House of Burgesses chamber in Williamsburg sensed it.

Edmund Pendleton had been elected chairman of the fifth and final Virginia Convention to meet between the fall of the colonial government and independence. Previously, as head of the Committee of Public Safety, he had overseen Virginia's military mobilization.

From the chair Pendleton looked out at many new faces. Of the 126 delegates, fifty had not served in any of the previous four conventions.[1] Pendleton had given prominent members their preferred committee assignments, but had then taken the unorthodox step of filling the remaining positions alphabetically by county. This opened up a great opportunity for new members and won Pendleton many friends.[2] One beneficiary was James Madison. In the Virginia Convention, the future author of the Bill of Rights would get his first opportunity to define and protect fundamental liberties.

If Madison hoped for a consequential entrée into public life, he would not be disappointed. He soon joined a unanimous convention in instructing Virginia's representatives in Congress "to propose to that respectable body to declare the United Colonies free and independent states absolved from all allegiance to our dependence upon the crown or Parliament of Great Britain." The resolution declared the colonies free to pursue foreign alliances. It authorized Virginia to confederate with other colonies, but not to cede authority over the internal affairs of Virginia to any new government.

Thus Virginia became the first colony to declare independence, and to instruct its members of Congress to seek the same for the American colonies as a whole. Bells rang out throughout the city of Williamsburg in recognition of independence, artillery was fired, and spontaneous celebrations began in the streets. Did the revelers realize that the next time they heard cannon it would be for a cause other than celebration?

The Virginia Convention prepared for war, while also taking on the responsibility of defining Virginia as a new and independent state. After the resolution on the colonies' independence, the next action of the Convention was to create two committees—one to prepare a "declaration of rights" and the other, a "plan of government."

George Mason, a delegate from Fairfax, was chairman of the former committee; he took the lead in authoring the Virginia Declaration of Rights. James Madison was a member of the committee and contributed to the creation of the Declaration. This enormously influential document of sixteen articles inspired the Declaration of Independence, as well as Madison's own Bill of Rights to the U.S. Constitution.

The Virginia Declaration of Rights recognized and guaranteed man's "inherent rights." It also established and codified other concepts that became important to American government, such as separation of powers, the right to jury trial, the prohibition of "cruel and unusual" punishment, the necessity of prior evidence for search-and-seizure warrants, and freedom of the press. The final provision of the Virginia Declaration of Rights guaranteed freedom of religion: "Religion, or the duty which we owe to our Creator and the manner of discharging it, can be directed by reason and conviction, not by force or violence; and therefore, all men are equally entitled to the free exercise of religion, according to the dictates of conscience; and... it is the mutual duty of all to practice Christian forbearance, love, and charity towards each other."

On June 7, 1776, in Philadelphia, Richard Henry Lee, acting on the instructions that Madison had voted for in the Virginia Convention, made a motion in Congress to declare the colonies "free and independent states."[3] A committee of five including Benjamin Franklin, John Adams, Thomas Jefferson, Robert Livingston, and Roger Sherman was appointed to draft a document setting forth the declaration of independence, should it be approved by Congress. Meanwhile, back in Virginia, on June 29 the Convention adopted "the first written constitution ever framed by an independent political society."[4] That constitution listed the offenses of the Crown against the colonies and declared the bonds between them "TOTALLY DISSOLVED."[5]

Only three days later, on July 2, the Second Continental Congress, by a "unanimous" vote (twelve states in favor, New York abstaining), declared the colonies free and independent. Writing to his wife the following day, John Adams pronounced, "The second day of July, 1776, will be the most memorable epoch in the history of America...it ought to be commemorated, as the day of deliverance, by solemn acts of devotion to God Almighty."[6] Indeed, it is a curiosity of history that America's birthday is celebrated on any other day.

On July 4, Congress adopted "The Unanimous Declaration of the Thirteen United States of America." The Declaration of Independence was chiefly the work of Jefferson, with major assistance from Adams and Franklin. (Originally, Jefferson was not even supposed to be a member of Congress, much less compose the Declaration. He was a replacement for Peyton Randolph, who had resigned to return to the Burgesses.)

Congress adopted a number of revisions to the committee's draft, but the passages that have been most remembered through the ages are nearly all those of the principal author.

> When in the Course of human events, it becomes necessary for one people to dissolve the political bands which have connected them with another, and to assume among the powers of the earth, the separate and equal station to which the Laws of Nature and of Nature's God entitle them, a decent respect to the opinions of mankind requires that they should declare the causes which impel them to the separation.
>
> We hold these truths to be self-evident, that all men are created equal, that they are endowed by their Creator with certain unalienable Rights, that among these are Life, Liberty and the pursuit of Happiness.

The Declaration of Independence presented a long list of complaints against King George III. These included making war upon Americans, "imposing taxes on us without our consent," denial of trials by jury, and harmful trade regulations. Jefferson's Declaration ends with an appeal "to the Supreme Judge of the world," and its signers, in support of the same, "with a firm reliance on the protection of Divine Providence...mutually pledge to each other our lives, our fortunes, and our sacred honor." The official, "engrossed" copy of the Declaration would not be created and signed by members of Congress until August.

During this period the Continental Congress was also considering how to formalize its authority. Up until now, Congress had convened for specific purposes and in response to events. A body formed to file formal complaints would now be charged with a different task entirely. As the former colonies hurtled toward independence and war with England, they would need some manner of organizing a common defense. Congress would have to coordinate the war effort among the thirteen states and attempt to obtain the support of foreign powers.

The idea of a confederation of the colonies was at least as old as the Albany Plan, which had been proposed by Benjamin Franklin in 1754. The Albany Congress, attended by seventeen delegates from seven colonies (and one lobbyist), considered a plan for a continental government to defend America during the French and Indian War. The plan they considered, however, in no way contemplated independence. Franklin had renewed his efforts for unity among the colonies in 1775, this time with independence in mind. Thomas Jefferson had responded favorably to Franklin's proposed "Articles of Confederation and Perpetual Union," but the reception in Congress had been decidedly cool. At that time reconciliation with Britain was the primary goal of most members; Congress refused even to vote on Franklin's plan. In fact, he was allowed to present his proposal to Congress only on the condition that no reference would be made to it in any of the journals.[7]

That was on July 21, 1775. Less than a year later, the mood in Congress was very different. With independence in sight on June 12, 1776, a committee was created, chaired by John Dickenson of Pennsylvania, "to prepare and digest the form of confederation."[8] The Dickenson Committee report, laid before Congress on July 12, 1776, was modeled closely on Franklin's proposal from the previous year.[9] The Articles of Confederation, then—the document establishing the Confederation in which the thirteen newly independent states would join to fight Great Britain—can be said to have sprung chiefly from the pens of two Pennsylvanians.

The debate over the Articles was characterized by the same divisions that would eventually, after America had finally won the independence Congress had just claimed, doom the Confederation and inspire Madison and the other delegates to the Philadelphia Constitutional Convention to draft a different form of federal government, one that would ensure "a more perfect Union." These were the same issues that would return again and again to bedevil the government under the Articles and that both Madison and Monroe would one day struggle with as members of the Confederation Congress. The Confederation—and the war—would be funded by "requisitions" paid by the individual state governments. But representatives defending the Articles in Congress disagreed over how to set the requisitions for the different states, and how to define the population on which the requisitions would be based. They differed about how many votes each state should have in Congress—whether it should depend on the states' monetary contributions, or not. They disagreed about how to settle disputes between the states about Western lands. And they differed on how many representatives should make a quorum, and where the capital should be—and even whether there should be one permanent capital, or not.

And while the Congress bickered, young men readied for war.

In August of 1776, Monroe's Third Virginia Regiment, along with the Fifth, was ordered to join Washington on Long Island.[10] The strong young man, now over six feet tall and broad-shouldered, had commenced his life of service. Monroe later described his public career in his memoirs. (He refers to himself throughout in the third person, in a tradition at least as old as Caesar's *Commentaries*.) "As Mr. Monroe had been employed, with little intermission, from the time that he entered into the army until his retirement in 1825 from the high office which he then held, and from a very early period, in the most important trusts abroad and at home, he was necessarily a party, in the stations which he held, to the great events which occurred in them, so far as they related to his own country; a spectator of many others on the interesting theatre on which he moved; and well acquainted with almost all which mastered that very interesting epoch." Like so many young men both before and after him, Monroe left the place of his birth for the first time in the company of armed compatriots, setting forth for a place distant and different from anything he had ever known.

The Third Regiment reached Washington's army shortly after the Battle of Long Island, which had seen two American regiments "nearly cut to pieces."[11] Monroe's company and three others under the command of Major Leitch and Colonel Knolton were sent to Harlem Heights to meet the advancing British. It was a vicious fight, in which both the major and colonel were killed. But the British were checked. After more than a year of training and spoiling for a fight, Monroe had seen war close up. It is an open question whether the sight of men trying to kill him, and the experience of leveling his musket to respond in kind, conformed to Monroe's excited expectations—or whether it ever has for any eager young man in a theater of war. After Harlem Heights, members of the Third Regiment were awarded the highest possible commendation by George Washington.[12]

Like the army and the country at large, Monroe admired George Washington. Years later he described the great general as

> an example to the world for talents as a military commander, for integrity, fortitude, and firmness under the severest trials, for respect to the civil authority and devotion to the rights and liberties of his country, of which neither Rome nor Greece have exhibited the equal. I saw him in my earliest youth, in the retreat through Jersey, at the head of a small band, or rather, in its rear, for he was always near the enemy, and his countenance and manner made an impression on me which time can never efface...a deportment so firm, so dignified, so exalted, but yet so modest and composed, I have never seen in any other person.[13]

Hero worship was a common thread that ran through Monroe's life, magnified by the early loss of his father. He constantly sought out the example of more experienced men—people who were respected and accomplished—and tried to emulate the qualities that made them so.

Washington would rely on his personal popularity after defeats at the battles of Long Island and White Plains and the captures of Forts Washington and Lee, which sent the rebel army retreating through the state of New Jersey. These reversals, Monroe observed, "put fairly at issue with the nation the great question whether they were competent and resolved to support their independence, or would sink under the pressure."

Washington's army had retreated across the Delaware River, taking with them every boat they could lay their hands on. The enemy was left without means of pursuit and assumed the fighting was done for the season. Washington needed to achieve victory, and quickly, or the war would be over before it had truly begun. The string of defeats had done nothing to raise confidence in the cause of independence in America or abroad. Worse yet, the enlistment of a substantial part of the army would end with the new year. So Washington made a bold plan. "The first attack," Monroe recorded, "was to be made on Trenton, on the result of which everything would depend."[14]

On Christmas Day, 1776, 2,400 of Washington's men re-crossed the Delaware River to prepare the assault. Lieutenant James Monroe eagerly offered to join the advance party of fifty men that would be led by Captain William Washington, a distant cousin of the general.[15] After landing, the advance party secured the main road that led from Trenton to Princeton to prevent the rest of the British army in New Jersey from learning of the attack. In the hours before the battle, Monroe and a group of men took control of an important street heading into town.[16]

Dr. Riker, a physician who lived outside of town, had not expected the call of history when he put out his candles and crawled into bed that Christmas night. But during the night he heard Monroe and his men outside, arose from his bed and, believing them to be British, scolded the intruders. When Dr. Riker learned they were Americans, however, he told them that he too was a patriot and brought them food. He also told Monroe, as commander, that he would join them in the action that was obviously afoot. "I am a doctor, and I may help some poor fellow," Riker said.[17] As it turned out, Monroe himself would be in dire need of the doctor's help.

In the first hours of December 26, 1776, the American army advanced on Trenton and ambushed their surprised enemy. The Hessians sounded the alarm, drums beat the call to arms, and Monroe remembered that "two cannon were placed in the main street to bear on the head of our column as it entered." Had the Hessians been allowed to fire their artillery, they could have ambushed the American troops on the narrow road and delayed them until the town had fully mobilized for defense. They might have wiped them out completely. If the Battle of Trenton held the balance of the Revolutionary War, this encounter on the road to that city held the balance of the battle. The cannons had to be captured.

Captain William Washington rushed forward and was struck down by musket fire. Lieutenant Monroe attacked as well, sending "the troops around the cannon to flight." Out of the repetitive pops of gunfire came the musket ball that hit James Monroe. The young lieutenant came to rest in the piles of new fallen snow, which were quickly stained scarlet around him. The eighteen-year-old Virginian lay dying on the road to Trenton, New Jersey, quickly bleeding out through his left shoulder. Perhaps Monroe thought of Virginia, and how improbable it was that he should lie dying so far from home. Maybe the sounds of gunfire that filled his ears reminded him of Spence Monroe, who had taught him how to hunt in his frontier boyhood. Both of his parents had died young, and for a moment it may have seemed that he would follow in their footsteps.

But Dr. Riker was quick with his clamp and stopped the bleeding, saving Monroe's young life. Without a professional doctor in his immediate presence, it is unlikely that Monroe would have survived his wound.

Monroe was carried from the battlefield and operated on by Dr. Riker and Dr. Cochrane, the surgeon general of the army. The next night he was taken to the home of the Coryell family, where he remained in bed for ten days. Each day, Riker stopped by to clean and dress Monroe's wound to prevent infection. After leaving the Coryell home, Monroe spent nine weeks in the home of Henry Wyncoops. He paid his doctor's bills from his own pocket, and would refuse a wounded soldier's pension from the government.[18]

While his body would recover, Monroe would never be the same. Gone was the brash young Virginian who had disparaged the troops of other states. When he left his blood in the snow before Trenton, James

Monroe became no longer just a Virginian but an American. For Monroe's fellow officers who "came from all the states," the effect of the war was to "break down local prejudices and attach the mind and feeling to the union."[19]

For his heroism at Trenton, Monroe was promoted to captain. Later in life, while writing his memoirs, his pride in his actions as a soldier shone through, even after all the intervening years. But Monroe was modest about his battlefield exploits in comparison with the accomplishments of the men in charge of directing the events of those momentous days for America: "In the great events of which I have spoke Mr. Monroe, being a mere youth, counted for nothing in comparison with those distinguished citizens who had the direction of public affairs." He believed the wartime statesmen were unequalled in history.[20]

April of 1777 was a month of disappointment for both Monroe the solider and Madison the statesman. Monroe's promotion to captain had become a burden; he was a high-ranking officer in a top-heavy army. With a scarcity of battlefield commands, he would have to raise his own troops. When Monroe was finally well, he returned to Virginia to do just that. Lacking a large personal fortune from which to pay soldiers, he resorted to appeals to patriotism. They did not get him far.

In the meantime, Virginians were having their first elections to the House of Delegates. Madison, as a member of the Fifth Virginia Convention, had automatically become a Delegate when the state Constitution was adopted. Now he would have to defend his seat. Charles Porter, an Orange County tavern owner, would be his opponent. Popular campaign tactics included plying the voters with food and alcohol—a practice prohibited by law but nonetheless widespread. By virtue of Porter's trade, the freeholders of Orange would perhaps be the fullest and drunkest on Election Day. Madison, for his part, would have none of it. He would follow the rules and not buy votes with food and drink. He appealed to the public based on his tenure in office, his early impact on the new state government, and his service in the Orange County militia. He was defeated.

Yet not everyone appreciated Porter's "generosity." His tactics would lead some voters in Orange to file a formal complaint, presented to the House on December 21, 1777:

> Mr. Charles Porter, one of the candidates at the election of delegates for the said county, on the 24th of April last, did, contrary to an ordinance of convention, make use of bribery and corruption during the said election, and praying that the said election may be set aside.[21]

The petition was referred to the Committee on Privileges and Elections, where it died. In his excellent biography of Madison, Ralph Ketcham points out that delegates who had obtained their seats by the same means Porter had used would naturally be reluctant to pursue this investigation.[22] The results would stand. But this would be Madison's last unsuccessful election.

Monroe wrote to one of his former captains about his own disappointment, "I am very unhappy in finding myself incapable of raising a sufficient proportion of men to take the field." Monroe had failed to raise troops to command, and he was desperate to get back to the action, where he was needed. He vastly preferred "that mode of life, attended with its usual fatigue and danger to the one in which I at present act."[23]

On August 11, Monroe rejoined the army in Bucks County, Pennsylvania. General Lord Alexander Stirling had invited him to serve as his aide-de-camp. It was far from the battlefield command Monroe sought, but he was back in the fight, in an important if unglamorous position. It was during this time that he first met the Marquis de Lafayette, a French nobleman and military officer who had been inspired by the American cause to join Washington's army. Though a year younger than

Monroe, Lafayette was serving in America as a general. Later Monroe remembered his friendship with Lafayette, "attended in the progress through life, in their respective stations, with the most interesting occurrences."[24]

As aide-de-camp Monroe was required to convey orders from Stirling to the troops serving under him in battle and when in camp or marching to take the orders of the commander in chief to Stirling.[25] Stirling, a wealthy New Jerseyan with a disputed Scottish title, was an exemplary general with the financial wherewithal to support a large company.

On August 25, Washington marched the army through Philadelphia for inspection by Congress: "The line extended six or seven miles."[26] Monroe would be present for the opening maneuvers of "the Philadelphia Campaign," a series of battles in which the British would attempt to take America's capital city while Washington fought to repel them.

Philadelphia was the second largest city in the English-speaking world, smaller only than London. It was easily the greatest city in America. Its loss would have enormous symbolic, political, and economic fallout. At least that's what Admiral Howe, leader of the British forces, believed. But Howe's very understanding of war—troops with brightly colored uniforms scheduling battles at preordained locations and times, in a jolly chasing game of "capture the flag"—would be tempered by what he experienced in America.

On September 11, 1777, Monroe experienced his first battle as an aide-de-camp. Howe's army had been making their way to Philadelphia rapidly. Washington was waiting for them, his divisions spread across the east side of Brandywine Creek. Rather than face the fortified Continentals head on, Howe and General Cornwallis crossed the creek far north of the American position, turned south, and came crashing down hard. The American right flank was completely surprised, including Stirling's brigade, which seems to have taken the worst of it. Lafayette was wounded, probably in sight of his friend Monroe.[27] Once the sounds of battle were heard downstream, a division of British and Hessian forces on the west side of the creek crossed and attacked in the center. The Brandywine ran red, and the British successfully took the east bank and captured the

American artillery.[28] The American lines, divided and squeezed in the middle and to the right, broke and retreated. It was a decisive British victory, but Washington still remained between Howe and Philadelphia.

Howe lured Washington north and himself slipped south toward Philadelphia. Belatedly, Lieutenant Colonel Alexander Hamilton wrote to John Hancock, the president of Congress, with this dire warning: "If Congress have not yet left Philadelphia, they ought to do it immediately without fail, for the enemy have the means of throwing a party this night into the city."[29] Howe took Philadelphia, but Congress simply reconvened in smaller Pennsylvania towns—York, and then Lancaster.

And life in the American capital was more than Howe had bargained for. He was in a hostile city and cut off from the rest of the British army. With the Delaware River in American hands, Howe could not be resupplied by water.[30] To protect his supply line over land, Howe dispersed three thousand men. Two battalions were sent to invade the town of Bilingsport, while four stayed in Philadelphia to hold the city. At Germantown, five miles north of Philadelphia, there were nine thousand British troops.[31]

With the English army dispersed in this way, Washington, whose instincts were toward bold, decisive offensive action, would attempt a knockout blow. The Americans marched quickly, covering twenty miles as the night of October 3 gave way to morning.[32] The Americans would strike at the heart of the British camp, taking the four main roads into town and meeting in the middle.

The battle of Germantown began at 5:00 a.m. on October 4. The intense fog made the coordination necessary to execute the brilliant but complicated plan difficult. One of the four American units was delayed at the "Chew House," a mansion of heavy stone occupied by British troops. The Americans eventually advanced without taking the building, but the delay had given the enemy critical time to mobilize.

The British counterattack was powerful and drove the Americans back. As the militia fled, Stirling held his men firm, their bravery the only barrier to an even more bloody retreat.[33] Still, the American army had, on the whole, acquitted themselves well, and very nearly won the day. If they had captured the nine thousand British troops in Germantown, the war would likely have ended then and there. Four years later, it was the capture of seven thousand British at York Town that ended major combat operations of the American Revolution and brought on negotiations for peace.

On October 16, the American army under Benedict Arnold and Horatio Gates won the decisive battle of Saratoga in upstate New York. Howe's Philadelphia campaign had cost the British dearly. "Gentleman" Johnny Burgoyne, the British commander at Saratoga, waited vainly for reinforcements that never came. As a consequence, fifty-eight hundred British surrendered after taking roughly a thousand casualties.[34] If Germantown had gone as Washington planned—and it nearly had—the two battles together would have delivered a death blow to the British and ended the war in 1777.

Though the American victory at Saratoga did not end the war, it was still crucial to the ultimate outcome. On the basis of victory there, the French decided that the Americans could win. The exhaustive diplomatic efforts of Americans in Europe, and on the battlefields of Pennsylvania and New York, would soon bring the nation of France fully into the war. French involvement was what America needed to win. It meant an army of experienced troops and officers, a reliable stream of financing, and ships to counter the British naval advantage.

On November 15, 1777, two decades after an American union was first conceived and over two years since it was proposed in Congress, the framework for a federal government was completed by that body and submitted to the states for approval. Under the Articles of Confederation, each state would have equal representation—because the small states would not join a union on any other terms. When the roll was called on the issue, only Virginia dissented. Under the Articles of Confederation, that state—the most populous one—would be no more powerful than Delaware.

By a close margin it was decided to apportion requisitions on states based on the value of land, including improvements.[35] Though each state would have only one vote, each would send not fewer than two representatives nor more than seven; these delegates would be term-limited to three years of service in any six-year period. Congress punted hard on the issue of the Western lands. The Articles prohibited Congress from regulating their boundaries; in fact, these would not be determined until after the dissolution of the Confederation and the establishment of a new United States under the Constitution.[36] (The West was such a contentious issue that it still delayed Maryland's ratification of the Articles until March of 1781.) All decisions on major questions would require nine of thirteen states. Amendments to the Articles would require the consent of every single state.

With the major questions decided and the fine print completed, Congress issued the Articles of Confederation to the state legislatures. The letter sent along with the plan reads more like an apology than anything else. The Articles were "the best which could be adapted to the circumstances of all."[37] In desperation and out of necessity, the states were slipping on a straitjacket that would nearly suffocate the new government. The Articles of Confederation were utterly unequal to the task of peace, and similarly unequal to the task of war. As one member pointed out, "a time of peace and tranquility" was the only "proper time for agitating so important a concern."[38] Peace and tranquility, however, were nowhere to be found.

As the Articles were presented to the states, Madison and Monroe both saw their fortunes improve. Monroe was promoted to major in November of 1777. And in the same month, Madison—his intellect and hard work recognized by his peers—was chosen to fill a vacancy on the Council of State. This body served as an advisory board for the governor and shared his executive authority. On the first ballot "James Madison, the younger, of Orange," received thirty votes to the twenty-one for his next closest competitor. On the second ballot he received sixty-one votes and achieved the needed majority.

Madison arrived in Williamsburg on January 14 to join the Council of State; Governor Patrick Henry administered the oath of office.[39] The wartime governor and Council, overwhelmed with work, wasted little time on formalities. Madison was immediately charged with responding to a letter from the Continental Congress. The suffering at Valley Forge was beyond imagination. Without an immediate infusion of supplies, the troops would "starve, dissolve, or disperse."

The Council agreed that the governor should appoint someone to purchase "pork, beef, and bacon" in northwestern Virginia and to obtain wagons to deliver these and other necessities, such as salt, to Washington's headquarters.[40] Though removed from the fighting, Madison was worried about his brother Ambrose, who was in the thick of the war, and about his many other friends whose lives depended on the honest and faithful service of public servants, including himself.

In Williamsburg, Madison lodged with his cousin, the Reverend James Madison, who had been appointed president of the College of William and Mary just a few months earlier. The Reverend Madison, only two years older than his cousin, was a well-educated and experienced college instructor who had been put in charge of the college when his predecessor was removed for loyalist sympathies.[41] The cousins lived together in the President's House, a Georgian red-brick mansion built in 1733. It has been the home of every William and Mary president except one.[42]

Monroe's quarters at the end of 1777 contrasted starkly with Madison's. Washington chose winter headquarters for his army in the most defensible position close to the enemy in Philadelphia. Valley Forge has been "a name associated with suffering since the winter of 1777–1778."[43] The terrible conditions there perhaps contributed to Monroe's disillusionment. "The principles on which the war is carried on now [are] entirely different from what it was at first," he wrote. "Patriotism, public spirit, and disinterestedness have almost vanished, and honor and virtue are empty names."[44]

Washington and his army of eleven thousand had arrived at Valley Forge on December 21, 1777. The nearest drinkable water was a mile away, and there were no accommodations. Shelter had to be built from scratch.[45] After miles of marching in polar temperatures, wearied from months of combat, and with stomachs that were completely empty, the fatigued soldiers at Valley Forge set about building a place to live. Without nails, wooden planks had to be notched to build their fourteen-by-sixteen-foot huts, where the soldiers would live in groups of twelve. Construction would not be completed until January 13.

On February 6, 1778, the Treaty of Alliance brought the French formally into the war. When the Americans at Valley Forge learned the news three months later, Washington proclaimed a day of jubilee for the entire army. There were military exercises, eating, drinking, and dancing to a band. As the worst winter of the soldiers' lives came to an end, there was hope that the worst of the war was behind them as well.

Monroe the warrior passed much of the time at Valley Forge reading books of poetry, which he eagerly shared with his friends. "'Tis the summit of fortitude and heroism to prevail over the views of this transitory life," he wrote, "and turn the mind on the more lasting happiness of that to come.... But while life remains, it is necessary you should have something more than mere repentance to amuse your thoughts on."[46]

Meanwhile, back in Virginia, Madison stayed busy on the Council, managing the state's wartime affairs. Gunboats were purchased, repairs to barracks were ordered,[47] and rum, wine, and sugar were sent to the army.[48] Rifles were sent to the Monongalia County Militia to fend off Indian attacks, and a prisoner of war camp was established in Charlottesville. The pardon power, which the Council exercised jointly with the governor, was used to grant a reprieve to two criminals previously set to be executed.[49] Correspondence went back and forth between the Council and House of Delegates in Virginia and the Virginia delegates in Congress, coordinating their efforts as best they could.

A bounty of five hundred dollars was placed on the head of Josiah Phillips, a laborer in Princess Anne County who had taken advantage of the war to lead an insurgency, stealing, pillaging, and committing murder against his countrymen. A bill of attainder (essentially a criminal conviction handed down by a legislature) was successfully sponsored by Jefferson, then serving in the House of Delegates; Phillips was ordered killed should he fail to surrender.[50]

On June 1, Thomas Jefferson was elected the second governor of the state of Virginia, commencing his first professional collaboration with Madison.[51] Friendship with Jefferson would be important in the lives of both Madison and Monroe; eventually the author of the Declaration of Independence would be instrumental in bringing these two close friends of his own together. But Madison may not have made the best impression on Jefferson at this time.

Madison's hat, which the style of the era required for public appearances, had recently been stolen; and like almost everything else during the war, hats were in short supply. The hatless Madison stayed in his room at the President's House for two days before finally paying a tailor an exorbitant sum for a hat because Williamsburg had no haberdasher. The hat was enormously large for him, and the 5'4" Madison attended the Council of State looking like a little boy playing dress-up, much to the merriment of his colleagues.[52]

In the summer of 1778, the king's peace commission, led by Lord Carlisle, arrived to offer terms to Congress. After the embarrassment of Saratoga, the trials of the Philadelphia campaign, and their plans to evacuate that city, the British decided to press now for the best terms they thought they could get. They offered the repeal of all the offensive acts that had followed the French and Indian War—in exchange for which

America would make peace and remain under British dominion. But despite the war (the hardships, the inconveniences, the violence and life-threatening deprivation) Congress would insist on nothing less than independence. Carlisle and the rest of the delegation returned to London, but two important events resulted from their visit.

The arrival of the peace commission caused Howe's resignation and replacement by Sir Henry Clinton. The peace commission told Clinton that a settlement would be impossible. He was authorized to fight the most brutal war he could to force American submission.

Clinton was willing. He was ready to fight a different kind of war. He began by preparing to leave Philadelphia. What was the point in holding the capital if the Congress kept moving? As Clinton prepared to leave the city, Washington and his generals planned their attack. General Charles Lee was put in charge of the assault, which would be carried out as the British were leaving the area near Monmouth Courthouse.

The fighting that followed was not only a missed opportunity for the Americans, but a near total calamity. Lee would end up court martialed for his lack of any apparent plan and failure to give orders. After an initial engagement through the pine trees of Monmouth, the Americans retreated. The American pursuers became the pursued as the British under Cornwallis turned and counterattacked.

Lord Stirling and James Monroe, temporarily serving as Stirling's adjutant general, were positioned on the left side of the American line and received the first blow of the counterattack. Stirling kept his men together and repulsed the British.

Monroe led a scouting party as close to the enemy lines as he could get. Around four in the afternoon he issued a critical dispatch to Washington. The British were regrouping and preparing to hit the Americans on the right, where Washington himself was positioned. Thanks to Monroe's timely warning, Washington was prepared and repelled the offensive.[53] And although he didn't know it yet, Monroe had just taken part in the last major combat he would see in the war he had joined in college.

When not thinking of war, Monroe had begun to spend more time thinking of women. Theodosia Prevost, whose husband had abandoned her to support the British, lived close to Philadelphia at the Hermitage, which had become a popular gathering place for American soldiers. James Monroe became one of her friends. In November, he wrote to her seeking guidance in pursuing a woman who had caught his attention. (In light of Mrs. Prevost's later marriage to Aaron Burr, her judgment in this arena is open to question.)

Monroe wrote, "A young lady who either is or pretends to be in love is, you know my dear Mrs. Prevost, the most unreasonable creature in existence." He complained of the numerous ways he might inadvertently give offense and took note of how easy it was for women to lose interest. Monroe asked Prevost to talk him up to the object of his affection on her upcoming trip to the Hermitage.[54]

In November of 1778, Governor Jefferson and the Virginia Council of State, including Madison, turned their attention from resupplying distant forces to preparing for invasion. The British had taken significant parts of Georgia, beginning the Southern Campaign that would define the remainder of the war. To that end, governor and Council agreed on an embargo against exporting meats. The food would be needed at home.[55]

Monroe, again serving as aide-de-camp to Stirling, never lost his desire for a battlefield command. On December 20 he tendered his resignation from the army effective January 12, 1779. He would return to Virginia in the hopes of obtaining a military command there. At Philadelphia Monroe obtained letters of recommendation from Stirling and Washington to present to the Virginia legislature in furtherance of his military career back home.[56] In August he was commissioned a lieutenant colonel of the State Line stationed in Williamsburg. But he was still without men, and neither Virginia nor Monroe himself had the resources to acquire them.

"I... desire as I began almost with the war, to serve to the end of it," he wrote. "They ordered me down in apprehension of an invasion which I believe will not happen." While Monroe waited, he enjoyed his private lodgings, spent time with the family of Colonel Dudley Digges, and enjoyed socializing with the women in town. Reading in the college library "forms the principal part of my amusement," he said.[57]

The restless Monroe began to feel that he was going nowhere fast. But he soon formed a connection that would change his life in ways he never imagined. As Madison had done beginning almost two years before, Monroe became close to Thomas Jefferson. Governor Jefferson, seeing promise in the young man, offered him a pupilage to study law. In this endeavor Monroe was joined by John Mercer, a William and Mary classmate who had been with him for much of the war. Mercer, like Monroe, had been promoted into the surplus of officers without men to command. Since Jefferson was not an active lawyer, his students were spared the drudgery of clerical work. Instead they served as his political aides and read thick treatises on law and the works of philosophers from antiquity to modernity.

Meanwhile, Madison had once again impressed his fellow public servants. On December 14, 1779, the Virginia legislature voted jointly to select their representatives to the Continental Congress. Madison and Joseph Jones, Monroe's uncle, were elected to fill vacancies in the state's delegation.

The twenty-eight-year-old sent his eager acceptance to Benjamin Harrison, Speaker of the Virginia House and the ancestor of two future U.S. presidents. Madison assured the Speaker that "as fidelity and zeal can supply the place of abilities the interests of my country shall be punctually promoted."[58] At a critical hour in the war for independence, Madison would assume his first role on the national stage.

Chapter Three

THE WORLD TURNED UPSIDE DOWN

"If these severe doses of ill fortune do not cool the frenzy and relax the pride of Britain, it would seem as if heaven had in reality abandoned her to her folly and her fate."

—James Madison

On his first trip to the North since leaving Princeton, Madison spent twelve days traversing bad roads under heavy rain.[1] He would shortly be making his debut in national politics, representing Virginia in the Continental Congress.

After arriving in Philadelphia on March 18, 1780, Madison found quarters at the home of Eliza Trist at the corner of Fifth and Market Streets.[2] Eliza ran a warm and convivial boarding house popular with many members of Congress. The Trists would become like a family to Madison. As his work continued to take him to Philadelphia, he never stayed anywhere else.

In preparation to represent Virginia in Congress, Madison had done his homework, undertaking a serious study of the nation's finances. The results were appalling. Congress had solved the problem of having no money by printing millions of dollars of worthless paper. Congress's credit was exhausted. Any future issue of currency would now have to be backed by the states.[3]

Upon arrival in Philadelphia, Madison wrote to Jefferson, offering a synopsis of his findings: "Our army threatened with an immediate alternative of disbanding or living on free quarter; the public treasury empty; public credit exhausted," as well as the private credit of patriotic purchasing agents; "Congress complaining of the extortion of the people; the people of the improvidence of Congress, and the army of both."

Madison thought that Congress was lacking in statesmen. Members voted for requisitions they knew their home states would never pay. The army was out of bread and would soon be out of meat, "without a shilling for the purpose, and without credit for a shilling." The only hope was for states to acquire the worthless paper money and reissue a new currency backed by their own resources. Or else, in Madison's estimation, "we are undone."[4]

As Madison struggled to cope with Congress's ruinous finances, the state government he had left behind in Virginia was preparing for a move. Williamsburg's proximity to the sea left it hopelessly vulnerable to the attack that would be coming at any minute. So Governor Jefferson and the rest of the Virginia government were moving inland to Richmond, the new capital.

And James Monroe was considering moving to Richmond at Governor Jefferson's personal invitation to complete his legal studies there. Joseph Jones strongly urged his nephew to do just that. Jefferson, Jones told Monroe, was "as proper a man as can be put into the office having the requisites of ability, firmness, and diligence. You would do well to cultivate his friendship." Jones also cautioned his protégé to get ready. The war was moving south.[5]

The practice of law was a dream that Monroe's father and uncle had shared for him, but it was a career in which Monroe himself had little interest. And not every adult advisor in his life agreed with his uncle's safe, practical advice. Charles Lee, the general at Monmouth, to whom Monroe had grown close during his service in the army, was entirely in sympathy with Monroe's preference for a career in public service: "There are few young men for whom I have a higher esteem and affection. I am extremely concerned that fortune has been so unkind as not to admit of your cultivating the talents which nature has bestowed on you to a greater advantage than your present situation seems to promise." Lee thought the law "a most horrid narrower of the mind."[6]

But Jones and practicality won out, for the present. Monroe had no hope of an immediate battlefield command. But if Virginia could raise a new regiment, proximity to Jefferson might be critical in securing one. Monroe, always in search of a mentor, had found in Jefferson someone worthy of his admiration. And what better place for an aspiring politician than the new seat of government? It was settled. Monroe was headed to Richmond.

Meanwhile, as a newly minted congressman in Philadelphia, Madison was elected by his colleagues to the Board of Admiralty, the committee charged with overseeing American naval efforts.[7] The Board's official actions reflected the impotence of the federal government. Having neither the money to buy goods nor boats to transport them, the Board denied navy Captain Abraham Whipple's three-month-old request for bread and flour. They did, however, commend his service and encourage him to keep up the good work.[8] The Board then recommended that Congress order the Continental agent in Boston to sell as much sugar and rum as he possessed to pay to finish building ships sitting unfinished in Portsmouth and Connecticut. (Congress ignored the report, and the ships were not finished until 1782 and 1783, respectively.)[9] Meanwhile, the eighteen-gun *Saratoga* sat idle for want of final riggings, and the frigate *Trumbull*, completely finished and with 120 men aboard, needed only additional food and cannon before it could be employed in the fight against the British.[10]

In a Christmas raid, a group of common criminals broke into a warehouse and stole all but three bolts of the national supply of canvas. The Board had previously directed that the canvas be sent where it was needed, but these orders had not been obeyed. The warehouse workers, for their part, apologized to the Board but proudly reported that they had found and killed two of the three thieves and had an excellent chance of finding the third.[11] The Board responded that, while this was nice, all they really wanted was their canvas back.

The Board was financially strapped, and in order to raise desperately needed funds they finally convinced Congress to order a Boston-based ship filled with sugar and rum to Philadelphia, where the goods could be sold at considerably higher prices. The trip put the ship and its cargo at significant risk of capture—a necessary risk, given the sorry state of the Board's financial affairs.[12] With no apparent irony, the Board designed a seal for the Admiralty with a Latin motto which translated means "Upholding and Upheld."[13]

On June 21, 1780, the Virginia legislature appointed Madison to a full term in Congress, meaning he would get to continue this kind of work for at least another year. The Virginia legislature wrote to its delegates in Congress to inquire where the state's requisition had gone, and Jefferson wrote a personal letter to Madison trying to clear up confusion about where three thousand new draftees from Virginia were to be sent.

Monroe would soon be receiving a more exciting assignment. Governor Jefferson and the Council of State wrote him stating their need "to employ a gentleman in a confidential business, requiring great discretion, and some acquaintance with military things. . . . It will call you off some weeks, to the distance of a couple hundred miles. . . . Will you be so good as to attend us immediately for further communications?"[14]

Six days later, Monroe received his mission.

The British invasion of the South had overwhelmed any resistance, and the city of Charleston, South Carolina, had fallen. Governor Jefferson anticipated that Virginia would be the next target. Jefferson assigned riders to Monroe, who would proceed to the front lines of the war in the Carolinas. Every forty miles Monroe was to station couriers who, riding by night, would convey information back to Virginia. Jefferson wanted to know of any troop movements as well as "the state and resources of our friends, their force, the disposition of the people, the prospect of provisions, ammunition, arms, and other circumstances, the force and condition of the enemy. . . . " Lines of communication were to be established with the governors of the Carolinas and the commander of the American forces. Jefferson was clearly on edge; he asked Monroe to send a message every fortnight whether or not there was any news.[15]

Monroe arrived in North Carolina on June 22 and met with Governor Abner Nash and General Richard Caswell. He wrote to Jefferson that six thousand men had embarked for Charleston under British General Sir Henry Clinton, leaving four thousand cavalry and six hundred infantry under Colonel Tarleton and Lord Cornwallis in North Carolina. Clinton had announced an amnesty for anyone who swore allegiance to the crown, but sentenced to death those who wouldn't. The rules of war respecting prisoners and civilians would not be honored in the Southern campaign.[16]

When Monroe's intelligence-gathering mission ended, he was not content to let it be the last of his military service. He continued to try to find a place for himself at the front so long as there was a war to be won. Even his former position as an aide-de-camp started to look better than missing further action altogether. Monroe wrote Lafayette inquiring whether he needed an aide, and if not, whether he would recommend Monroe to General Benjamin Lincoln.[17] But Monroe's heroic efforts to get back into the war were frustrated at every turn.

He had also tried unsuccessfully to sell some of his land to finance a trip to Europe, where he was considering finishing his studies. Despite these setbacks, Monroe was coming into his own and feeling good about the future. When he had last failed to gain a command—in the time between his recovery from Trenton and his rejoining the army before Brandywine—Monroe had contemplated retiring to private life. This time he was determined on public service, in politics if not in the army. Monroe stayed the course, he said, largely because of Jefferson's influence: "Your kindness and attention to me in this and a variety of other instances has really put me under such obligations to you that I fear I shall hardly ever have it in my power to repay them. But believe me in whatever situation of life the chance of fortune may place me, no circumstance can happen which will give me such pleasure or make me so happy... whatever I am at present in the opinion of others or whatever I may be in the future has greatly [arisen] from your friendship. My plan of life is now fixed, has a certain object for its view."[18]

While the main front of the war had moved south, Philadelphia was still subject to shocks and alarms. In September of 1780 an epidemic terrorized Congress and the people of the city. "The Flux" had a mortality rate that "exceed[ed] anything ever remembered," and took the wife of Joseph Reid, president of Congress.[19] The government was further shaken by the defection of General Benedict Arnold to the British. An effigy of Arnold was paraded through Philadelphia holding a mask while a man dressed as the devil followed shaking a purse of coins. Ultimately, the mock Arnold was burnt to the delight of all. "Thus with one act faded the laurels of a hero," observed Madison of Arnold's treachery, "and the appellations of Arnold must be everlastingly changed for a representative of the blackest infamy."[20]

During this period Madison for the first time took on an issue that would consume his career for a decade and constantly threaten to break apart the nation. He was chosen as chairman of a committee to elaborate on previous instructions given to John Jay, the Ambassador to Spain. That country had joined the war against Great Britain as an ally of France. Congress hoped to create a direct alliance with Spain, to prevent Spain from making a separate peace with England, and perhaps to obtain a loan from the Spanish government. The difficulty was that Spain possessed New Orleans and wanted exclusive control of the Mississippi River.

The report of Madison's committee, written in his hand, asserted the claim of the United States to that river, citing the 1763 Treaty of Paris, Article VII, which had ended the French and Indian War: "That part of the world, shall be fixed irrevocably by a line drawn along the middle of the River Mississippi . . . provided that the navigation of the river Mississippi shall be equally free, as well to the subjects of Great Britain and those of France, in its whole breadth and length, from its source to the sea . . . vessels belonging to the subjects of either nation shall not be stopped, visited, or subjected to the payment of any duty whatsoever." The committee report deemed the United States to be the successor in interest to British rights under the treaty.

The committee further recognized the claims of numerous states to parts of the Mississippi; it simply was not Congress's river to bargain away. Additionally, the law of nations required the innocent passage of troops and individuals through nations at peace. "If the right to a passage by land through other countries may be claimed for troops which are employed in the destruction of mankind," Madison wrote, "how much more may a passage by water be claimed for commerce which is beneficial to all nations."[21]

On October 25, Madison's friend David Jameson in Virginia wrote to him with the news he had been dreading: "We are invaded." The British had landed at Newport News and taken the city of Hampton. The invaders had fortified Portsmouth and made incursions down the river to Suffolk, easily taking possession of that city.[22] Even with the state legislature still short of a quorum, Virginia rallied to repel the attack.[23] A bounty was raised for enlistments, and militia were deployed to halt the advance. In Congress, Madison was added to the committee to correspond with the commander of the American forces in the South.

In a November 10, 1780, letter to Madison from Richmond, Joseph Jones took the opportunity to brag on his nephew, Colonel James Monroe—perhaps bringing him to Madison's attention for the first time.

Monroe was commanding a three hundred-volunteer horse and infantry unit in defense of Virginia. At the time, Madison could not have guessed the significance that this young officer would have for his political career and the future of America.[24]

But a volunteer unit such as the one Monroe was serving with mobilized in response to an immediate threat and disbanded just as suddenly. A permanent command of regular forces could be obtained only with substantial resources from himself or Virginia. Monroe, apart from volunteering where he could, would continue to search vainly for a role in the war and spend most of his time in idleness.

At a juncture when the states desperately needed unity, the Mississippi issue could be counted on to be divisive. On November 18, 1780, Georgia delegates moved to empower John Jay, Congress's Ambassador to Spain, to yield the Mississippi if no separate peace would be made between Spain and Britain, and if the deal could be used to gain a substantial grant or loan to finance the war effort.[25]

Georgia and South Carolina, which were largely controlled by the enemy, were terrified by the doctrine of *uti possidetis,* or "as you possess," which holds that each side keeps the territory it has at the end of a conflict unless otherwise spelled out by treaty. If peace came without a decisive American victory, the two southernmost states might remain under British control. And bringing in Spain as an ally of the United States, not only of France, would all but guarantee independence—whereas Spain's quitting the war entirely could well doom the American cause. The British were actively negotiating a separate peace with Spain, dangling the Mississippi as a reward.

But Madison did not believe that peace should be bought with the territorial rights of the states. He suggested that states eager to sell out others for their perceived immediate self-interest would find no one standing with them when their own rights were challenged.[26]

Throughout the Southern campaign, Madison's attention drifted to his native land. In his first known statement on slavery, Madison criticized Virginia's proposal to enlist soldiers by paying them in slaves, asking, "Would it not be just as well to liberate and make soldiers at once of the blacks themselves as to make them instruments for enlisting white soldiers? It would certainly be more consonant to the principles of liberty which ought never to be lost sight of in a contest for liberty."[27] Madison's idea went nowhere; it would still prove controversial nearly a century later when blacks were mustered to fight in the Civil War.

On New Year's Day, 1781, Washington was instructed by Congress to distribute his forces to defend against the Southern invasion.[28] The same day, American soldiers mutinied in Morristown, Pennsylvania, killing two of their own officers. They were starving, inadequately clothed, and unpaid and had been forcibly kept beyond their enlistment.

Madison received frightening news from Virginia. Jefferson informed the delegates in Philadelphia that the British had burned five tons of gunpowder. Virginia had already sent gunpowder south; stores were getting perilously low.[29] The government fled Richmond, barely before the traitor Arnold marched in with fifteen hundred men, destroying the public buildings of the city as well as foundries for producing arms, munitions, and rum.[30] Virginia was in a state of terror. No one knew when the British would strike, or where, or what their objectives were. Nor could Virginians always tell friend from enemy. A traitorous state militia colonel was caught just in time to prevent him from delivering his thousand men to the British.[31]

On January 2, 1781, the Virginia legislature had voted to maintain the American states' rights to the Mississippi.[32] But in desperation Congress voted to revise Jay's instructions. He could now cede the Mississippi below the thirty-first degree of northern latitude (just north of New Orleans, the area controlled by Spain), but only at the insistence of Spain, and only if Spain would grant permission for navigation above that latitude. Jay was further instructed to get a free port below the thirty-first from which Americans could ship goods into the Gulf of Mexico.[33]

On February 3, Madison introduced a measure to create an impost, a tax on imports, which would require the unanimous consent of every state legislature. He argued that it was "indispensably necessary to the support of public credit and the prosecution of the war." The measure, which would take effect on May 1, would assess a tax of 5 percent of the value of all items imported into the states. Congress would be empowered to collect and appropriate the impost.[34] If Madison's tax passed in the states, the revenue would come not a moment too soon. Britain, Congress learned, was planning to borrow sixteen million pounds sterling and deploy ninety-two thousand marines to finish the war.

In March of 1781 the Articles of Confederation, first recommended to the states in 1777, were finally ratified by all thirteen states. Maryland, the last holdout, had participated in the Continental Congress but had waited to ratify. The urgency of war pushed them toward formal ratification. The Continental Congress was now the Congress of the Confederation. As the former had already adhered to the rules proposed in the Articles, nothing would change. Meet the new government: same as the old government.

Samuel Huntingdon of Connecticut was the president of Congress when the Articles were ratified and remained in that position for nearly four more months. But the president of Congress had less power than the average colonial Speaker of the House. In July, Thomas McKean became the first president elected after the Articles went into effect. McKean would soon resign to resume a much more important position: associate justice of the Pennsylvania Supreme Court.

On March 13, 1781, twelve days after Maryland's ratification, Madison introduced a radical amendment to the Articles. Madison's amendment would have required states that ignored their federal responsibilities or refused to be bound by decisions of Congress to be compelled to do so by use of the army or navy or by the seizure of exported goods. Noncompliant states would also be subject to trade sanctions.[35] The entire war effort had been jeopardized by states refusing to pay their share. "Without such powers," Madison wrote Jefferson, "the whole confederacy may be insulted and the most salutary measures frustrated by the most inconsiderable state in the union."[36] However necessary, this measure would get nowhere with the states.

French ships and guns headed to reinforce Virginia. They would carry twelve thousand troops to join another twelve thousand under the command of Lafayette.[37] All sides, it seemed, were converging on the birthplace of British America for the final act of the war.

In April, Jefferson wrote the Virginia delegation in Congress that at least four thousand British soldiers were at Portsmouth. The war in Virginia, he noted, had put a complete stop to any sort of commercial activity.[38] Supplies were desperately needed: "It is impossible to give you an idea of the distress we are in for want of lead. Should this army from Portsmouth come forth and become active (and as we have no reason to believe they came here to sleep) our affairs will assume a very disagreeable aspect."

Meanwhile, Massachusetts had rejected Madison's 5 percent impost on the ground that it was too high. Madison sat on a committee to hear their petition.[39] When the hostilities had been confined to Massachusetts, that state had eagerly accepted the assistance of the others. Now that the focus of the war had shifted to other states, funding the effort had ceased to be a priority in Massachusetts.

On April 28, the British troops took the city of Williamsburg.[40] On May 14, Jefferson informed his delegates to Congress that the Virginia assembly had fled from Richmond to Charlottesville. As spring turned to summer, the latest in a list of shifting Virginia capitals fell to the British.

On June 4, Jack Jouett arrived in Charlottesville after riding through the night with an urgent message for Governor Jefferson. He had spotted the British forty miles away—and closing in. Jefferson and all but the lieutenant governor and seven legislators escaped just in time, avoiding a tremendous setback for the defense of Virginia. Richard Henry Lee, Speaker of the House, described the situation: "Without either executive or legislative authority," he wrote, "everything in the greatest possible confusion. . . ."[41]

And the push into Virginia continued. Six thousand British soldiers were serving under Cornwallis and Arnold. But Lafayette's army was in Orange and Culpeper counties, waiting to link up with General Wayne. When their joint forces marched toward the British lines, Cornwallis fell back to Williamsburg.

Madison was disgusted with the conduct of the British. "Every outrage which humanity could suffer has been committed by them," he wrote a friend. "Desolation rather than conquest seems to have been their object. They have acted more like desperate bands of robbers or buccaneers than like a nation making war for dominion." British soldiers had committed "rapes, murders, and the whole catalogue of individual cruelties." Madison considered this "a daily lesson to the people of the United States of the necessity of perseverance in the contest."[42]

The Virginia legislature managed to reassemble in Staunton and elected Thomas Nelson as governor to replace Jefferson, whose term had expired during the legislature's relocation. On August 1, Madison shipped a barrel of sugar and a bag of coffee to his father, and a number of books to his sister "Miss Fanny." He had been gone from Virginia for over a year now and certainly must have been concerned for them. Perhaps this small gesture would provide them some comfort in a time of troubles.

On August 3, Governor Nelson notified the congressional delegation that the enemy had landed on the York and Gloucester shores. The two towns border the York River close to where it meets Chesapeake Bay, Gloucester on the north side of the river and York on the south side. The British had dug in and begun to build fortifications. It was here that they would make their stand.

On September 4, Madison and the members of Congress reviewed French troops in the command of Generals Washington and Rochambeau as they marched past the Pennsylvania State House on their way to Virginia. British Admiral Hood sailed with thirteen ships from the West Indies to New York, which was still held by the British, joined up with eight other ships there, and put out to sea again. Madison noted somberly that "there is little doubt that this activity is directed against the mediated junction."[43] Events were coming quickly to a head.

The French admiral, Comte de Grasse, signaled his intention to take his fleet to the Chesapeake Bay. Throughout the war, the British had used their naval superiority to devastating effect. They had blocked trade, captured ships, and easily moved their forces from one part of the continent to the other, while the Americans were run ragged following them on foot. But now the French navy had leveled the playing field. And with a British encampment divided by a river and facing the bay on the east, the maritime aspect of this final showdown would be crucial.

Spain, meanwhile, used the opportunity of the pending battle in Virginia to attack British possessions—in Gibraltar and Minorca. Madison was livid, and more determined than ever not to retreat from the Mississippi. "Yet we are to reward her with a cession of what constitutes the finest part of America," he argued sarcastically.[44]

As chairman of the Committee on Retaliation, Madison devised a solution to end the atrocities against civilians. The committee produced a resolution that British officers held as prisoners of war would answer with their lives. The Department of War was ordered to put to death as many officers as they judged necessary "on the first authentic notice of the burning of any town or village."[45]

Monroe made one final attempt to rejoin the war. He wanted to serve in Virginia's militia, in order to "play a small part in bringing about the event we all so anxiously wish for." Governor Nelson, however, told him that the militia was fully officered.

With the invasion of Virginia came the closure of the courts and the cessation of all legal proceedings. Monroe, it seemed, could be neither a warrior nor a lawyer. His fallback plan was to sail aboard a vessel leaving November 10 or 12, headed for France—to continue his education in Europe. He asked Jefferson for letters of introduction to Franklin, Adams, and Jay, serving as ministers in Europe. He also asked for advice about where to live. Since leaving Richmond at the time of the British invasion of that city, Monroe had led "a very sedentary life upon a small estate I have in King George," reading every single book recommended him by Jefferson.

While in Europe, Monroe hoped to acquire a broad education in the liberal arts, not just the law: "This if not profitable will be agreeable for surely these acquirements qualify a man not only for public office," but also give him the opportunity to entertain himself[46]—as when he had spent the horrific winter at Valley Forge reading poetry.

Jefferson was happy to make the introductions. He also encouraged Monroe to learn as many things as he could while abroad: "They may be of use to you when you shall become a parliamentary man, which for my country and not for your sake, I shall wish to see you." In this exchange, Monroe and Jefferson shared their optimism about the coming fight at York Town.

On October 5, Virginia's Governor Nelson wrote his delegates in Congress from the "Camp before York." On the north side of the river, at Gloucester, the British troops under Banastre Tarleton were attacked, and Tarleton himself was dismounted and wounded. A major was killed, along with fifty other men.[47] And on the south side of the river, near the town of York, on October 19, the battle of York Town commenced.

The following day, the governor sent the Virginia delegates in Congress the best news in memory. "It is with infinite pleasure I congratulate you on the reduction of York and Gloucester, and the capture of the whole British army under Cornwallis.... This blow, I think, must be a decisive one, it being out of the power of G.B. to replace such a number of good troops."[48]

The normally reserved Madison was ecstatic. "If these severe doses of ill fortune do not cool the frenzy and relax the pride of Britain, it would seem as if heaven had in reality abandoned her to her folly and her fate."[49]

Cornwallis, feigning sickness, had his subordinate, General Charles O'Hara, lead the defeated party in surrender. The English incredulously approached the victors, their "slow and solemn" steps accompanied by a tune that tradition holds to be "The World Turned Upside Down." There could not have been a more fitting soundtrack.

O'Hara apologized for Cornwallis's absence to General Washington, who politely directed him to his own subordinate, General Benjamin Lincoln, for further instructions. And the British soldiers laid down their arms, purportedly to the steady, martial drumbeat and the fife playing a song that captured the feelings of everyone on that great field of battle.

If buttercups buzzed after the bee,
If boats were on land, churches on sea,
If ponies rode men and if grass ate the cows,
And cats should be chased into holes by the mouse;
If the mammas sold their babies
To the gypsies for half a crown;
If summer were spring and the other way round,
Then all the world would be upside down.[50]

Chapter Four

THE IN-BETWEEN DAYS

"Is it to be peace or war?"
—Jacquelin Ambler

In the telling, the story of how the Americans won their independence seems to end on the fields of York Town. But the period from York Town to the official peace was longer than two years. Washington's astounding victory brought on a stalemate, not peace.

During that stalemate, the fatal weaknesses of the Continental government under the Articles of Confederation were laid bare. Congress had responsibility, but no authority. It could not force the states to pay requisitions, so it could not meet the country's needs, much less pay down its debts. This period would see Congress unable to enforce its own rules for membership—and federal foreign policy frustrated by the sheriff of Chester County, Pennsylvania. It would also see Congress itself flee Philadelphia to escape from a mob of soldiers demanding their back pay. The issues that emerged in this strange and disjointed period of stalemate would eventually forge a political alliance between Madison and Monroe, then break that alliance, and ultimately shape the U.S. Constitution and Bill of Rights.

York Town did prove fatal to further military conquests by the British and signal the end of major fighting. But there were significant issues to be resolved. The British were still firmly in control of significant parts of the country, including the cities of Charleston and New York. Washington had planned on retaking these cities by siege. But the departure of the French navy, which had been instrumental at York Town, frustrated that ambition, even if the unstable American government could have financed such an effort. It was as though two boxers in a ring suddenly lost the ability to strike each other. James Monroe's political career would commence in these in-between days, with America suspended between war and peace. James Madison, in Congress, would spend this time in increasingly futile efforts to make the government under the Articles of Confederation adequate to the needs of an independent country.

Edmund Pendleton, the Virginia elder statesman Madison frequently corresponded with while in Congress, wrote him with the results of the legislative elections back home. There would be many "new members, amongst others are Monroe and John Mercer, formerly officers, since fellow students in the law and said to be clever."[1]

The twenty-four-year-old Monroe would represent King George County in the upcoming 1782 session of the House of Delegates. He had used General Washington's strong letter of recommendation, which had failed to get him a command in the Virginia military, in his first campaign for office. Monroe wrote Washington his thanks: "The introduction you gave me some time since to this state for the purpose of attaining some military appointment to place me in the service of my country...although it failed in that instance has availed me in another line."[2] There is no telling whether Washington approved of Monroe's repurposing his letter, or if he raised an eyebrow at his own unwitting endorsement of Monroe's bid for office.

In Richmond, Monroe avoided the temptations that might be pitfalls to a young legislator. He rented a house with a friend and ventured to town only when business required, otherwise spending his time buried in books.[3] Monroe's remarkable war record, his successful study of the law under Jefferson, and the words of praise from Washington had been sufficient to initiate his service in government. His plans to visit Europe had fallen through again when the ship he had planned to travel on cancelled the journey, but a voyage of a different sort had commenced with high tides and fair winds.

As Monroe's political career was just beginning in Richmond, Madison was still struggling with the recalcitrant Mississippi problem in Congress. Madison chaired a committee that authored a report on Jay's negotiations with Spain. The Spanish had been warned in September of 1781 that if they waited until the "vicissitudes, dangers, and difficulties of a distressing war" has passed, America would never relinquish its claims to the Mississippi.[4] "The surrender of the navigation of the Mississippi was meant as the price of the advantages promised by an early and intimate alliance with the Spanish monarchy."[5] It was unthinkable to Madison that the Mississippi should be ceded to Spain now.

The government's system of finance was still an absolute wreck, with nobody even certain how bad things were. As a first step toward making sense of the mess, Madison successfully passed a motion ordering the Superintendent of Finance to determine the debts owed by the United States and to report to Congress every six months on money borrowed and bills of credit issued during that period.[6] Madison also passed a resolution charging the Superintendent to send the state legislatures "a representation of the alarming prospects which their neglect to comply with the…requisitions of Congress has produced." As of May 20, the states had contributed $5,500 dollars in 1782, one-fourth of what was necessary to fund government operations for a single day.[7] Congress sent delegations to personally lobby legislatures for funding.[8]

Madison also presented a motion asking states to send their representatives: "Business of the greatest consequence is often delayed or retarded for want of sufficient representation in Congress."[9]

He had been away from home for over two years. "It has at no time been more difficult for me to fix my probable return to Virginia," Madison wrote his father. "Anxious as I am to visit my friends, as long as I sustain a public trust, I shall feel a principle which is superior to it."[10] The times were filled with rumors of more war. Thirty British ships arrived in New York, their purpose unknown.

Though there was not yet peace, life in various quarters of America began to return to normal. Assisting in Virginia's post-war transition was James Monroe who, after a short time in the legislature, was appointed to the Council of State in June of 1782. He would again credit Washington's letter of recommendation for his appointment. Because the beloved general thought highly of him, others were predisposed to do so as well.

One of the great difficulties faced by states in 1782 was the need to maintain soldiers in readiness in case peace negotiations failed. The Commissioner of War for Virginia requested two hundred men from the Montgomery and Washington County Militia. The Council also authorized the sale of all public bacon, though the proceeds would still not provide enough for the state's soldiers to eat.[11] The state's lead mines, which had been torn apart to rush materials to the munitions factories, would soon be unusable unless repaired.[12]

Virginians were terrified that war might be renewed, and many felt their state would again be the central theatre of action. Governor Benjamin Harrison[13] wanted to be able to call on four thousand soldiers at a moment's notice and needed support for the troops stationed at York Town.

Ordinary matters of businesses also needed tending to. As the legislature returned to business as usual, clemency was recommended for soldiers accused of manslaughter, as well as for a twelve-year-old boy convicted of grand larceny. The Council and governor also oversaw the issuing of professional licenses. Ironically, one of the first items of business before the Council after Monroe joined it was a recommendation that the governor grant him a law license, in light of his successful examinations.[14]

Despite his success in politics, Monroe was still agitating for adventure. He began a correspondence with George Rogers Clark, commander of the Virginia forces in the Northwest Territory who had routed the British in the West during the revolution. "[I] have some thoughts of turning my attention toward your quarter and perhaps sometime hence removing there myself," Monroe wrote.[15] As a veteran, he was entitled to a certain acreage of the Western lands.

In the meantime, Monroe and the Council agreed to send 150 soldiers with ten days' provisions to Fort Pitt after receiving a letter from Congress with intelligence that the fort was about to be attacked and would be lost unless immediately reinforced.[16] The fort was reinforced, a British spy witnessed its reinforcement, and the attack was called off.[17] Instead the British turned to Hanna's Town, which they completely leveled.[18] The governor and Council also handled relations with Indian tribes and granted the Catawba Nation food, clothing, and gunpowder after receiving their delegation.[19] Money was authorized for treaties with other Indian tribes as well.[20]

Like the rest of America, the Council was looking for propitious signs from the other side of the Atlantic. They scoured the king's speech to the mayor of London for clues to the intentions of the British government. Monroe had not given up on his dream of traveling to Europe. He fancied the idea of employment with the American delegation there after the peace, perhaps as an aide to Jefferson, who would likely be one of the new ambassadors.

As Monroe was feeling his way, trying to chart a successful course in public life, he wrote to Jefferson seeking his advice "upon every subject of consequence."[21] He also wrote his friend John Mercer who had entered the legislature with him and was now serving in Congress: "You are young and reputation is only to be acquired by filling with ability those offices in which the public place you." He mentioned one of Mercer's colleagues, a man they both saw as a role model. "Mr. Madison I think hath acquired...reputation by a constant and laborious attendance upon Congress."

Monroe had already begun to learn some of the hard lessons of politics. He continued in his letter to Mercer, "I must here observe that political connections are but slender ties between men, that they commence mutually in a respect for talents and the opinion of the public...that these connections will rather be strengthened than weakened by the same cause. It is not to these connections that we are to look for the good offices of friendship: in an intercourse with the world the heart is steeled with insensibility...those who had been educated together have a different kind of tie and more natural claim to the good offices of each other and with but few here have you or myself connections of this kind."[22]

Meanwhile in Philadelphia, Madison was attempting to organize the dysfunctional federal government. He and John Witherspoon, his college president now serving alongside him in Congress, worked to establish five committees of five members each to oversee finance, foreign affairs, war, marine, and post office departments.[23] With his proposed impost still not passed by the states, Madison moved successfully to instruct John Adams to procure a loan in Europe. Adams was ultimately able to obtain one from the Dutch for five million guilders at 5 percent interest.[24]

The difficulties of trans-Atlantic travel meant at least a two-month delay learning about developments in Europe. British negotiator Henry Grenville had arrived in Paris authorized to treat with all belligerents. It was rumored that the king would agree to independence, but nobody could be certain.

The British abandoned Savannah. It was believed they would leave Charleston next.[25]

And the civic institutions of the new republic began to take shape. Madison continued to develop as a statesman. He learned of *Commonwealth v. Canton*, a court case in Virginia that posed a unique question:

Did a state court have the power to invalidate an act it judged to be unconstitutional? The House of Delegates had attempted to issue a pardon for three prisoners, but the Virginia Senate had not concurred. The prisoners claimed that the House had given them their freedom. The Court of Appeals, including Judges George Wythe and Edmund Pendleton, determined that it could, in fact, reverse the action of the House of Delegates as unconstitutional—setting a legal precedent that would be crucial for the future of constitutional government in America.[26]

Congress's financial state worsened, and the Rhode Island legislature adjourned without even considering the impost proposed by Madison and recommended by Congress. In response, Congress sent a delegation to try and reason with them. The Rhode Island representatives responded to Congress with a list of objections. They claimed that the tax would weigh hardest on commercial states, that the tax collectors would be employees of the federal government unaccountable to Rhode Island, and that the tax itself would represent a "danger to public liberty" from the power of the federal government.[27]

So long as Rhode Island took this position, the unanimous consent required to amend the Articles would never be attained. A state with a population of barely fifty thousand would have veto power over the affairs of a continent of nearly 2.4 million people.[28] The possibility that the states would support the federal government with requisitions was nil. Pennsylvania was insisting that its requisitions be directed toward Pennsylvania creditors of the national government.

In November of 1782, a letter appeared in the *Boston Gazette* revealing the secret loan obtained by Adams in Europe.[29] This leak sealed the fate of the impost. Congress was relying on the dire financial situation to walk the impost over the finish line in Rhode Island and Georgia. The revelation of the foreign loans completely undercut the urgency of the moment. According to the *Gazette*, the sender of the letter was a resident of Providence. The congressional delegation from Rhode Island fell under immediate suspicion.

Madison was assigned to the committee that investigated the matter. They instructed the Secretary of Foreign Affairs to write the Governor of Rhode Island to inquire into the source of the leak. The investigation was cut short, however, when Congressman David Howell confessed on the floor of the Congress. Howell offered a vigorous defense, claiming that his duty was to Rhode Island alone and that the investigation and this debate were improper. His colleagues were outraged. Those that did not abuse him or challenge him to duels froze him out. His situation was untenable, and Howell returned for a time to Rhode Island.

If one man became the personification of the weakness of Congress, it was David Howell. Later, when he had reached the three-year term limit imposed by the Articles of Confederation, Howell nevertheless sought and won reelection. (Rhode Island, always charting its own course, chose its members of Congress by election of the people, not of the legislature.) Congress once again held a debate on the subject of David Howell. The issue seemed straightforward; the Articles limited members' terms of service to three years within a six-year period. Since all agreed Howell had exceeded the term limit, he was asked to leave.

Howell not only refused. He became a cause célèbre among opponents of the Confederation throughout the states. With no authority to remove him, Congress had simply embarrassed itself.

The Howell affair was emblematic of the sorry state of American affairs in 1782. France and the United States were finding it increasingly difficult to negotiate as one. Madison noted the truism: "The closest friends on a rupture are apt to become the bitterest foes."[30]

While Madison watched the impost sink, the debts of the United States, estimated to be about $40 million, continued to mount.[31] At the beginning of 1783, two representatives of the army, Ogden and Brooks, came to Congress to try to settle arrears in pay. Ogden and Brooks had come to ensure that with the prospect of peace their concerns and those of their fellow soldiers would still be addressed. Congress first responded by asking what would happen in the event no pay could be advanced. That wasn't the message Ogden and Brooks were hoping to take back to their battle-hardened, hungry, and apparently forgotten comrades.[32] Instead of holding back wages, Congress ordered the Superintendent of Finance to pay the army as soon as possible and then asked the states to turn in their arrearages from August 1780 onward.[33] The Articles had given Congress complete accountability without the power to fulfill its monumental responsibilities.

As the war continued to wind down, George Washington issued a passport to British officials to bring supplies to their prisoners of war held in Pennsylvania, Maryland, and Virginia. The shipment landed at Wilmington, Delaware, and all went as planned until an unfortunate encounter with the sheriff's department of Chester County, Pennsylvania. The sheriffs ignored Washington's passport and impounded the wagons. Their ostensible excuse was that the British were planning to sell the goods illegally, rather than use them to aid their starving soldiers in American custody. A committee with Madison at the helm was established to look into the affair. The members of the committee concluded that the only option was to repay the British out of the common treasury. So weak was our national government at the time that it could be thwarted by the greedy sheriff of Chester, Pennsylvania.[34]

Virginia, having previously passed the impost bill, suddenly repealed it—costing Madison the high ground in Congress. If the crisis in government finances persisted, he feared that "the foundations of our independence will be laid in injustice and dishonor," resting as they did upon the backs of unpaid soldiers and other patriots.[35] Madison considered other ways to raise the money. A poll tax—a per-person assessment—was forbidden by the Maryland Constitution, and therefore that state legislature could never agree to it. The $40 million dollar debt continued to mount at 6 percent interest. The interest payments alone were $2.4 million each year.[36]

Concern that the British might decide to renew the war persisted, and Madison calculated that America would need at least $600,000 to mount any kind of defense. Coupled with the interest on the debt, this made revenue of at least $3 million absolutely necessary.

Madison considered a number of solutions, including a half dollar tax on a barrel of salt, which was consumed in small amounts by many and "in great quantities by none." He estimated the salt tax would yield $1 million annually. Another possible source of revenue was a land tax of one dollar per hundred acres, which would bring in $500,000 or perhaps even $1 million. An impost would bring in $500,000, but in the event of peace with Britain, that number could climb to $3 million.

Madison rejected the idea that states already collecting the impost should have their requisitions reduced accordingly. The states were divided between those supplied by ships and those supplied by land because they lacked deep harbors. Since the impost tax would be passed on to consumers, it would be manifestly unjust to credit the amount collected back to, for example, South Carolina, which received goods into its ports and then exported them to North Carolina, where the citizens would actually foot the bill.[37]

Complicating the debate in Congress were the instructions by which various state legislatures had bound their delegations. Delegates in Congress were employees of the state legislatures. In almost every case they were chosen by the legislatures, and they were even paid out of state treasuries. When the state legislatures gave instructions, their delegates in Congress could do no other. Delegates to Congress could be recalled by the states at any time and for any reason, and they needed to be reappointed by the legislatures every year.

After Congress spent a week in February debating the subject of revenue, Madison felt that "we seem only to have gone round in a circle to the point at which we set out...the only point on which Congress are generally agreed is that something ought to be attempted, but what that something ought to be, is a theorem not solved alike by scarcely any two members."[38] Madison told his family that Congress was just as uncertain as they were about the future of the country: "Every day almost brings forth some fresh rumor."[39]

Congress decided to commit the revenue issue to a committee of five, including Madison and Alexander Hamilton. The committee proposed a 5 percent tax on imports, a 5 percent tax on goods condemned in a court of admiralty (when an individual captured a British ship but then had to bring the cargo to court to gain proper title), and various taxes on salt, wine, sugar, brandy, rum, and tea. The money would be earmarked specifically for the interest and principal on the debt, and the taxes would last for only twenty-five years. To address state concerns about collection, the report included a significant compromise. States could choose the collectors of the impost, who would be removable by Congress. If states attempted to stonewall by not choosing anyone, Congress would have the right to choose instead.

On March 12, Captain Joshua Barney arrived in Philadelphia, having sailed from France on the ship *General Washington.* He carried a short letter from Benjamin Franklin indicating that preliminary articles of peace had been signed and would go into effect once France and Britain had concluded terms.[40]

The articles of peace themselves came a month later.[41] Independence was recognized, and all British claims to the territory of the thirteen states relinquished. Seizures of American vessels would come to an end, and both sides would enjoy reciprocal trade. British forts would be handed over, Americans would have free access to the Atlantic, and there would be a mutual amnesty. British citizens would have their property returned and their pre-war debts honored.[42]

Madison must have wondered whether, if the British knew what he knew, they would have agreed to terms so generous. In March of 1782, Washington sent Congress two anonymous fliers that were circulating through the military. One such exhortation called for soldiers to "assemble for the purposes of seeking by other means, that justice which their country showed no disposition to afford them." The business community, it appeared, was fanning the flames among the army, hoping to incite violence that might result in repayment of commercial creditors.[43]

In a Virginia Council of State meeting on April 19, Governor Harrison announced that "a general peace has taken place between the belligerent powers." The Council ordered the soldiers to be dismissed, their guns to be collected, and the paymaster to compensate them.[44] Monroe could not have helped but consider all that he had seen and done leading up to this happy result.

Matters in Congress were in disarray, but Madison's personal affairs were taking on a new, more favorable aspect. William Floyd, a congressman from New York and a signer of the Declaration of Independence, boarded with his family at the Trists' house along with Madison. His daughter Catherine, or Kitty, was nearing the age of sixteen, when she would be presented to society and eligible for marriage.[45]

Before negotiations had been concluded in Europe, it had been proposed to send Jefferson to join the delegation there. Jefferson had traveled to Philadelphia to be ready in case the appointment, which seemed all but certain, came. There he joined his friend Madison in the Trist boarding house.

The Floyds, Jefferson, Madison, and the other boarders considered themselves "family," enjoying evenings together filled with interesting conversation and laughter.[46] Kitty, though young, was well educated, a woman of "more than usual beauty and of irrepressible vivacity."[47] The charming young woman had an unprecedented effect upon the notoriously stiff and serious Madison, and he had—for the first time in his life—an interest that could compete with his important public duties.

Madison was in love with Kitty Floyd, and it seemed to all their friends that the object of his affection loved him in return. Jefferson certainly believed this to be the case and was eager to facilitate the match, which, as he wrote to Madison later, would "give me a neighbor whose worth I rate high" and "render you happier than you can possibly be in a single state."[48]

Jefferson raised the issue with Kitty and informed Madison that he "was able to convince [himself] that she possessed every sentiment in your favor which you could wish." And when peace eliminated the need for Jefferson in Europe and he returned to Virginia, he asked Madison to pay his compliments to "Miss Kitty particularly."[49] Madison was pleased to inform his friend, "Your inference on that subject was not groundless. Before you left us, I had sufficiently ascertained her sentiments. Since your departure the affair has been pursued. Most preliminary arrangements although definitive will be postponed until the end of the year in Congress. At some period of the interval I shall probably make a visit to Virginia." Jefferson was thrilled at the news of his friend's engagement.

At some point, the two lovers walked down the streets of Philadelphia to the studio of artist Charles Willson Peale. He painted miniature portraits, and each was sealed with a lock of the other's hair. Madison and Kitty exchanged them to be reminders of each other when they were apart.

Madison must have believed that things could only get better. He was at the height of his influence in Congress. He received his first letter from Washington, recommending one of his majors for an appointment to the delegation at London or Versailles. Addressed to Madison and only one other member of Congress, this letter from the commander in chief is a mark of the recipient's excellent reputation.[50]

A committee that Madison chaired and Hamilton also served on published an "Address to the States" detailing the scope of the debt and the increasing interest and demonstrating what revenue could be expected from approval of the impost. This appeal ended with the encouragement that the money would go to a good cause: it would repay France (which had made the victory possible), individuals in other countries who had believed in the United States, soldiers who had risked their lives, and American patriots who had put their private credit at the service of their country.[51]

On April 25, Madison cheerfully recorded in his notes on the proceedings of Congress, "The writer of these notes absent till Monday, May 5."[52] Madison was traveling with William Floyd and his daughters to New Brunswick, New Jersey. The spring weather would have made it a beautiful journey for Madison and his future family. As they passed the town of Princeton, perhaps Madison showed Kitty where he had gone to college and, like a good alumnus, discussed their children following in his footsteps. The girls likely stayed with family in New Brunswick. William Floyd went on to New York to see if he could get access to his estate on Long Island, which had been held by the British since the first days of the war.[53] On May 2, Madison headed back to Philadelphia to attend to business and await word from his bride-to-be.[54]

Public matters were not going as swimmingly as Madison's private affairs. A regiment of one hundred men under the command of Colonel George Baylor mutinied and marched from South Carolina to their home state of Virginia to obtain redress for their grievances. Governor Harrison wrote the delegates in Congress, "They really are a band of heroes, who have performed a great and meritorious service, and I am satisfied would not have taken this rash step if their sufferings had not been very great."[55]

Madison was encouraged by friends in Virginia to continue his service in Congress. He politely declined. "Staying in Congress does not coincide with my plans following November," he wrote.[56] Madison had now been working for three years on the business of his country. The Articles of Confederation limited terms in Congress to three years of service out of any six-year period. Still, the Articles had not been ratified by all states until March of 1781. Congress had conducted itself as though bound by them prior to that date, yet there was legitimate disagreement about when the term limits had officially gone into effect. But having left so much undone in Congress, and aware of the indispensible role he played there, Madison would likely not have stepped down had he not believed himself to be term-limited from continuing to serve.

On June 7, 1783, James Monroe was selected by the legislature to replace James Madison in Congress.[57] For a one-year term (not to begin until the fall) Monroe would join his uncle Joseph Jones, his mentor Thomas Jefferson, and his best friend John Mercer in the Virginia delegation.[58] A more exciting entrée to national politics was scarcely imaginable for the twenty-five-year-old veteran. Monroe's career was following the same path as Madison's: service in the House of Delegates, on the Council of State, and in Congress.

Meanwhile, on June 19, unrest in the army boiled over when eighty soldiers entered the city of Philadelphia, captured the arsenal, and surrounded the Pennsylvania State House, pointing their muskets menacingly in the windows of Congress. Inside, the members frantically discussed what should be done while outside the soldiers drank heavily and cursed loudly.[59] There was some concern that the soldiers might kidnap and ransom members of Congress or loot the national bank. Members who dared to step outside were confronted by the angry soldiers.[60]

State governments were little help. The executive of Pennsylvania refused to provide assistance or call the militia for Congress's protection. For their own safety, members of Congress fled to Princeton like common deadbeats. After this shameful incident, Washington wrote a letter to the executive of each state begging for some kind of action to provide justice for his men. But even in Virginia the legislature adjourned without taking action on his request.

While Pennsylvania was offering Congress little support, Virginia had been hard at work on a proposal to make Williamsburg the national capital. The Virginia legislature offered $100,000 to build thirteen hotels, a presidential palace, the capitol, and all the public buildings. In Williamsburg, or anywhere along the Potomac River, Virginia would cede five miles square to the national government.[61] Their first proposal had been made earlier, on April 10. Along with Maryland, they offered to cede a "small tract of territory...in the neighborhood of George Town on Potowmack."[62] Madison believed this was the best course of action, "to unite" with Maryland "in offering a double jurisdiction."

Nearly every Virginian of importance was eager to have the capital, but Pendleton was an exception: "No doubt there are advantages in the great circulation of money wherever Congress sit, yet I am not so old fashioned to think that overbalanced by another thing which circulates with it and need not be named....I doubt if Philadelphia would not have a good bargain to give up all advantages on this head to be restored to the morals her citizens possessed in 1775."[63] In the end, Annapolis, Maryland, was chosen as the next capital of the Confederation.

Madison's thoughts were firmly fixed on the next stage of his life—his marriage, and his return to Virginia. Madison would not join his colleagues in Princeton for the remainder of the session before July 1, and he wrote, "[M]y preparations for leaving Congress will keep me much of the remainder of my time."[64] His near perfect attendance now became a near perfect absence. Madison was always sure, however, to be present when his vote would be decisive.

Ironically, the government of the United States was now housed in Nassau Hall of the College of New Jersey in Princeton, where Madison had lived and learned for three years. Congress met in the very library where Madison had poured himself into his studies. When Madison was in Princeton to attend Congress, he was forced to share a room of ten square feet, with a bed and no desk, with Joseph Jones while his belongings remained in Philadelphia. He began one letter from Princeton, "My situation here for writing is so incommodious, that you must excuse my brevity."[65] The dorms, it seemed, were not now as livable as they seemed when he was "perfectly pleased" with his "three years confinement" as a college student.

On July 28, Madison wrote of "a disappointment in some circumstances which must precede my setting out for Virginia."[66] Kitty, it seemed, had failed to write as expected—or worse yet, had said something in a letter to create uncertainty in the engagement.

But the days during which America was suspended between two possible futures were over, and those days would soon be over for Madison as well.

Chapter Five

THE TEDIOUS SESSIONS

"Of all machines, ours is the most complicated and inexplicable."

—Thomas Jefferson

Kitty's dismissal of Madison came in a letter that was sealed with rye dough.[1] It is thought that Peale's miniature of him, which Kitty had carried with her, was returned at the same time. Another man had taken Madison's place. William Clarkson, a young medical student in Philadelphia, had pursued Kitty in his absence; and an older woman in Trist's boarding house who befriended Kitty encouraged her in the direction of the younger man.[2]

Her father was disappointed to lose such a promising son-in-law, but what was done was done. After his marriage to Kitty, Clarkson became a minister of the Presbyterian Church and died at age forty-nine during the presidency of James Madison. There is nothing to record whether Kitty ever regretted her choice in light of Madison's subsequent career, and her near miss at becoming First Lady of the United States. But the story of her engagement to Madison has been handed down among her descendants to the present day.

On August 11, 1783, Madison wrote Jefferson with the news: "At the date of my letter in April I expected to have had the pleasure by this time of being with you in Virginia. My disappointment has proceeded from several dilatory circumstances on which I had not calculated. One of them was the uncertain state into which the object I was then pursuing had been brought by one of those incidents to which such affairs are liable. The result has rendered the time of my return to Virginia less material, as the necessity of my visiting the state of New Jersey no longer exists. It would be improper by this communication to send particular explanations, and perhaps needless to trouble you with them at any time."

When Madison retrieved this letter from Jefferson a half-century later, he violently blotted out the next passage with ink. What can still be deciphered reads as follows: "An...agst...is in general an impediment...of...to them. Character will &c...which every...the...of being demanded of them. Toward the capricious...for a profession of indifference at what had happened, I...do not...forward and have faith in a day of some more propitious turn of fortune."[3] It is clear from the passage that Madison's dismissal had been most unceremonious.

Jefferson, the young widower who had placed such great hopes in Madison's happiness, was surely disappointed. The act of consoling a friend after a painful breakup is so human, it is hard to imagine these men engaged in that process. But on August 31, Jefferson wrote from Monticello, "I sincerely lament the misadventure which has happened, from whatever cause it may have happened. Should it be final, however, the world still presents the same and many other resources of happiness, and you possess many within yourself. Firmness of mind and unintermitting occupation will not long leave you in pain. No event has been more contrary to my expectations and these were founded on what I thought a good knowledge of the ground, but of all machines ours is the most complicated and inexplicable."[4]

Madison would soon be leaving Congress, headed for an uncertain future.

Monroe, on the other hand, had the entire world before him. He had met with approval for his public service, and he eagerly awaited the beginning of his term in Congress. In August of 1783 he was chosen by two prominent Virginians to arbitrate a dispute over land.[5] Although licensed to practice law, Monroe still needed to be admitted separately to the various courts in the state. On October 4, he wrote, "Tomorrow I shall qualify at the bar of the general court. I do it merely to have the name of a lawyer behind me. And about the 20th of the month shall [set] out for Congress."[6]

Meanwhile Madison was busy attending to loose ends. When he had first come to Philadelphia in March of 1780, he had brought with him a slave named Billey. Billey had for three years lived in a city of free blacks in a state where gradual emancipation was taking place. Madison examined the legal options for setting Billey free, unable to "think of punishing him by transportation merely for coveting that liberty for which we have paid the price of so much blood, and have proclaimed so often to be the right, and worth the pursuit of every human being."[7] Billey and Madison would stay in touch through the years; in a September 6, 1788, letter to his father, Madison indicated that he still knew the whereabouts of his former slave and current friend.

On September 12, Congress in Princeton received the European dispatch dated July 27, reporting that the Treaty of Paris, which would end the war, had still not been officially signed.[8] A final peace would not be ratified during Madison's tenure in Congress. He had spent the course of the war in public life, serving with only one interruption. But final peace would be left for another Congress and another day.

This and other matters would have to be taken up by others. Madison wrote his "Notes on Congress' Place of Residence" for Jefferson, who he hoped would champion the issue of a Virginia location for the capital in the next Congress. Madison's "Notes" compared the Potomac site to its competitors including Kingston, New York, and the falls of the Delaware River.[9] Philadelphia, meanwhile, was willing to do nearly anything to win Congress back. Pennsylvanians now expressed their regret at having failed to protect Congress from the mutineers and considered impeaching the governor to prove that they meant it.

Jefferson traveled to Philadelphia, and left on the road south together with Madison on November 22, 1783. He had written to Monroe that he and Madison would ride together, arriving in Annapolis on the twenty-fourth.[10] They no doubt talked about Madison's broken engagement, as well as about the scientific issues that fascinated them both—Buffon's groundbreaking research on the origins of the universe[11] and questions about the effects of distance from the equator on calculations of the earth's temperature.[12]

Madison probably left Annapolis for Virginia on November 27, while Jefferson stayed to serve in Congress, which was now meeting in Maryland's capital.[13] Madison had been urged by Pendleton, and no doubt others, to run for the Virginia legislature that spring. He could make a contribution on the state level, even on the national issues that had occupied his time in Congress. On his way home to Orange, Madison stopped at George Mason's house to get a sense of Mason's position on the impost and the cessation of Virginia's Western lands to the federal government; he found that his friend was not opposed to either.[14]

While Madison headed south, Monroe was headed north. He arrived in Annapolis before December 6. Monroe wrote, "I am called on a theatre to which I am a perfect stranger. There are before us some questions of the utmost consequence that can arise in the councils of any nation; the peace establishment, the regulation of our commerce, and the arrangement of our foreign appointments. Whether we are to have regular or standing troops to protect our frontier or leave them unguarded."[15]

Delegates of only six states were present on December 11. The definitive treaty of peace with Great Britain had been signed and was transmitted to Congress for ratification. The embarrassment of the Philadelphia mutiny had stoked rumors that Britain would renew the war, a dreadful possibility that now looked less likely.[16]

On December 23, 1783, more than two years after York Town, Washington appeared before the members of Congress who had assembled in the Maryland State House to receive his message.[17]

The room was rapt with attention while Washington spoke. He began, "Mr. President, The great events on which my resignation depended having at length taken place, I have now the honor of offering my sincere congratulations to Congress, and of presenting myself before them, to surrender into their hands the trust committed to me, and to claim the indulgence of retiring from the service of my country."[18] Washington concluded,

> I consider it an indispensible duty to close this last act of my official life by commending the interests of our dearest country to the protection of Almighty God, and those who have the superintendence of them to his holy keeping.
>
> Having now finished the work assigned me, I retire from the great theatre of action, and bidding an affectionate farewell to this august body, under whose orders I have so long acted, I here offer my commission, and take my leave of all the employments of public life.[19]

Monroe recorded the scene in his autobiography, his enthusiasm for the general undiminished by the passing years: "It could not fail to excite the sensibility of Mr. Monroe to reflect that he had served as a lieutenant under him only a few years before."[20] In that room filled with adoration for Washington, Monroe probably wanted to jump from his seat to show everyone just how well he knew the general. As a member of the civil authority, Monroe was now receiving the resignation of the military commander under whom he had once served.

John Marshall may have spoken for everyone when he wrote to Monroe, "At length the military career of the greatest man on earth is closed...when I speak or think of that superior man my full heart overflows with gratitude."[21] Even King George III, when informed that Washington planned to retire, doubted the report and remarked that relinquishing power would make the general "the greatest man in the world."[22]

Meanwhile, Madison was trapped at home at Montpelier, now under a heavy snowfall. He was craving good books to read; he wrote to Jefferson asking him to find him the names of booksellers in London and Paris.[23]

When Jefferson wrote back, he included the news of strange bones discovered in South America and told Madison about a meteorology experiment that he and the Reverend Madison were conducting. The two were recording daily temperature measurements to determine the source of warm weather. Jefferson encouraged Madison to obtain a thermometer so that he could assist in their research.[24]

Ratifying the final peace with Britain would take the votes of nine states. The delegates were panicked; the Treaty of Paris stipulated a March 3 deadline to both ratify and deliver notice of ratification. Serious consideration was given to a ratification vote by fewer states than required, in the hope that no one would notice. Jefferson, fulfilling his duties as a senior statesman, scotched a notion that would have forever cast doubt on the legitimacy of the treaty (and thus the peace). At long last, on January 14, nine state delegations were present in Congress, and the Treaty of Paris was unanimously ratified. It was now too late for notice of ratification to cross the Atlantic by the deadline. Congress had to hope that Britain had lost the appetite for continuing the war.[25]

For James Monroe, the American War of Independence had come full circle. He had participated as a young student in the earliest agitations of the war, been present with Washington in many of the great scenes of battle, and nearly forfeited his life to secure victory at Trenton. He had been at the battles of Brandywine, Germantown, and Monmouth and led men in defense of Virginia. Now he was a member of Congress voting to approve the final peace. The young student who had raided the Governor's Mansion would scarcely have believed that in such a short span of time America would be free—and that he would have a vote on the matter.

Under Jefferson's wing, Monroe attended balls and socialized with the members of Congress and their families, as well as with other dignitaries in Annapolis. What the congressional session itself lacked in educational value, Monroe gained from the social circuit which, under the tutelage of his former law instructor, provided him with perhaps more valuable lessons.

Though Congress must have at times seemed like a series of parties uninterrupted by business, Monroe was continually guided by a seriousness of purpose. He wrote of these days in his memoir, "The theatre on which Mr. Monroe was now placed was a very important one. It was important not only to his fellow citizens, but to the whole civilized world, because the people were called on to make a fair experiment of the practicability of free government and under circumstances more favorable to their success than were ever enjoyed by any other people."[26]

Though the newly independent America was beset with desperate problems, Monroe still believed that his country was the setting in which liberty could best prosper. He brought youthful energy to a Congress exhausted by the insoluble dilemmas of the war years.

And service in Congress gave Monroe something else, too—the opportunity to see his country's political problems from the federal perspective. Jefferson (undoubtedly in reference to Monroe among others) wrote, "I see the best effects produced by sending our young statesmen here. They see the affairs of the Confederacy from a high ground; they learn the importance of the union and befriend federal measures when they return. Those who never come here, see our affairs insulated, pursue a system of jealousy and self interest, and distract the union as much as they can."[27]

In a rare burst of activity, Congress chose John Jay as the Foreign Minister and appointed Jefferson ambassador plenipotentiary to conclude commercial treaties in Europe.[28] Measures were also taken to make peace with the Indian tribes who had sided with the British.

Meanwhile, each state was adopting its own commercial regulations and fighting trade wars with other states. On such a large and bountiful continent, with so many industrious people engaged in so many varied pursuits, the benefits of free trade would have been enormous. But Congress was utterly powerless to prevent the interstate bickering.

Monroe would later write, "These considerations urged Congress to call on the states for an enlargement of the power of the general government to enable it to manage the whole concern, for local as well as the general interest."[29] A committee asked the states to invest Congress with the power to regulate trade for fifteen years. America had become subject to discriminatory trade practices from other countries, especially Britain. European nations knew they could act with impunity because Congress could not retaliate and the states were too fractured to agree upon a common solution. Even if twelve states raised tariffs against Britain, the thirteenth state would reap enormous gains by offering Britain lower rates for imports. As long as Congress lacked the power to establish a rational and unified trade policy, the American people would continue to suffer economically.

Jefferson departed for Europe, and Monroe bid farewell to his mentor. In many ways Jefferson's absence was a good thing for Monroe. He would be forced to step out of his friend's shadow, feel his way around national politics, and stand on his own two feet. Monroe bought the books that Jefferson had brought to Annapolis. But otherwise he had little from the man to guide him. He later wrote to Jefferson, "I very sensibly feel your absence not only in the solitary situation in which you have left me but upon many other accounts."[30]

Jefferson dreamed of retiring in Virginia upon his return, with two of his best friends close to him. Monroe had already been talked into the plan. "What would I not give [if] you could fall in the circle," Jefferson wrote to Madison. "With such a society I could once more venture home and lay myself up for the residue of life, quitting all its contentions which grow daily more and more insupportable." He offered Madison free use of his library at Monticello. Jefferson's collection of books, which was ultimately acquired by the United States to start the Library of Congress, was no small incentive. Jefferson knew well that Madison was a cautious, hesitant man, and he gave him a gentle nudge. "Think of it. To render it practicable only requires you to think it so. Life is of no value but as it brings us gratifications. Among the most valuable of these is rational society. It informs the mind, sweetens the temper, cheers our spirits, and promotes health." Jefferson mentioned a 140-acre farm close to Monticello that was for sale.[31]

But at least in the immediate future, Madison's plans were not for rural retirement. He was seriously considering returning to the legislature, a place he understood with people he knew. Patrick Henry wrote to Madison, encouraging him to end his brief time on the sidelines: "Although…some respite might be demanded for the present, yet I must tell you I think several matters of the greatest moment forbid it. Is not the federal government on a bad footing? If I am not mistaken you must have seen and felt that it is.... How mortifying is it to see a rich harvest of happiness and laborers wanting to gather it in?"[32]

By March Madison had made his decision to serve, and in April of 1784 he was elected to the House of Delegates. He had earned a first-rate reputation during his time in Congress. Seven years after casting him aside for meat and beer, the voters of Orange put Madison back in the Virginia House of Delegates. He arrived in Richmond in the first week of May, as the legislature prepared for the session.

On hand to observe the carnival atmosphere was Johann David Schoepf, a German medical doctor who had come to America in 1777 to serve as physician to the Hessian soldiers. Schoepf was fascinated by the strange new world around him. After the war, he took an extensive journey through the new United States. He would later publish a book, *Travels in the Confederation*, which was widely read throughout Europe.[33] He found Richmond a "town on the hilly banks of the James

River," with "hastily built and unimpressive wooden houses."[34] The capital consisted of 280 houses, he estimated, with two thousand inhabitants.[35] He was fascinated not only by the strange animals and plant life of the Americas, but also by the political culture he found here.

Schoepf's writing shocked European sensibilities and provide a humorous and interesting window into this early American legislature. He painted a picture of an assembly without decorum, people coming and going, talking when others had the floor, bringing up irrelevant issues, dressed as though they were hunting or tobacco farming.

If Madison had read Schoepf's book, he might have said, "Yes, but you should see our Congress."

Schoepf observed,

> Among the orators here is a certain Mr. Henry who appears to have the greatest influence over the House. He has a high-flown and bold delivery, deals more in words than in reasons, and not so long ago was a country schoolmaster. Men of this stamp, either naturally eloquent or become so through their occupation, as e.g. lawyers, invariably take the most active and influential part in these Assemblies; the other members, for the most part farmers without clear and refined ideas, with little education or knowledge of the world, are merely there to give their votes, which are sought, whenever the House is divided into parties, by the insinuations of agreeable manners and in other ways.[36]

Schoepf's observations set forth the difficulties Madison would have in undertaking the serious work to be done.

On May 19, Henry Tazewell introduced in the House seven resolutions, all of which would further the national interest. One of them, for example, would have given the federal government power to regulate the export of goods to countries in the absence of a trade treaty. Tazewell's proposals are believed to have been drawn up by Madison.[37]

Another issue of concern to Madison was the "revision of statutes," first introduced by Jefferson while he served in the House. The laws of

Virginia were a mess—unorganized and badly drafted. Madison supported a wholesale revision to the laws of the state so that they could be easily located, understood, and applied.[38]

On June 4, the clergy of the Episcopal Church petitioned to be established the state religion of Virginia. They asked to be deeded all property previously belonging to the Church of England and requested authority to regulate all spiritual matters within the Commonwealth.[39] The petition was referred to the Committee on Religion, of which Madison was a member. Despite Madison's best efforts, the committee recommended the establishment of the Episcopal Church as the state's official religion, and a bill to that effect was introduced on June 16. The House of Delegates adjourned on June 30 without taking action.

"The friends of the measure did not choose to try their strength in the House," Madison wrote Jefferson. "Extraordinary as such a project was, it was preserved from a dishonorable death by the talents of Mr. Henry. It lies over for another season."[40] Though Henry had urged Madison to serve in the state legislature, the two men would not be allies on the question of religious establishment in Virginia.

Meanwhile in Annapolis, before adjourning until fall, Congress set up a Committee of the States pursuant to Article IX of the Articles of Confederation, with one representative from each state to conduct the affairs of the national government during the interim. Jefferson believed that Monroe would be Virginia's representative on the Committee. "[Monroe] wishes a correspondence with you," he wrote Madison from Paris, "and I suppose his situation will render him a useful one to you. The scrupulousness of his honor will make you safe in the most confidential communications. A better man there cannot be."[41]

As it happened, Monroe's position on the Committee of the States in 1784 did not in fact render him useful to Madison—or to the country at large. The Committee of the States met one day and immediately adjourned until June 26.[42] When they reconvened with barely the numbers needed for a quorum, some members moved to adjourn again. The majority of the Committee, not wishing to abdicate their responsibility, voted adjournment down. Committee members who did want to leave did a simple head count, realized their departure would bring the number below a quorum, and decided to go home.[43] Serious members of the Committee, including Monroe, were absolutely appalled.

Thus during the summer and fall of 1784, the United States had no operative federal government. If the British had renewed hostilities or if the Spanish had declared war over the Mississippi, weeks might have been lost before a common response could be organized.

Both Madison and Monroe used their recess to travel. Monroe would finally see the Western country. He had made plans to travel north through Albany, see the Great Lakes, and return through the Ohio country. Before his new assignment to Europe, Jefferson had planned to be his travel companion.[44] After arriving in New York, Monroe considered traveling to Montreal, Quebec, and perhaps Detroit. He wanted to examine the Western forts that the British had not relinquished. Monroe romanticized travel and could hardly wait to see these new places and the adventure they promised.

"It is possible I may lose my scalp," Monroe wrote in a letter to a friend, "but if a little fighting and a great deal of running will save it, God knows they shall not be wanting and particularly the latter." He even had romantic designs. "[T]he Indian women I am told are handsome and some of their young girls are tall, quiet, majestic, and susceptible of the influence of all powerful love. For that little villain is not contented with giving pain and torturing the feelings of those who live in the civilized world, of being the cause of routs, tumults, quarrels, ill-blood and sometimes the shedding of blood...he ranges also in the desert and wilderness and preys upon the heart of many a portly savage."[45]

If he did meet an Indian woman, Monroe fancied, "if she did love me how could I refuse to kiss her hand, for I believe if any woman in the world gave me convincing proofs I possess her affections she would acquire mine." In the same letter, Monroe asked about the women in

Annapolis. "The ladies have not a greater admirer of their charms than myself."

On his travels from Albany, the romantic Monroe encountered the Vaughan family and was smitten with one of the daughters. The young woman wrote to a friend about her admirer, "Poor Colonel Monroe! The man is in despair; he has written a letter [indicating that] he lost his heart on board the Albany sloop.... I fear his love did not meet with a return.... He is a member of Congress, rich, young, sensible, well read, lively, and handsome." She appealed to the friend for advice: "[H]is being your choice will have great influence upon me, and stop me often when I might be saucily inclined, for at present he is more the object of my diversion than admiration."[46]

By August 19 Monroe had traveled to Schenectady. The British were still firmly in control of their forts. Monroe heard and believed that they were receiving secret orders to maintain their posts in violation of the Treaty of Paris.[47]

In Schenectady, Monroe met a man named Taylor who was a successful trader with the remote Indian tribes. Taylor was taking a party west with him, and Monroe, who found the idea of leaving the beaten path with an experienced guide exciting, joined in the expedition.

The Taylor party, now including Monroe, entered Ontario at Fort Oswego, journeyed along the eastern coast of the lake, and traveled to Fort Niagara, where Monroe received an unusual invitation to dinner.[48] On account of that invitation, Monroe would narrowly escape death a second time.

Colonel Arent DePeyster, the British commander of the Fort, was eager to meet Monroe, the young member of Congress and veteran of the recent war. DePeyster was hospitable, and the two men, meeting to enjoy a hot meal in a heated room, probably discussed their experiences in the war and the interesting state of affairs both in Europe and in America.[49]

During the course of their conversations, DePeyster tried to convince Monroe to change his travel plans. The British governor of Detroit had been embittered by his imprisonment by Governor Jefferson at Williamsburg during the war. DePeyster warned his new Virginian friend that he risked becoming the object of retaliation if he traveled west with the Taylor party.[50]

Monroe, young and headstrong, at first resisted DePeyster's warning. Monroe had fought the British at close quarters and lived to tell about it. He did not want to give up the rest of the journey that he had waited so long to take and was looking forward to so eagerly. But Monroe continued to dine with DePeyster throughout his stay in Niagara, and eventually the colonel was able to convince Monroe to take his advice. He persuaded Monroe to travel by the eastern side of Lake Erie to the Allegheny River and from there to Pittsburgh and safety. DePeyster even sent a detachment of Indians who had come under his influence with Monroe to protect him.[51]

And at the ferry's landing in Pittsburgh, Monroe was greeted with shocking news. Taylor's party had been massacred. They had unknowingly made camp near an Indian village. The party went to sleep in the quiet wilderness of the frontier, but apparently the residents of the village mistook their intentions. During the night, the Indians killed them one after another, leaving only two survivors.[52] The news must have shocked Monroe. The happy group of explorers with whom he had traveled, who had been alive just days ago, were dead. And but for DePeyster's persistent warnings, Monroe would almost certainly have died with them. Once again, a small twist of fate had kept Monroe alive. "This narrow escape from destruction," he later wrote, "forming an interesting incident in Mr. Monroe's life, it is thought not improper to notice it."[53]

Madison had traveled north during the recess, too. In Baltimore, he ran into the Marquis de Lafayette, who wanted him to accompany his party to Fort Stanwix by way of Boston. Stanwix would be the site for a historic treaty with the Indians, and the marquis was eager to be a witness. The staid Madison was not used to being the center of attention, but as members of Lafayette's party, he and his comrades were made much of throughout their travels. Madison sent news articles about their journey to Jefferson in Europe, asking that they be republished in France to show the allies how much Americans valued French support.[54] Lafayette was lionized throughout the states by Americans well aware that independence would never have been won without French help.

The group took a barge up the North River and visited the Oneida Indian nation. At Fort Stanwix Madison learned of Monroe's journeys ahead of him; he wrote Jefferson that "Colonel Monroe had passed Oswego when last heard of and was likely to execute his plan."[55]

The next session of the Confederation Congress met in Trenton on the first day of November, 1784, with Monroe present. His last visit to that town had been in secret, in the early hours of the morning in December of 1776, with the war for independence in the balance. It was here, on the road to Trenton, that Monroe had first cheated death. Arriving in the same town to serve in Congress, he knew there was much to be done before the fruits of the soldiers' and patriots' sacrifices would be secure.

Congress attained a quorum on November 30, and America had a government again five months after the ignoble end of the Committee of the States. Monroe had seen and learned much during the recess. He had viewed the incredible beauty of Niagara Falls but had also observed the dangers under which the new nation was operating. The British were keeping their forts and working closely with the Indians.[56] Their reason, he learned, was that the colonies were out of compliance with the terms of the peace treaty.

The peace had called for Americans to repay the British the debts they had incurred before the war. But the states were not complying. Virginia had passed a law, championed by Patrick Henry, preventing the use of state courts for the collection of debts to the British. Without a national court system, British creditors were without legal recourse.[57] Monroe chaired a committee that examined the issue and condemned the British for violating Article VII of the treaty regarding posts and fortifications.[58]

Monroe and his friend and old fellow student John Mercer had brought new youthful energy to the Virginia delegation in Congress. But they were facing the same intractable problems that Madison had wrestled with for years. From Congress Mercer wrote Madison, who was in Richmond for the fall session of the House of Delegates, "In my judgment, there never was a crisis, threatening an event [outcome] more unfavorable to the happiness of the United States, than the present. Those repellent qualities the seeds of which are abundantly sown in the discordant manners and sentiments of the different states, have produced great heats and animosities in Congress now no longer under the restraint imposed by the war."

Europeans believed that America was "verging fast towards anarchy and confusion," and Americans in Europe were asking whether their country had anything resembling a government at all.[59] Mercer was not finished delivering bad news. Several states had not even considered paying their requisitions for 1784. In other cases, legislatures had taken up the issue only to formally decline to pay. "I believe no other plan, short of divine wisdom, and not protected by the providence of God, would meet the unanimous concurrence of these states... a year's interest will soon be due in Europe... without a shilling to pay."[60]

During Madison's jaunt with Lafayette, the Frenchman had let him know that Spain was determined to deny America the use of the Mississippi.[61] Madison's first initiative during the October session of the House of Delegates was a resolution instructing Virginia's delegation in Congress on the issue. The first part of Madison's proposal had to do with American settlers who were acting lawlessly against the Spanish. Congress, Madison proposed, should pass a law allowing extradition for citizens who committed crimes against other nations, lest they provoke the Spanish into a war.

The second part of Madison's proposal resolved, "It is essential to the prosperity and happiness of the western inhabitants of this Commonwealth, to enjoy the right of navigating the river Mississippi to the sea, and that the delegates representing this state in Congress, ought to be instructed to move that honorable body to give directions... to forward negotiations to obtain that end, without loss of time."[62] Based on these instructions, Monroe, Mercer, and the rest of the congressional delegation passed a resolution appointing a Minister to Spain to ensure the free navigation of the river.

In addition to the problem of the Mississippi, Madison passed some of the very first veterans' legislation introduced in America, awarding a Virginia state pension "to all regular or militia officers and soldiers who have been wounded or otherwise disabled in the service of their country" in an amount deemed appropriate by the governor and Council.[63]

There was serious work to be done, little of which was being addressed either in Congress or in the Virginia legislature. For both Madison and Monroe the vacation was over, and they struggled mightily in their respective roles to take care of their country's business. Madison would refer to this time in the legislature as "the tedious session" on no fewer than three separate occasions.[64] Monroe surely felt the same way about his fruitless session in Congress, a weak and detested body wholly unequal to the great tasks before it.

It was during this time of great frustration that the two statesmen found common cause and a sympathetic ally and friend—in each other.

Chapter Six

MADISON AND MONROE

"I beg of you to write me weekly and give me your opinion upon these and every other subject which you think worthy of my attention."

—James Monroe

"I wish much to throw our correspondence into a more regular course."

—James Madison

By the autumn of 1784, Madison and Monroe had heard of one another often from their many close mutual friends, but they had yet to establish a friendship. Jefferson was an intimate of each man, he was eager to have both relocate near Monticello, and earlier that year he had suggested a confidential correspondence between the two men. Madison was also very close to Monroe's uncle Joseph Jones, with whom he had served in the Convention of 1776 and in Congress, even living with him in the ten-foot-square room in Princeton. Madison had also previously corresponded with John Mercer, Monroe's best friend from college and the war.

Madison and Monroe may even have met the previous June, while they were both members of the "Constitutional Society," the purpose of which was "preserving and handing down to posterity, those pure and sacred principles of liberty...from the happy event of the late glorious revolution...by giving free and frequent information to the mass of people, both of the nature of them, and of the measures which may be adopted by their several component parts."[1]

This illustrious group, which included Madison, Monroe, Edmund Randolph, Joseph Jones, and Patrick Henry, among others, was dedicated to such measures as "the surest mode to secure republican systems of government from lapsing into tyranny." Unfortunately, recorded minutes are extant only from the Constitutional Society's first meeting. If Madison and Monroe did make one another's acquaintance as members of the Constitutional Society, the records of the meeting have been lost.

It wasn't until November 7, 1784, when he was back from his nearly fatal trip west and waiting for Congress to convene in Trenton, New Jersey, that Congressman James Monroe penned his first letter to Delegate James Madison. Seated at his desk, quill in hand and inkwell before him, Monroe could not have known that he was commencing a correspondence that would last for five decades, establish one of the great friendships of his life, and play a role in the founding of the United States under the Constitution.

"Dear Sir," he began, "I enclose you a cipher which will put some cover on our correspondence." By accident or avarice, it was too easy for letters to fall into the wrong hands. Cryptography to allow for communications of a personal or politically sensitive nature was a common practice of the time. The cipher Monroe sent was a separate document containing ninety-nine words, each corresponding to a number. They included "Thomas Jefferson," "John Adams," and the kings of Spain and France, as well as "war," "peace," "defense," "prepare," and "states." Using this code, the two correspondents could communicate freely about the sensitive matters they were addressing in their work. Monroe reported that only five states were present in Congress, a fact which came as absolutely no surprise to Madison.[2]

Before even receiving a reply, Monroe sent a second more detailed letter to Madison. "I beg of you to write me weekly and give me your opinion upon these and every other subject which you think worthy of my attention," he wrote. Monroe, who was twenty-six—seven years Madison's junior—was hoping to learn everything he could from his new friend.

Monroe's second letter told of an incident involving a high-ranking French diplomat peacefully going about his business on a street in Philadelphia. A French citizen, upset with some decision of his government, decided that the best way to express his frustration was to approach the diplomat and punch him in the face. This case of common assault soon became an international affair, with the French demanding custody of the attacker. The offender was punished severely, with a two hundred-dollar fine and a two-year prison sentence, but the French insisted that they should be able to mete out justice themselves. Monroe also shared what he had learned of the western defenses and Indian policy and lamented what had happened to the Committee of the States.[3]

A week after his first letter to Madison, Monroe received a reply expressing regret that the two men had not been able to travel together from New York and congratulating him on surviving his close brush with death and returning unharmed to Trenton. Madison wrote that his own travels "extended neither into the dangers nor gratifications of yours." Monroe received many such letters of congratulation, with one missive declaring that "hereafter you may certainly consider yourself as one of heaven's favorites, for to what else can we impute you being in the land of the living (when all your comrades were lost) but the interposition of providence."[4]

The continuing correspondence between Madison and Monroe was characterized by reports of the latest developments in Congress and in Virginia government. These letters stand as some of the most important accounts of what transpired in the two governmental bodies at the time. In his first letter to Monroe, Madison reported that a statewide tax to fund the teaching of Christianity, known as the general assessment, had been proposed in the House of Delegates.[5] The general assessment and the bill to establish the Episcopal Church as the official church of Virginia would ignite a pivotal debate on the proper relationship between religion and government in the next session of the House.

For all its failings, the federal government under the Articles of Confederation did establish a popular and generally effective postal service. Monroe's second letter from Trenton reached Madison in Richmond in only ten days.[6] Ironically, Madison and Monroe were using the one effective service of the federal government to share their exasperation at that government's many failures.

While waiting for Congress to act on his extradition proposal, Madison created a mirror resolution for Virginia. Madison applauded Monroe's efforts to spearhead the issue on the federal level: "We are every day threatened by the eagerness of our disorderly citizens for Spanish plunder and Spanish blood."[7] Since many of the settlers antagonizing the Spanish were within Virginia's jurisdiction, Madison hoped his bill in the House of Delegates could stave off a conflict. As was characteristic of Madison's time in the Virginia legislature, he was using his position to help strengthen the national interest. The term limits provision of the Articles prevented him from returning to Congress for at least two more years. What would those years bring? The machinery of government under the Articles of Confederation seemed ever more obviously inadequate for the needs of America.

The states, enjoying the blessings of the successful Revolution, were refusing to contribute toward repayment of the soaring national debt and in some cases openly mocking the Congress. Congress, needing unanimous consent of the states to regulate trade, received affirmative votes from only four of the thirteen.[8] States with active trade and manufacturing contingents, such as Massachusetts, were the hardest hit by the disarray in America's commercial affairs. The American negotiators in Europe were having trouble concluding commercial treaties since they lacked authority to bind the states. The British continued oppressive trading measures against America, with heavy taxes and in some cases outright prohibitions on imports from America. Meanwhile, Britain flooded America with inexpensive goods that no American state could tax in return without being undercut by another state.

Connecticut had resorted to the creative measure of voting a 5 percent impost on all goods imported from abroad—or from Rhode Island. The impost would commence when the remaining eleven states adopted the impost recommended by Congress. Perhaps, it was hoped, this measure could prevent Rhode Island from holding out while the other states did not.

In Massachusetts, where the first shots of the revolution had been fired, a second, constitutional revolution was beginning. In 1785, the Massachusetts Assembly became the first state legislature to call for a convention of the states to revise the Articles of Confederation, which they deemed inadequate.[9] This initial state proposal to amend the Articles went nowhere. It was no more significant to the events that followed than the skirmishes at Lexington and Concord were to the Revolutionary War. But a seed had been planted.

A convention of this kind was already being discussed with growing seriousness in Congress. Monroe's friend Mercer wrote to Madison, "For my part I have no hopes but in a convocation of the states." Mercer expected a motion for such a convention to be introduced in the next Congress.[10]

On Christmas Day, 1784, Madison wrote his friend Richard Henry Lee, who had returned that year to Congress. He confessed, "I have not yet found leisure to scan the project of a Continental Convention with so close an eye as to have made up any observations worthy of being mentioned to you. In general I hold it for a maxim that the union of the states is essential to their safety against foreign danger, and internal contention; and that the perpetuity and efficacy of the present system cannot be confided on. The question therefore is, in what mode and at what moment the experiment for supplying the defects ought to be made."

The cautious Madison was slow to warm to the concept of the Constitutional Convention, in connection with which he would ultimately perform the greatest, most enduring acts of his public life. In April of 1783, when Hamilton had made a motion in Congress for a new convention, Madison had done nothing to assist him.[11] At that time Madison still believed that the most serious failings of the Articles of Confederation would be solved if the states would simply pass the impost and expand the trade power. By the dawn of 1785, however, it was obvious that the federal government would have neither one. Mercer, Lee, and others had come to believe that a convention was the last and best hope for America's survival, and Madison was coming to the same conclusion.

Madison's letters to Monroe included matters ceremonial as well as substantive. He wrote one letter to his friend explaining that the legislature of Virginia had recently fêted Lafayette and Washington and voted to create a statue of Washington and a bust of Lafayette. These two works of art, the former of which was sculpted by Jean-Antoine Houdon and boasts an inscription by Madison himself, can still be seen on display in the Virginia capitol in Richmond, built in 1788. Marble busts of Madison and Monroe—among other Virginians who reached the summit of American political life—would one day join them.

But in the days before they were marble, both Jameses of Virginia were terribly concerned with the uncertain course of their country. On the day Monroe received the letter mentioning the Washington statue, Madison was trying to overhaul the state court system and stop Virginia from seizing British property. Meanwhile, Monroe was trying to prevent a war with Spain while maintaining the Mississippi River for America. Two men taxed with the burdens of a nation, they no doubt snuffed out their candles at the end of the day, crawled beneath their covers, and worried about what tomorrow would bring.

At the end of December, Monroe wrote to Madison that Spain had presented Congress with claims of its exclusive rights to navigate the Mississippi. He sought his friend's advice: should Adams, Jefferson, or someone new be the ambassador to Spain to resolve this issue?

The next session of Congress convened in New York in January of 1785, and Monroe rented "three very excellent rooms in a convenient house, in a fashionable part of town," with his friend Samuel Hardy, a Virginia congressman the same age as himself. The increasingly experienced and sure-footed Monroe was emerging as a leader, if not the leader, of the nationalist cause in the Congress. Before Lafayette returned to France at the end of his grand tour through America, he penned a letter to Madison telling him so. "Our friend Monroe," he wrote, "is very much beloved and respected in Congress."[12]

In the issues he championed, Monroe was in many ways Madison's heir, picking up the unfinished works of the elder statesman. The two were also partners, working in tandem and in total agreement about what needed to be done to advance the national cause. When Madison in the House of Delegates passed an instruction to the Virginia delegation in Congress to create an ambassadorship to Spain to secure the Mississippi, it was Monroe who chaired the committee. Monroe also chaired a committee which drafted "instructions to the U.S. Minister to Spain," restricting the ambassador from treating away the river, and detailing the states' legal and historical rights to the same.[13] Monroe was encouraged in his efforts by his partner and predecessor in the role of the Mississippi's champion. "The use of the Mississippi is given by nature to our western country," Madison wrote, "and no power on Earth can take it from them."[14]

John Jay, decidedly unsympathetic to the cause of the Mississippi, was appointed Secretary of Foreign Affairs, a post which had been vacant during the previous year. His acceptance was contingent on the capital's planned relocation to New York, his home city.[15]

Monroe participated in a committee report on the settlement of the West. Commissioners would be appointed to negotiate with Indians and to make temporary treaties for the purpose of trade. French and Canadians who, having previously held Virginia citizenship, were now living in the West would take an oath to the Union. An announcement that the Western land would be surveyed was to be published in newspapers as quickly as possible, and offices would be opened for selling it. Anyone who simply seized land would be removed.[16]

Monroe successfully passed a resolution raising seven hundred men to protect settlers on the frontier.[17] Fascinated by the West, and apprised of its dangers during his travels, he also shared the belief of Madison and other nationalists that it held out unlimited promise for America. Land sales in this uncharted territory were expected to help pay off the national debt, and the successful settlement of this region would make America—already the size of France and Spain combined—one of the largest and most prosperous nations in the world. Monroe's success in sending troops to the area was hard won, given Americans' deep suspicions about standing armies during peacetime. It was also a vital step in the development of a region that Monroe would promote for the rest of his life.

Meanwhile, Jay bristled under the yoke of his instructions. He complained to Congress in February, just two months after accepting the Foreign Affairs portfolio, that he did not have the authority he needed and expected. Jay made veiled threats to quit.[18]

In March of 1785, Lafayette wrote Madison of his efforts with the French government to resolve the Mississippi issue: "I am every day pestering government with my prophetics respecting the Mississippi." He promised to discuss the issue with the new French ambassador to Spain.[19]

The same month, Monroe served on a committee that proposed an amendment to Article IX of the Articles of Confederation. The committee published a report suggesting that Congress should have exclusive power over defense measures, treaties and alliances, sending and receiving ambassadors, regulating trade between states and foreign countries, and laying duties on imports and exports.[20] Congress did not act on the report.

Monroe, along with the rest of the delegation, saw the cessation of Virginia's claims to the West through to completion. This measure was indispensable to consolidating the Union. In the case of the states' Western claims, their eyes were bigger than their stomachs. Virginia, like the other states with plans for the West, had found the giant territories unwieldy, expensive, and impossible to manage. The western part of Virginia, then known as the Kentucky district, had long since been preparing to separate and become its own state with Virginia's blessing. The legislature approved the final plan for Virginia to cede its claims after reimbursement for its protection of that area during the Revolution and thereafter. Monroe and the Virginia delegation in Congress steered this arrangement successfully to passage. A committee of three, consisting of one member from Congress, one chosen by Virginia, and a third chosen by agreement of the other two, would determine the amount of the reimbursement.[21]

Monroe also worked on the establishment of a national capital. In a letter to Governor Patrick Henry, the Virginia delegates to Congress indicated their support for "a federal town. If we reason from experience, we are inclined to think many disadvantages must arise, from the residence of Congress in a great commercial city, a city more especially under the jurisdiction of a particular state."[22]

The Virginia legislature entered into a compact with Maryland to clear and expand the Potomac and to settle jurisdiction and navigation on the river. Washington was appointed as Virginia's representative to settle these issues.[23]

Madison wrote to Monroe in April that Massachusetts was pushing Rhode Island to accept the impost. He was hungry for information from the national government, the place where his true interests lay. "What other measures are on foot or in contemplation for paying off the public debt?" Madison asked. He wondered if any of the states were paying their share. It was clear that Madison increasingly valued Monroe's friendship and their political connection. "I wish much to throw our correspondence into a more regular course," he said.[24] Madison's next dispatch included a more developed cipher, which Monroe had requested some time before.

During the 1740s, the American colonies had been swept by an evangelical Christian revival known today as the First Great Awakening. When the movement reached the frontier in Hanover County, Virginia, it divided the family of Patrick Henry. Henry's mother and his maternal grandfather, Isaac Winston, became "born again."[25] Winston hosted traveling preachers and church services at his home and financed the construction of religious "reading houses." Patrick Henry's father, John Henry, remained loyal to the Church of England, in which Patrick's uncle served as the local rector. Needless to say, the divide caused tension among family members. John Henry even had his father-in-law hauled into court and fined for avoiding Anglican services.

For Henry, who was born in 1736, the evangelical revival and its aftermath were probably an early childhood memory. Henry accompanied his mother to the powerful sermons of the traveling preachers and was expected to recite their lessons during the carriage rides home.[26] It was likely during these times that Henry, the greatest orator of his age, would first witness the power that the spoken word could have on people. Yet Patrick Henry would also remember that his father and uncle had characterized the new religious movement as a threat to the established church and the good order of society.[27] Ultimately, Patrick adopted the views of his father and uncle and considered the "dissenters" a threat to public morality and civil order.

This conflict between the establishment and the growing religious minority in Virginia would split the commonwealth as it did the Henry family. It would also determine the result of the 1789 congressional election between Madison and Monroe—and result in the First Amendment to the Constitution.

Baptists made up the largest group of dissenters in Virginia. When they had first appeared in the colony, they were "viewed by men in power as being beneath their notice." But as the Baptists grew in number, "men in power strained every law in the Virginia Penal Code to obtain ways and means to put down these disturbers of the peace, as they were called."[28]

The first known imprisonment of Baptist ministers in Virginia occurred in 1768 in Spotsylvania County, in the future 5th Congressional District twenty years before the race between Madison and Monroe. Three ministers were arrested and charged with disturbing the peace. The prosecutors brought evidence that the accused had preached the gospel to strangers. The magistrate, uncomfortable with hearing such a politically charged case, offered what he thought was a reasonable compromise: the ministers were to agree to stop preaching for a year and a day, and all charges would be dropped.

But the ministers refused to agree to stop preaching the gospel, and the persecution became worse. Baptists were arrested for worshipping in private residences, incarcerated, and often beaten and whipped. Imprisoned Baptists continued to worship and preach from their jail cells. Rather than become embittered or curse their captors or doubt their God for not protecting them, they sang hymns, prayed out loud for their persecutors, and thanked Jesus that they were merely in prison, and not in hell.[29]

In the years that followed, dissenting preachers were consistently arrested and brought to trial throughout Virginia. According to one history, these arrests were so common that "time and space would fail to enumerate them all."[30] Legal oppression of the dissenters gave license for private persecution as well. Without fear of punishment, people would interrupt services, ride their horses through the river while baptisms were being performed, and assault church members.

This was the Virginia in which Madison was raised. He could not help but feel sympathy for people who wanted the right to worship in peace and according to the dictates of their consciences. While at Princeton he had lived in a colony with significant religious toleration and attended school with people who were members of many different Christian denominations. When he returned to Virginia, he was increasingly appalled by the systematic attempts to control religion.

In October of 1776 the Virginia legislature had defunded the Church of England—not to disestablish religion in the colonies, but to cut ties with the British. Before the Revolution, taxes had been collected to support the Church and clerical salaries had been paid by the colonial government. The break with England had brought about an effective, if unintended, disestablishment of religion in Virginia. But by 1784, efforts to use tax dollars to support teachers of the Christian religion were back. Henry and other supporters of religious establishment believed that morality in the commonwealth had declined since the Revolution; they saw state-funded religion as a tool for reversing the moral decline. Henry argued that the public would benefit from the revitalization of the church, and thus of public morality, and that therefore the public should also bear the financial burden of supporting the church.

Madison saw this debate as fundamental to Virginia's future, and he brought his usual level of focused, meticulous preparation to it. He was always a well-prepared participant in any debate, researching the history of each issue and exploring all of the possible arguments that might be offered for and against a measure.

The words of the debate were not recorded, but Madison's notes provide insight. If Virginia could tax citizens in order to support the church, Madison argued, then religious matters could become subject to the courts' jurisdiction. Should Virginia courts really be deciding disputes among believers? What edition of the Bible should be used: Hebrew, Septuagint, or Vulgate? Which books are canonical and which apocryphal? What is the proper way to understand salvation and forgiveness of sin? Should religious teachers preach salvation by faith or by works?

These were matters of individual conscience, Madison believed, not for courts or lawmakers to decide. Man has a propensity for religion, Madison argued, and state sanction is not necessary for its promotion. Besides, state-established religion was highly susceptible to corruption.[31]

As Madison fought his own battle on religious freedom in Virginia, he cheered Monroe for defeating a measure that would have allowed state-sanctioned religious denominations in the Western territory. It had been proposed that each township in the West set aside a parcel of land, the proceeds from which would be used to finance the religious activities of a majority of the residents. Madison was firmly opposed:

> How a regulation, so unjust in itself, so foreign to the authority of Congress, so hurtful to the sale of public land, and smelling so strongly of antiquated bigotry, could have received the countenance of a committee is truly a matter of astonishment.
>
> Who does not see that the same authority which can establish Christianity, in exclusion of all other religions, may establish with the same ease any particular sect of Christians, in exclusion of all other sects?
>
> Whilst we assert for ourselves a freedom to embrace, to profess and to observe the religion which we believe to be of divine origin, we cannot deny an equal freedom to those whose minds have not yet yielded to the evidence which has convinced us. If this freedom be abused, it is an offense against God, not against man.[32]

The bill would make civil authorities the arbiters of religious truth, "an arrogant pretension falsified by the contradictory opinions of rulers in all ages, and throughout the world...an unhallowed perversion of the means of salvation."[33] Religion, Madison pointed out, has both existed and flourished not only without the support of human laws but in spite of active opposition from them, and not only during the period of miraculous aids to belief, but long after the Christian faith had been left to the ordinary care of Providence. State-sanctioned religion, Madison believed, led non-believers to see faith as an institution that needed secular support because it was too weak to stand on its own. Government, he felt, "will be best supported by protecting every citizen in the enjoyment of his religion with the same equal hand which protects his person and his property."[34]

On December 3, 1784, a House of Delegates committee chaired by Patrick Henry had produced a formal bill for the assessment of taxes to support the Episcopal Church in Virginia.[35] Madison had succeeded in postponing the final vote on the assessment until November of 1785. He had also proposed a resolution to distribute twenty-four copies of Henry's bill in each county in Virginia, along with a list of its supporters and opponents and an appeal to the citizens to make their viewpoints known. Madison didn't yet have the votes to stop the assessment, but he knew that if he could engage public opinion, he could influence the House elections of April 1785. At the same time, Madison voted for a bill he desperately opposed: the establishment of the Episcopal Church in Virginia. Choosing Jefferson as his confessor, he wrote, "A negative of the [establishment] bill would have doubled the eagerness and pretexts for a much greater evil—a general assessment—which, there is good ground to believe, was parried by this partial gratification."[36]

In April of 1785, Madison was focused on the elections for the House of Delegates, which would decide the outcome of what Madison wrote Jefferson would be a "warm and precarious" battle over church and state in the next session.[37] Before the formalization of political parties, elections turned heavily on personalities. Voters typically knew their candidates well, lived in the community with them, and selected representatives who had the best qualifications and personal characteristics to represent them. But in 1785 Madison and his allies succeeded in running a rare issues-based campaign.

Madison wrote a "Memorial and Remonstrance against Religious Assessment," which was published anonymously and distributed widely throughout Virginia. The pamphlet would be among the most famous documents in the history of American religious freedom. As news of the proposed assessment and church establishment spread throughout the Commonwealth, so did the organized opposition. The Baptists and other dissenters bearing the scars of years of state-sanctioned persecution mobilized to defeat candidates who supported establishment.

The dissenters in Culpeper flexed their muscles to unseat a delegate who supported establishment. Culpeper would later be the largest county in Virginia's 5th District where Madison and Monroe ran for a place in the First Congress under the Constitution. Madison's success in winning support from the dissenters in 1789 would ultimately secure his victory over Monroe. And it was Madison's backing of religious freedom in 1785 that made those dissenters his supporters. For the time being, however, Madison was pleased to report to Monroe that many new members of the legislature had won elections by campaigning against the general assessment and establishment of religion, while a number of incumbents had lost their seats for supporting these measures.

In the same letter, Madison also told Monroe about his ideas for promoting commerce. He lamented that the variety of currencies used in the thirteen states created barriers to trade. He was also concerned about a lack of uniform standards for weights and measures. People who wanted to do business across state lines could not be quite certain either what they were paying or what they would get in return. "Do not Congress think of a remedy for these evils?" he asked. Madison suggested that length could be calculated from a pendulum vibrating seconds at the equator, and that weight could be standardized around a cubical piece of gold or something similar.[38] While so many members of Congress neglected vital matters of interest to all America for parochial concerns, Madison, even in Virginia, continued to look for federal solutions to the problems in the states.

Monroe replied with the news that Don Diego de Gardoqui, the Spanish ambassador who had been sent to negotiate the matter of the Mississippi, was expected to arrive in New York at any time. Benjamin Franklin was leaving his post as ambassador to France, and it was expected that Jefferson, already in Europe, would be his replacement. Monroe also wrote of his success in moving Congress to recommend that the states of New York, Connecticut, New Jersey, and Pennsylvania raise soldiers for the protection of settlers on the frontier. Monroe was making great strides on the issue of the development of the West. Unsettled Western lands would be surveyed and sold, measured in townships of one square mile. Negotiations with the Indians were also under way to increase trade and limit the dangers that made the West unattractive to potential settlers. Monroe believed the sale of lands to the west would "soak up all of the debt to the east." In the meantime, Congress was considering a requisition of $3 million from the states to cover the interest on the debt.[39]

Madison was pleased to hear about Monroe's work on Western policy. He wrote back that the Kentucky district of Virginia would soon be petitioning the legislature for a separation. Madison also shared the interesting news of a "state" formed from the "back country of North Carolina that is organized, named, and has deputed representatives to Congress." This was the short-lived "Republic of Franklin," in territory that would eventually become part of Tennessee.*

Monroe was fully engaged in the great events of the day, as he had always wanted to be. As he walked to the post office to retrieve his mail, he was no doubt recognized and acknowledged with respect as a prominent member of Congress. When he opened and read his mail, however, he did not always meet with such respect in his correspondence.

Throughout the spring of 1785, Monroe's uncle Joseph Jones was pushing him in a direction Jones thought more practical than public

---

* On August 23, 1784, a convention was held at which the counties of Washington, Greene, and Sullivan, North Carolina, declared independence, forming their own constitution and government. North Carolina had given these counties to Congress in partial payment of their debt. The leaders of the self-proclaimed State of Franklin negotiated with Congress and Spain to preserve their independence, but ultimately gave in and accepted the authority of North Carolina, which promptly ceded the counties back to Congress. Tennessee would eventually include these counties and others to the west. John Sevier, governor of the Republic of Franklin, became Tennessee's first governor. See James Gilmore, *John Sevier* (New York: D. Appleton and Company, 1887).

service. "If you have serious thought of pursuing the law as a profession it will be necessary you turn your attention to it," his uncle wrote. "Without a sufficient stock of law knowledge you would be wrong to attempt to practice."[40]

Like any parent (or surrogate parent, in this case) giving advice, Jones was not content to send just one letter. His "encouragement" arrived in a steady drip. Following up after his first letter, Jones wrote in another, "I sometime mentioned to you that if it was your real design to undertake the law, the sooner you did it the better."

Jones also employed the time-honored tactic of comparing Monroe unfavorably to his friends. Monroe's old school-fellows Marshall and Mercer, now out of public life, were both distinguishing themselves at the bar. Jones believed that the practice of law required his nephew's full attention. "As a man engages to do with the woman he marries," he advised, "cleave only unto her. It is a business that requires both our time and attention, and unless these are bestowed on it, neither profit or reputation will be gained. In short, it is high time you fixed your course in this life." Public life had its satisfactions, but no public office "can be deemed profitable. They provide for the day, so long as we are able to work. But if a family are to be attended to, or the infirmities of age provided for, a man should extend his views somewhat beyond the present moment and acquiring what is barely necessary."[41]

In a third letter, Jones wrote that Richmond, where Monroe had wanted to settle, was saturated with lawyers, but that three or four outlying counties were less stocked with competitors. In Fredericksburg, lots and houses were reasonably priced; Jones suggested Monroe relocate there. He also said that if Marshall or Mercer, who were considering locating in a less competitive county, moved there first, Monroe should drop the idea.[42]

While Jones remained unconvinced that his nephew was making the right professional choices, Monroe continued to gain respect as a congressman and statesman. During the summer of 1785, that respect was affirmed when a boy carrying a letter from Jefferson in Paris knocked on Monroe's door. The young man, just about eighteen years old but preternaturally poised, introduced himself as John Quincy Adams.

Adams, who had joined his father in Europe on missions in France and the Netherlands and served as a secretary to Francis Dana while the latter was ambassador to Russia, had just returned to the states for the first time in seven years. He was looking to continue his career of public service, and Jefferson had chosen Monroe of all the members of Congress to receive this letter of introduction. Jefferson praised the boy for his "abilities, learning, application, and the best of dispositions."[43] This was Monroe's first introduction to the man who would eventually serve as his Secretary of State and succeed him in the American presidency.

On June 21, Madison sent Monroe a copy of the Virginia religious establishment bill, and the two men discussed traveling together. True to form, Monroe was impulsive while Madison was extremely cautious. "The part of your letter which has engaged most of my attention is the postscript which invites me to a ramble this fall," Madison wrote. "I have long had it in contemplation, to seize occasions as they may arise, of traversing the Atlantic states as well as of taking a taste of the western curiosities." Madison always sounded as though he were the kind of person who would consider every possible objection to an idea. Such obstacles, or excuses, can be found in every situation, but Monroe was as quick to look past them as his friend was to see them.

As Kentucky prepared for statehood, former Virginia legislator Caleb Wallace solicited Madison's opinions on the new state's constitution. Madison's response, written less than two years before the Philadelphia Convention, offers a window into his thinking about the structure of government.

Madison liked the format of the Maryland Senate, in which fifteen members were elected for five-year terms. The other chamber, he felt, should not be too numerous; its membership should be capped. Madison believed that legislative powers should be indefinite, and that it was better to prohibit legislators from certain acts (such as interference with religion, taking away juries, and passing ex post facto laws) than to delineate all of the government's powers. Madison also supported the idea of a Council of Revision to review bills before they become law in order to maintain the uniformity and consistency of the laws.

Madison's theory of executive power was incomplete and would more or less remain that way into the Philadelphia Convention. He did know, however, that the Virginia executive, who was dependent upon the legislature for every move, was "the worst part of a bad Constitution." Judges, he believed, should hold their places during good behavior, with generous salaries not subject to reduction during their tenure. These ideas would eventually make their way into the U.S. Constitution.

Monroe wrote in July from Congress, where Gardoqui had arrived from Spain and presented his credentials from the king and where states were still not sending their requisitions. He was still interested in traveling with Madison, perhaps during the upcoming recess. "What say you to a trip to the Indian treaty to be held on the Ohio, sometime in August or September. I have thoughts of it and should be happy in your company."[44]

Monroe was solidifying his position as a leader of the nationalists in Congress. On July 13, 1785, he made a motion "for vesting the United States with power to regulate commerce between the United States and foreign nations and between the states themselves." Interestingly, though Monroe would oppose the Constitution of 1787, he pointed to this motion in later years as "the first volume of the laws of the United States, among the preparatory acts leading to a change of the system."[45]

On July 18, a committee of Congress reported what funding would be necessary in 1785 and called on a requisition from the states. Monroe would later write, "The ill effect was seriously felt and great apprehensions entertained, if a reliance should be placed on requisitions only, that the sums called for and indispensably necessary would not be furnished, and in consequence the public faith be violated and the government, failing in all its duties, be dishonored and shaken."[46]

The two friends would not after all travel together during the 1785 recess. Madison journeyed to Philadelphia and up to New York, just missing Monroe, who by the time of Madison's arrival had left to observe the treaty negotiations on the Wabash. Throughout his trip, Madison was increasingly pessimistic that the present government would ever have powers sufficient for its responsibilities. He wrote Jefferson, "Congress have kept the vessel from sinking, but it has been by standing constantly at the pump, not by stopping the leaks which have endangered her.... The present plan of Federal government reverses the first principle of all government. It punishes not the evil doers, but those that do well."[47]

Madison and Monroe, manning their respective stations in Congress and in state government, had done their best to keep America afloat. But federal government under the Articles of Confederation was a leaky ship that took in water as fast as they could bail it out. It was time for statesmen to turn their attention to mending the flaws in the ship's fabric.

Chapter Seven

A PRAYER FOR AMERICA

"It has been a year of excessive labor and fatigue and unprofitably so."

—James Monroe

The table of the Virginia House of Delegates groaned beneath the weight of the petitions that had flooded in from across the Commonwealth. Madison's "Memorial and Remonstrance against Religious Assessment" and a number of similar publications had rallied the tide of public opinion against a general assessment to support the Episcopal Church with taxes on the people. That dreaded tax, placed before the legislature with such fanfare and debated with such a passion in that body and throughout Virginia, was allowed to die a quiet death.

The supporters of religious establishment had put everything into a punch that landed wide of its target. Madison seized the opportunity to deliver a knockout blow. With the general assessment dead and its champions chastened or defeated, Madison reintroduced the Virginia Statute of Religious Freedom.

Madison sensed that the time for the bill, initially drafted by Jefferson in 1777 and proposed to the Virginia legislature two years later, had finally come. The act begins, "Whereas almighty God has created the mind free.... Be it enacted by the General Assembly, that no man shall be compelled to frequent or support any religious worship, place, or ministry whatsoever, nor shall be enforced or restrained, molested, or burdened in his body and goods, nor shall otherwise suffer on account of his religious opinions or belief; but that all men shall be free to profess, and by argument to maintain, their opinion in matters of religion, and that the same shall in no wise diminish, enlarge, or affect their civil capacities."

The statute ends with an acknowledgment that future legislators could undo the work of the men who had created it, but insists that it is a representation of something more permanent than civil law. "[W]e are free to declare, and do declare, that the rights hereby asserted are of the natural rights of mankind, and that if any act shall be hereafter passed to repeal the present, or to narrow its operation such act will be an infringement of natural right."

Madison wrote Jefferson that his Statute of Religious Freedom had finally become the law of Virginia. "The steps taken throughout the country to defeat the general assessment, had produced all the effect that could have been wished. The table was loaded with petitions and remonstrances from all parts against the interposition of the legislature in matters of religion."[1] Madison proudly noted, "The enacting clauses passed without a single alteration, and I flatter myself have in this country extinguished for ever the ambitious hope of making laws for the human mind."[2]

The Statute of Religious Freedom was celebrated throughout Europe, hailed and envied as a tremendous achievement in the story of mankind. Jefferson later noted that only this act stood to counter arguments in Europe that America was backward and divided. Madison, who had felt compelled to support the religious establishment in the previous session, now took the opportunity to successfully support its repeal.

From these historic achievements on religious freedom, Madison returned his focus to national issues. He sponsored a resolution instructing Virginia congressmen to vote to give the federal government the authority to regulate commerce for twenty-five years. Washington wrote him in support: "The proposition in my opinion is so self evident that I confess I am at a loss to discover wherein lies the weight of the objection to the measure. We are either a united people, or we are not. If the former, let us, in all matters of a general concern act as a nation, which have national objects to promote, and a national character to support. If we are not, let us no longer act a farce by pretending it to be."[3]

When the Virginia legislature amended the bill to only thirteen years, Madison voted against it. Thirteen years of authority to tax commerce would not allow Congress to pay the national debt. It would only give a false assurance that something to that end had been accomplished.

On December 9, 1785, Madison wrote to Monroe, "It is more probable that the other idea of a convention of commissioners from the states for deliberating on the state of commerce and the degree of power which ought to be lodged in Congress, will be attempted."[4]

This time in the Virginia House of Delegates saw both victory and defeat for Madison. He had pushed Virginia's compliance with the national requisition, which, Monroe wrote, "does the highest honor to the state," and "gives an additional assurance of the strength and permanence of the federal government."[5] But Madison's attempt to repeal Henry's policy of banning the British from collecting debts in Virginia failed.[6] Closing the door to these creditors was a blatant defiance of the Treaty of Paris and gave the British an excuse for their own noncompliance. It was also, simply put, unfair. Why should a Virginia merchant who had accepted a shipment of goods from Britain in 1775 be relieved of his duty to pay for what he had bought simply because there had been a war in the interim? On this issue, Madison was able to pass only an amended bill that would be utterly useless. It would not go into effect until Congress notified the governor that the British had fully complied with the treaty, and even then the governor could still choose to suspend the law at any time.[7]

Madison, like other delegates who had served in Congress, was suspected of having "gone Federal." Thus any measures he introduced to strengthen the national government were met with suspicion by those unfriendly to federal power. It is widely believed that a motion for a convention of states that was presented to the House of Delegates by

John Tyler Sr. (a member whose son and namesake would serve as president) on January 21, 1786,[8] was actually drafted by Madison.[9] The bill, which was passed and sent to other states in the hope that they would follow suit, named Annapolis as the place for that meeting.[10]

Madison, along with his friends Edmund Randolph, George Mason, and five others were chosen to represent Virginia at this convention of the states. Its stated purpose was to "take into consideration the trade of the United States...to consider how far a uniform system in their commercial regulations may be necessary for their common interest and their permanent harmony."

At the end of the session, Madison updated Monroe: "If importance were to be measured by the list of the laws which has produced, all preceding legislative merit would be eclipsed...if we recur to the proper criterion no session has perhaps afforded less ground for applause."[11] In light of the deaths of establishment and general assessment, and the passage of the momentous Statute of Religious Liberty, it is remarkable that Madison could see this as anything less than a session of mixed results. But Virginia's failures in promoting the national interest—even in light of the call for the convention at Annapolis—were sufficient for him to judge the whole session a failure.

Monroe had begun his congressional service in 1783, so the term limit in the Articles of Confederation would end his tenure in less than a year. Monroe wrote to his uncle about the possibility of serving again in the House of Delegates. But he was also ready to accede, at least in part, to his uncle's urgings that he devote time to the practice of law. The Virginia legislature had cut yearly sessions from two down to one, which would begin in October. Thus if Monroe were elected to the legislature, he would still be able to ply his trade as well as continue his public service.

Perhaps one reason for Monroe's acquiescence to the career Joseph Jones had been urging on him was his affection for Elizabeth Kortright, the daughter of a wealthy New York merchant. The tall dark-haired beauty had accepted Monroe's proposal for marriage, and he would soon have a wife and, in time, a family to support.

Jones, aware of his nephew's impending marriage, offered these kind words to Monroe: "Sensibility and tenderness of heart—good nature without levity—a moderate share of good sense with some portion of domestic experience and economy will generally if united in the female character produce that happiness and benefit which results from the married state, and is the highest human felicity a man can enjoy and he cannot fail to enjoy it when he is blessed with a companion of such a disposition.... You have reached that period of life to be capable of thinking and acting for yourself in this delicate and interesting business...."[12]

Monroe had chosen well. His marriage would be a genuine and enduring love match. He wrote later that his wife "has been the partner of all the toils and cares to which he has since been exposed in his public trusts abroad and at home." These duties were great, he acknowledged, and "it would be unpardonable to withhold, that it was improbable for any female to have fulfilled all the duties of the partner of such cares, and of a wife and parent, with more attention, delicacy, and propriety than she has done."[13]

On February 11, Monroe wrote Madison cryptically about his upcoming nuptials. "If you visit this place shortly," he told his friend, "I will present to you a young lady who will be adopted a citizen of Virginia in the course of this week."[14] Unable to pry his mind from his duties, Monroe also included some discussion of the impost in his letter.

On his wedding day, February 16, Monroe again took time to write his friend in Virginia. The inadequate powers of the federal government were very much on his mind, even on that day.[15] Richard Henry Lee wrote Madison on February 16 as well, joking, "Monroe becomes Benedict this evening"—the latter's name already synonymous with "traitor."[16]

Madison was quick to congratulate his friend. Monroe was seven years younger than he, and his wedding must certainly have been a bittersweet reminder of Madison's own broken engagement. On the eve of his thirty-fifth birthday, marriage must have seemed like a happiness that was increasingly beyond his reach. "A newspaper," Madison wrote, "has verified to me your inauguration into the mysteries of wedlock.... You will accept my sincerest congratulations on this event, with every wish for the happiness it promises."[17]

Monroe had been preparing for candidacy for the Virginia state legislature, as well as for marriage. He would run in the election to represent King George County, where he owned land. A Colonel Taliaferro, a prominent man of Italian descent, would effectively serve as Monroe's campaign manager. Taliaferro believed that it was "indispensably necessary" for Monroe to "be in the county before the election and attend it when made. The people are discontented and will not be prevailed on again to elect an absent person."[18] He urged Monroe to write letters to various prominent citizens of the county asking for support, but he continued to point out that only Monroe's physical presence in the district would assure victory: "I still hope you will attend the election in person...your presence will ensure you a majority of votes, and absence will I fear make it doubtful."

Taliaferro also repeated a rumor he had heard: "There is a report circulating in this neighborhood that a certain member of Congress was lately wounded in New York by the little god cupid at the instance of a belle dame of that city. Can you tell me what is the gentleman's name?"[19]

On March 2, Monroe wrote Jones to announce his marriage: "Agreeably to the information I gave you in my last, the Thursday ensuing I was united to the young lady I mentioned." He wrote also of their honeymoon in the country, a brief respite from the mounting challenges in Congress.

His marriage seems to have inspired Monroe to focus on his personal finances, which had previously held little interest for him. In his wedding-day letter to Madison, Monroe proposed a business partnership to purchase land in the Mohawk Valley which could later be sold for a tidy profit.[20]

Madison, always eager for financial security, loved the idea. He wrote, "The vacant land in that part of America opens the surest field of speculation of any in the U.S. Its quality is excellent, its communication with the sea is almost, and in time will be altogether by water alone."[21] The cash-poor Madison asked Monroe to spot him the initial payment, or else to go ahead on his own. Madison also proposed visiting the land together in May or June.[22]

Monroe graciously advanced Madison's share of the down payment of $675. The friends were now on their way to being the proud owners of nine hundred acres, which they would possess outright after paying the full purchase price of $1.50 per acre.[23]

In August, Madison headed north to inspect their purchase while Monroe was held up in Congress. Madison wrote his friend about the good soil and the property's safe distance from the frontier and proximity to the Hudson River. Madison had consulted Washington about the purchase; the great man had told him that if he had had the money, he too might have had an interest in investing in the land.[24] The private collaboration of Madison and Monroe, if not their public one, seemed to be bearing fruit.

Monroe's interest in finance, however, extended beyond his private life. Before his wedding Monroe had sat on a committee that was working to remedy the precarious state of the nation's finances. Interest on the foreign debt was now $440,252 a year, and execution of the basic functions of government alone would take $2,508,327. Taking on additional loans was not an option in light of the ruinous state of American credit, and printing worthless paper money, which would only hurt American creditors by devaluing the dollar, was not an option either. The committee recognized that requisitions were completely unreliable. They decided that the only viable option was to levy an impost to keep the government functioning.

During March of 1786 Monroe was part of a congressional delegation to New Jersey. The state had expressly refused to pay the requisition for the previous year until certain demands were met, and even then, only after the other states had paid their contributions.

Madison and Monroe shared each other's disgust over the matter. Madison wrote,

> Is it possible with such an example before our eyes of impotence in the federal system, to remain skeptical with regard to the necessity of infusing more energy into it? A government cannot long stand which is obliged in the ordinary course of its administration to court a compliance with its constitutional acts, from a member not of the most powerful order, situated within the immediate verge of authority, and apprised of every circumstance which would remonstrate against disobedience. The question whether it be possible and worthwhile to preserve the Union of the states must speedily be decided one way or other. Those who are indifferent to its preservation would do well to look forward to the consequences of its extinction. The prospect to my eye is a gloomy one indeed.[25]

While Monroe had been in Congress and away from Virginia, Taliaferro had continued to tend to the election back home. On May 4, he wrote Monroe with unwelcome news: "Sorry and concerned most sincerely I am to tell you, that you were left in the minority by four votes only."

Monroe's opponent Daniel Fitzhugh had returned from Europe only three weeks before the canvass and had run at the behest of his father. Taliaferro believed that Monroe would have had the win if a certain Colonel Wallace had not pushed his prominent brother to campaign hard against Monroe under the belief that, if elected, Monroe would replace him as Collector of the Rappahannock Port. Monroe had also become a victim of rumors that he would not return in time for session or, worse, that he intended to stay in New York permanently after his marriage. Several of Monroe's friends had also abandoned him. Taliaferro wrote, "Some persons that you expected to be active in your interest were I assure you quite other way upon the occasion. I never was more chagrined in my life...and more especially when the interest of the men I love and admire is at stake. I know my county men will see their error but then I lament that they cannot rectify it."[26]

It is a phenomenon as familiar to any candidate today as it was to James Monroe in 1786. Many of those he relied on had simply failed to deliver. Undoubtedly some of those were the most vocal in proclaiming their fidelity to him and his ambitions.

Madison was quick to commiserate with his friend on the loss: "I regret much that we are not to have your aid. It will be greatly needed I am sure."[27]

Monroe was undoubtedly disappointed, but he was sanguine in light of other considerations. He was finding the married state a happy one. "I have formed the most interesting connection in human life, " he wrote on May 11. Defeated in King George County, Monroe decided to move to Joseph Jones's house in Spotsylvania County and practice law. He would be the only attorney in a good-sized town, with the closest competition miles away in Marlborough and Caroline Counties. Spotsylvania was also fertile ground politically, providing a good opportunity for another run at the legislature.

But in the meantime there was much to be done in Congress before Monroe could return to Virginia. He continued his work on Western policy, authorizing Congress to choose governors, councilors, judges, and other officers to serve as the executors over the new territories. As parts of the West gained a certain population, they were authorized to elect a general assembly; when they reached the population of the least numerous of the original states, they would then be admitted as new states.[28] Monroe also helped create the Indian Department to facilitate good relations with native tribes.

Monroe continued to be appalled by Congress's lack of effectiveness and the states' irresponsibility. "We have twelve states on the floor and yet do little or nothing.... No money comes into the public treasury, trade is on a wretched footing, and the states are running after paper money," he wrote Madison.[29]

Rhode Island had issued reams of worthless paper money and had devised a method for forcing people to honor their currency. They outlawed treating the paper notes as anything less valuable than specie. Rhode Island's businesses responded by closing their doors instead of trading their valuable goods and services for paper.

John Jay seemed resolved to give the Mississippi River to Spain despite his instructions. In fact, rather than carrying out Congress's instructions to him, Jay was actively courting members of Congress to support his position on the Mississippi. Monroe believed there was an "intrigue on foot under the management of Jay to occlude the Mississippi supported by the delegation of Massachusetts.... I have a conviction in my own mind that Jay has managed this negotiation dishonestly."[30]

The Mississippi issue evoked a severe sectional split. The Mississippi River served as the western border of states including Virginia, and a number of other states laid claim to land on other parts of the river. To representatives in favor of western expansion, the river was essential for transporting goods and people along the frontier. The Northern states, however, had active seaports and could easily ship and receive goods. Thus they saw holding onto the Mississippi as risking a war over a distant and unutilized territory. Northerners also felt that if they could cut the West off from development, they could keep the population center in the North. Jay and his supporters dreamed of commercial benefits that might be realized by trading the Mississippi away, but Spain never offered anything of value in return for the river.

Sectional tensions were so high that committees in New York were planning for a separation of the states, with a confederation of the North.[31] It was the most serious crisis the postwar government had faced.

In July, with Monroe's time in Congress running out, Jay requested a committee be appointed and fully empowered to direct him on all issues. In addition to having support from Massachusetts, Jay appeared to have support within the New York, New Jersey, and Pennsylvania delegations. Congress responded by forming a committee to determine how to answer Jay's request for a committee. It was decided that Congress as a whole should consider the issue with Jay present. Jay addressed a secret session of Congress on August 3, 1786.

The whispers and rumors were now confirmed on the floor of Congress. Jay argued for ceding the Mississippi for a period of twenty-five to thirty years.[32] He believed that without a treaty Spain would soon begin blocking American trade. With a treaty, however, Spain could provide assistance in dealing with other countries, in particular with the Barbary States in Northern Africa that plagued American shipping. Jay further argued that claiming the right of navigation was distinct from having actual use of the river. Spain was already restricting the use of the Mississippi, he argued, and therefore America had already lost control.[33] Jay believed the United States would gain commercial advantages by giving up something he argued they did not have and did not presently need—besides avoiding a war he felt they would not win.[34] Massachusetts moved to repeal Jay's instructions and give him the power he wanted, to give away the Mississippi.

Monroe readied himself for the biggest battle of his career. He wrote, "We have and shall throw every possible obstacle in the way of the measure.... This is one of the most extraordinary transactions I have ever known, a minister negotiating expressly for the purpose of defeating the object of his instructions, and by a long train of intrigue and management seducing the representatives of the states to concur in it."[35]

The debate over the Mississippi called into question, once again, the effectiveness of the Articles of Confederation. A supermajority of nine states was necessary for any treaty to be approved. But on August 29 seven Northern states voted in favor of repealing Jay's instructions. And they argued that the vote of only seven states was sufficient to remove the restraints previously imposed by nine states. Monroe and his supporters forcefully disagreed.

On the authority of the seven votes, Jay wrote Gardoqui of his new powers to "make and receive propositions."[36] Thankfully, Gardoqui rejected the proposal that the United States would cede the Mississippi to Spain only temporarily, and the negotiations stalled.

Throughout the crisis, Monroe was in close contact with Madison, using him as a sounding board for his plans.[37] Madison encouraged Monroe to maintain the high ground, and not to offer compromise: "If the temper and views of Congress be such as you apprehend, it is morally certain they would not enter into the accommodation. Nothing therefore would be gained and you would have to combat under the disadvantage of having forsaken your first ground." Compromise would also be rejected by Spain, Madison argued, which would only use Monroe's offer as a starting point for all future negotiations.[38]

Monroe was good to his word in throwing up every possible road-block to Jay's plans. But he did propose a compromise, allowing Jay to offer a 2.5 percent *ad valorem* tax to Spain on all American exports passing through New Orleans.[39] Monroe also tried to change the location of negotiations from New York to Spain. By the change of venue Monroe hoped to transfer jurisdiction over the matter from Jay to someone like Jefferson who was already serving in Europe.[40] In addition, Monroe approached the French ambassador, who promised to forward to his government Monroe's request that France recognize America's right to navigate the Mississippi. Monroe also attempted to embarrass Jay and his allies by moving to publish the secret session journals—to no avail.[41]

In response to the seven-vote "repeal" of Jay's instructions, Monroe introduced a resolution declaring that only nine states could actually remove them.[42] In any case, it was beyond dispute that the approval of nine states would be necessary to approve a treaty. Since that number could not be had, the issue would be left at a standstill.

While Monroe defended the Mississippi, Madison was engaged in an even more desperate battle.

Chapter Eight

THE ANNAPOLIS DISASTER AND THE ROAD TO PHILADELPHIA

"The efforts for bringing about a correction through the medium of Congress have miscarried. Let a convention be tried."

—James Madison

"That the present era is pregnant of great and strange events, none who will cast their eyes around them, can deny."

—George Washington

Madison and Monroe looked past their recent disappointments to the upcoming convention in Annapolis, which flickered, if dimly, as a beacon of hope.

"What is thought of this measure where you are?" Madison wrote to Monroe in the spring of 1786.

> I am far from entreating sanguine expectations from it, and am sensible that it may be viewed in one objectionable light. Yet on the whole I cannot disapprove of the experiment. Something it is agreed is necessary to be done, towards the commerce at least of the U.S., and if anything can be done, it seems as likely to result from the proposed convention, and more likely to result from the present crisis, than from any other mode or time. If nothing can be done we may at least expect a full discovery as to that matter from the experiment, and such piece of knowledge will be worth the trouble and expense of obtaining it.[1]

Were the convention at Annapolis to fail, it would not be for lack of preparation by Madison. His "Notes on Ancient and Modern Confederacies" are the fruit of an exhaustive study on the organization of governments throughout world history. Madison's particular focus, not surprisingly, was on the attempts of diverse and distinct political units to join in functional confederations. Madison examined these governments from every possible angle—representation and suffrage, the raising of armies and the waging of war, the regulation of weights and measures, the collection of taxes. He gave Jefferson in Paris *carte blanche* to buy and send him any book in Europe that might be helpful in his research.[2] Immersed in the history of confederacies from the Lycian League to the Helvetic Confederacies to the German Diet, Madison carefully considered what form was best suited to the challenges of the United States. As he read about the failed confederacies ancient and modern, Madison must have wondered whether America would soon be added to the list.

The weak Amphictyonic League had been undermined by Alexander the Great's father, Philip of Macedon, who had used the Greek city-states' jealousy of one another to conquer them. Britain was playing on the same weakness in America, punishing American exporters in the confidence that all thirteen states, behaving as separate actors, could not retaliate. Spain was also busy pitting Northern and Southern states against each other in its attempt to wrest the Mississippi from America.

One characteristic of the failed governments Madison studied, from the Achaean League to the Belgic Confederacy, was paralysis. They were unable to get things done. The Achaeans required the agreement of ten of twelve members, and the Belgic Confederacy required unanimous consent. The Belgic Confederacy consisted of fifty-two independent cities and seven provinces. Thus foreign powers and enemies needed to co-opt only one city or province out of fifty-nine to get their way.[3] It was exactly what both Madison and Monroe had continually experienced in Congress. A minority of states, or even one single state, putting regional concerns above the common good, could prevent the government from acting.

From his place in Congress, Monroe had done what he could to ensure success at Annapolis. He wrote the president [the chief executive] of New Hampshire to encourage New Hampshire to send delegates. Monroe explained, "I have looked forward to that convention as the source of infinite blessings to this country. However expedient it may be to extend the powers of Congress, yet recommendations from that body are received with such suspicion by the states that their success, however proper, may be always doubted. . . . I therefore earnestly hope your state and all the eastern [northern] states will send representatives to the convention."[4]

On September 1, 1786, Monroe was part of a congressional committee sent to Pennsylvania to encourage that state to adopt the impost amendment. The issue of the Mississippi was in such a critical state at the time that Monroe extracted promises from other members of Congress not to act on it in his absence. In fact, the tension and distrust in Congress were so great that Monroe felt promises were not sufficient. He took Rufus King, Jay's strongest supporter in Congress, with him to Philadelphia to ensure that Americans' rights to the Mississippi were not dealt away by Congress in New York while he was negotiating in Philadelphia.[5]

Monroe wrote to Madison, who was heading for Annapolis and the convention, "I have always considered the regulation of trade in the hands of the US as necessary to preserve the Union," he said. "Without it, it will infallibly tumble to pieces... I consider the convention of Annapolis as a most important area in our affairs... requiring your utmost exertions."[6]

Madison arrived in Annapolis September 4, 1786, and lodged at George Mann's tavern, which would also be the site of the convention. Four days later, he wrote to his brother that only two other commissioners were present.[7] On September 11, Madison wrote Monroe that only Delaware, Virginia, and New Jersey were fully represented. Two commissioners from New York and one from Pennsylvania were also in attendance. "Unless the sudden attendance of a much more respectable number takes place," he wrote, "it is proposed to break up the meeting, with a recommendation of another time and place, and an intimation of the expediency of extending the plan to other defects of the Confederation."[8]

John Dickinson, formerly of Pennsylvania and now of Delaware, was unanimously chosen as chairman. In 1777, Dickinson had been the principal author of the Articles of Confederation. At fifty-three, he had served as the president of both Delaware and Pennsylvania, as well as in Congress. He could fairly be said to be the most senior statesman in the room.*

Once the chairman was chosen, each member presented his credentials, which were read aloud. The roll call was short, consisting of five states and twelve delegates. For Madison, Hamilton, and the other nationalists in the room, the sparse attendance at the conference must

* Delaware had never been a separate colony from Pennsylvania. "The Lower Counties" had their own colonial legislature but were still part of Pennsylvania. The two shared a Royal Governor, and it was not extraordinary that they should have a common executive as separate states. L. S. Mayo, *John Wentworth, Governor of New Hampshire: 1767-1775* (Harvard University Press, 1921), 5.

have been maddening. They had not had unreasonably high expectations of this convention. But Annapolis had offered a possible way out of the morass the states were in, and barely anyone had even bothered to attend.

A committee was appointed to draft a report, and the Annapolis Convention adjourned for two days. On September 13 the members reconvened and the report, drafted by Hamilton, was debated and revised. The Annapolis Report began by detailing what had happened there—or more precisely what had failed to happen. Yet, it succeeded in expressing a sentiment that is still remembered. It read, "Deeply impressed, however, with the magnitude and importance of the object confided to them on this occasion, your commissioners cannot forbear to indulge an expression of their earnest and unanimous wish, that speedy measures may be taken, to effect a general meeting of the States in a future convention, for the same and such other purposes as the situation of public affairs may be found to require."[9]

Though the mandate of the Annapolis Convention had been limited to trade and commerce, the delegates called for "digesting a plan for supplying such defects as may be discovered to exist...." The seriousness of those defects, they claimed, had reduced the United States to a situation "delicate and critical," which called for "an exertion of the united virtue and wisdom of all members of the Confederacy." The report was transmitted to the legislatures of those states which were represented, to Congress, and to the executives of those states not present.

To his last hour in Congress, Monroe was engaged in the cause of strengthening the union. On October 7 he wrote Madison of his attempts to get the Annapolis report considered by a committee.[10] Monroe had proven himself as a leader in Congress on the critical issues of tax and trade, the national debt, developing the West, and protecting the territorial integrity of the United States. He had arrived in Congress a twenty-five-year-old bachelor, a novice in national politics. Three years later, he would be leaving with a significant record of achievement, in the company of his wife and best friend.

On October 13, James and Elizabeth Monroe headed south for Virginia. Whatever enthusiasm Monroe had ever felt for the law was already gone before he set foot in a courtroom. "I should be happy to keep clear of the bar if possible," he wrote to Jefferson, "and at present I am wearied with the business in which I have been engaged. It has been a year of excessive labor and fatigue and unprofitably so."[11]

"You wish not to engage in the drudgery of the bar," Jefferson wrote to Monroe. "You have two asylums from that. Either to accept a seat in the council, or in the judiciary department." But Jefferson, to whom Monroe looked for an older, wiser perspective, also offered a piece of wisdom that the newlywed was surely beginning to realize for himself. Nothing compares "with the tranquil happiness of domestic life," Jefferson wrote. Monroe did not come to the practice of law with enthusiasm, but it was necessary to support his domestic happiness, and he succeeded in it. Monroe began building a substantial law practice in the fall of 1786. "His success at the bar was gratifying to him, and the prospect of future profit very favorable," Monroe would one day write of his younger self.

Madison, in Richmond for the October session of the House of Delegates, wrote Washington that the Annapolis report would soon be considered by the Virginia legislature.[12] Washington, for his part, could not conceal his disappointment with what had transpired in Annapolis. He hoped the national government "may be considered with that calm and deliberate attention which the magnitude of it so loudly calls for at this critical moment: let prejudices, unreasonable jealousies, and local interest yield to reason and liberality. Let us look to our national character, and to things beyond the present period. No morn ever dawned more favorable than ours did—and no day was ever more clouded than the present."

Washington hoped that Virginia would take the lead: "Without some alteration in our political creed, the superstructure we have been seven years raising at the expense of much blood and treasure, must fall."[13]

The Constitution that ultimately emerged from the Constitutional Convention in Philadelphia would produce the most severe split among the leaders of Virginia, separating families and friends and dissolving close and long-standing alliances. The friendship between Madison and Monroe would not be immune from this division. In light of what was to come, it is worth noting that the bill to appoint delegates to the Convention of 1787 passed the Virginia House of Delegates unanimously.

The legislature resolved that "[it] can no longer doubt that the crisis is arrived at which the good people of America are to decide the solemn question, whether they will by wise and magnanimous efforts reap the just fruits of that independence which they have so gloriously acquired... or whether by giving way to unmanly jealousies and prejudices, or to partial and transitory interests they will renounce the... blessings prepared for them by the Revolution, and to furnish its enemies an eventual triumph over those by whose virtue and valor it has been accomplished."[14]

Seven commissioners would be elected by a joint ballot of the House of Delegates and the Virginia Senate, "to assemble in convention in Philadelphia: and to join with them in devising and discussing all such alterations and further provisions as may be necessary to render the Federal Constitution adequate to the exigencies of the union."[15]

Madison would make one of his most significant contributions to the Constitutional Convention at Philadelphia before he ever arrived there. The dearth of preeminent characters had been a great failing of the Annapolis Convention, and Madison was absolutely determined to secure Washington's presence in Philadelphia. As a universally respected and beloved figure, Washington in attendance would guarantee the meeting legitimacy and encourage other statesmen of high caliber from every state to participate.[16]

Washington understood the significance of his presence at the Convention and indicated his interest. "Although I have bid a public adieu to the public walks of life, and had resolved never more to tread that theatre," on such a critical matter, if his presence was thought useful, he would oblige. But Washington pointed to a serious problem that might prevent his attendance. An unforeseen obstacle had put the decision "out of my power."[17]

Washington had initially been expected to speak at the Society of the Cincinnati convention. As chance would have it, the Society was meeting in Philadelphia at the same time as the planned Constitutional Convention. The Society of the Cincinnati, founded in 1783 to promote the ideals of the Revolution, was named for the great Roman general who had returned to private life on his farm at the end of his service to Rome. Membership was restricted to French and American military officers who had served in the war for a certain number of years or were serving at the close of the conflict. (Men who had been killed in combat were awarded posthumous membership.) Family of deceased Society of the Cincinnati members inherited membership by primogeniture. The Society was the subject of enormous controversy on account of its exclusivity. For that reason, Washington had come up with a pretense for declining the invitation to speak at their convention and serve as their president. If he attended the Philadelphia Constitutional Convention after telling the Society of the Cincinnati that he was unavailable, he would insult the officers of his army.

Madison understood Washington's dilemma. But, Madison urged, "it was the opinion of every judicious friend whom I consulted that your name could not be spared from the deputation to the meeting in May in Philadelphia." Washington's attendance would signal that Virginia was in earnest about the project while also serving as "an invitation to the most select characters from every part of the Confederacy" to attend.[18]

On December 4, the Virginia legislature began naming commissioners to the Philadelphia convention.[19] The issues with the Society of the Cincinnati, Madison conceded, could "as little be denied, as they can fail to be regretted." But the convention was so important that nobody would criticize Washington for his attendance. Madison closed with a "wish that at least a door could be kept open for your acceptance hereafter, in case the gathering clouds should become so dark and menacing as to supersede every consideration, but that of our national existence or safety." He cautioned Washington against bowing out prematurely. After all, with only three of Virginia's seven openings filled, the governor could name Washington to a vacancy at any time.[20]

Madison had been absent from national politics for three years. Edward Carrington, then serving in Congress, attempted to give his friend a summary of what was going on there: "I cannot learn that Mr. Jay is proceeding in the business of the Mississippi. He probably will wait to see the countenance of the new Congress. If he can assure himself the cover of a bare majority, I believe he will make the treaty, and rely upon the timidity of some of the dissenting states for the ratification."[21]

But by February of 1787, Madison was back in New York and once again a member of Congress. He and Monroe both regretted that the urgency of Madison's attendance there had prevented him from visiting Monroe in Fredericksburg.

Monroe trusted Madison above his other friends in New York to help him handle some outstanding issues he had left unresolved there. "A Mr. Coghill in King Street engaged to make some furniture for me," Monroe explained. He asked Madison to "examine it" and, if it didn't measure up, "reject it. Tell him I decline taking it, for if it is not of the best kind I had rather have none." Monroe asked Madison to cover the bill for the furniture with the money he owed Monroe for their land purchase and to "send the furniture to me," with a bill for anything that exceeded Madison's debt.[22]

Madison also checked in on Monroe's in-laws. They were well, he reported, "but full of complaints against your epistolary failures.

I became your apologist as far as I could, but have agreed to give you up if you do not give future proofs of repentance and amendment."[23]

Madison presented his credentials to Congress on February 12, 1787, and immediately set to work to have that body sanction the upcoming meeting in Philadelphia. He received pushback from members who felt that such a convention violated the Articles, but Madison could not be discouraged. He succeeded in persuading Congress to approve the Philadelphia Convention. And the congressional recommendation would give legitimacy to the proceedings there, as well as to their final product.

With this important business out of the way, Madison went to judge Monroe's furniture. But "having little confidence" in his "judgment of cabinet workmanship," Madison enlisted fellow members of Congress William Grayson of Virginia and William Bingham of Pennsylvania to join him. As they walked through the streets of New York, perhaps they laughed at the absurdity of their task. Three men charged with conducting the nation's affairs were applying their combined expertise to judge the quality of household furnishings. At least it was a job they could see through to a conclusion, unlike virtually every issue they had to deal with in Congress. They agreed that the workmanship met the terms of the contract. "The aspect of the furniture does not I own entirely please my eye," Madison wrote Monroe, but "no particular defect appears in the workmanship. It is to be considered too that mahogany is one of the few things which appears worst when new."[24]

In his letter reporting to Monroe about the furniture, Madison included updates on the progress toward the convention, including the recommendation by Congress and the fact that New York, Massachusetts, and Connecticut would likely be represented there.[25] He also updated Monroe on Shays' Rebellion, then burning in the western lands of Massachusetts. Soldiers who had helped win the Revolution but had not been paid by Congress were being sued and having their property confiscated to pay their debts. Men who had risked their lives for their country were now losing their land because of congressional inaction. Rather than suffer this indignity, some former soldiers banded together to close down courts, halt foreclosure proceedings, and prevent the confiscation of their farms. The rebellion was quashed by the Massachusetts militia, thousands of rebels were arrested, and many were killed. This horrible tragedy would serve as a bloody reminder that the country could not continue to travel the road it was on.

Eight days after arriving in Congress, Madison wrote to Edmund Randolph, now serving as the governor of Virginia. "Nothing of consequence done," he told his friend.[26] His next update to Randolph was similarly bleak. "Our situation is becoming every day more and more critical. No money comes into the federal treasury. No respect is paid to the federal authority; and people of reflection unanimously agree that the existing confederacy is tottering to its foundation." At least there was consensus on something. Madison feared that a monarchy might even rise up out of the ashes of the confederacy.[27]

Randolph, a close longtime friend of Madison's, had served with him during his first term in Congress and in the Annapolis Convention. He was now serving as Madison's co-conspirator in the plot to get Washington to Philadelphia by any means short of kidnapping. Randolph wrote to Madison that he would "press in warmest terms our friend at Mount Vernon to assent to join us." He then wrote to Washington, "It is my purpose to take you by the hand."[28] As Washington's former aide-de-camp and personal attorney, Randolph could allow himself liberties that others would not dare take with the general.

While Congress did nothing, Madison wrote, "The general attention is now directed toward the approaching convention." Every state had chosen delegates—with the predictable exception of Rhode Island.[29]

Madison wrote to Washington with unfortunate news and some prophetic analysis: "I hear from Richmond with much concern that Mr. Henry has positively declined his mission to Philadelphia. Besides the loss of his services in that theatre, there is danger I fear that this step has proceeded from a wish to leave his conduct unfettered on another theatre where the result of the convention will receive its destiny from his omnipotence."[30] Henry would abstain from any role in shaping the Convention, content to sit back and wait for the final result.

There was good news, however, in a letter from Randolph. "General Washington," Randolph wrote triumphantly, will "agree to go to Philadelphia if his health will permit." But first the general would go to the Society of the Cincinnati to apologize for refusing their presidency.[31]

"I am glad to find you are turning your thoughts towards the business of May next," Madison wrote Randolph. He included his latest thoughts on what was needed to strengthen the national government. Interestingly, though the mandate for the convention was only to revise the Articles, Madison was already contemplating drafting an entirely new document. He envisioned incorporating the best of the Articles into a new constitution, rather than simply revising the old one.[32]

Madison suggested a bicameral legislature selected by the people or state legislatures, with total authority where uniform measures were necessary, and a veto over the laws of the states, as well as a federal judiciary. Madison was still surprisingly unsure about the proper makeup of the executive. "To give the system proper energy," Madison suggested having it ratified by the people, not the state legislatures. The legislatures, after all, had been the great obstructionists against all measures aimed at solving problems on the national level. Madison wrote a similarly worded letter to Washington.[33]

Just as he had for his "Notes on Ancient and Modern Confederacies" before the Annapolis Convention, Madison began meticulous research for the Philadelphia Convention. But he titled his new notes "Vices of the Political System of the United States."[34] Madison listed twelve areas of deficiency, including states' trespassing on each other's rights as well as on the prerogatives of the federal government under the Articles; the failure of requisitions from the states to fund the federal government; the lack of concerted action where common interests required it; and a lack of security against internal violence such as Shays' Rebellion.

Meanwhile, Madison helped draft a summons requiring Jay to appear before Congress and report on the status of the Spanish negotiation.[35] Madison was taking up once again the role Monroe had played in Congress in the three years of Madison's absence—champion of the United States' rights to the Mississippi, statesman working to assure that the federal government would meet its obligations, banner-bearer for the national interest.

In April of 1787 Jay complied, updating Congress on his talks with Gardoqui and addressing the increasing Spanish-American violence along the river.[36] Jay said ominously that the United States had a decision to make: "wage war with Spain, or settle all differences with her by treaty, on the best terms in their power." If it was to be war, the United States must prepare without delay.[37] Congress most certainly did not want war, but could not agree on what it did want. Therefore, the issue remained unresolved.

In the spring of 1787, Monroe won election to the House of Delegates, defeating Mann Page, who had opposed allowing Virginians to pay their state taxes in tobacco.

Monroe's only surviving letter to Elizabeth comes from this time. The newlyweds were apart for the first time, and finding the separation painful. Monroe and another young delegate, Edward Carrington, were discussing taking a house in Richmond where they and their wives could be together during session. In the meantime, Monroe wrote to Elizabeth urging "fortitude and patience, however painful or afflicting." But he hoped that the future would hold "little occasion to exercise this kind of fortitude…hope we shall be able…to surmount those difficulties which the severities of fortune had imposed on us in our commencement, to avoid a separation for such a length of time." The temporary separation was necessary because James Monroe was a man of duty; he felt it "essential to my character here and of course to my prospect of extricating ourselves from our present embarrassments, that I show the public I can attend to business."[38]

Madison congratulated Monroe on his victory in the election. "I hear with great pleasure that you are to aid the deliberations of the next assembly," he wrote.[39] He also made arrangements to ship Monroe's furniture to Norfolk. With that important business behind him, James Madison headed for Philadelphia and the Constitutional Convention.

Madison arrived in Philadelphia on May 3, 1787, staying once again in the guest house of Eliza Trist, at the corner of 5th and Market Streets. He could hardly have failed to remember how happy he had been there at the height of his courtship of Kitty Floyd, in the company of Jefferson and Kitty's family. The house had been full of cheerful companionship then, and Madison's life had been filled with happy prospects for the future. The city was quiet now, with Congress long since gone. Delegates to the convention were slow to arrive. In the silence before the convention, Madison was forced to confront his fears. Would it end like Annapolis? Would it all be for absolutely nothing?

Chapter Nine

GREAT EXPECTATIONS

"We all look with great anxiety to the result of the Convention at Philadelphia."

—James Monroe

The Annapolis Convention had been an utter failure. But hopes for a more perfect union of the states had survived that disaster. A new convention had been planned. The development of a unified national government would rest on the shoulders of delegates to the Philadelphia Convention.

On May 23, Monroe wrote Madison to offer encouragement: "My leisure furnishes me with the opportunity, but the country around does not with materials to form a letter worthy your attention. We all look with great anxiety to the result of the Convention at Philadelphia. Indeed it seems to be the sole point on which all future movements will turn. If it succeeds wisely and of course happily, the wishes of all good men will be gratified. The arrangement must be wise, and every way well concerted, for them to force their way through the states."[1]

But Madison was "daily disappointed" by the lack of attendance. "Every reflecting man becomes daily more alarmed at our situation," he wrote.[2] What if poor attendance doomed the Philadelphia Convention to failure as it had doomed Annapolis? Would there be another chance for the United States?

Still Madison, always meticulously prepared and disciplined in the pursuit of his aims, would gain what benefit he could from consulting with those delegates who had arrived. He talked and dined with the delegates present in Philadelphia and worked hard to unite the Virginians around his plan. Madison and his home state delegation met every day in the run-up to the Convention. Their preparation would amplify their influence in the proceedings.

Finally on May 25, 1787, the Convention at Philadelphia reached a quorum.[3]

Madison was impressed by the caliber of those in attendance and took their prestige as a sign that both they and those who had sent them were taking the Convention seriously. "It contains in several instances the most respectable characters in the US and in general may be said to be the best contribution of talents the states could make for the occasion," Madison thought. "But the labor is great indeed; whether we consider the real or imaginary difficulties, within doors or without doors."[4]

On May 27, Washington was the unanimous choice to chair the Convention. The only other possible choice among the Philadelphia delegates, or anywhere in America, was Benjamin Franklin. Franklin was now eighty-one years old, and the Philadelphia Convention would be his last service to his country. Franklin himself had intended to nominate Washington for chairman, but infirmity had prevented him from attending that day. Instead, the motion nominating the great Virginian originated with another Pennsylvania delegate, signaling a conciliatory beginning to the endeavor.

Washington's prestige was absolutely necessary to success at Philadelphia. But Madison provided the historical research, the broad knowledge of political philosophy, and above all the thorough preparation and planning that made the ultimate results of the Constitutional Convention possible.

Throughout the Convention, Madison sat directly in front of the chairman, front row and center. He was never absent, even for a day, nor for more than a fraction of an hour.[5] And it was his plan for a new constitution for the United States that would be the basis for the delegates' debate.

As so often in Madison's career, whenever he deemed it helpful to the cause he was espousing, he would introduce his own proposals through someone else. On May 29, in the first substantive action the Convention had seen, Edmund Randolph of Virginia took the floor to offer fifteen resolutions. The resolutions Randolph offered had been drafted by Madison and reflected his extensive research and his philosophy about the structure and powers of government.

Edmund Randolph, in the words of Georgia delegate William Pierce, was "a force of eloquence...a most harmonious voice." As governor of Virginia, and as a powerful orator, Randolph was the natural choice to present what became known as the Virginia Plan. Randolph opened his address by lamenting that it should fall to him rather than someone with more experience to begin. But as Virginia had originated the call for a convention, the state was obligated to offer its proposal, and as the governor, the task of presenting it had fallen to him.

Randolph discussed the many failings of the Confederation, while praising its creators as having done their very best under difficult circumstances. Randolph declared the need to amend the Articles to make them suitable for the purposes of "common defense, security of liberty, and general welfare." He then introduced the resolutions one by one.

The Virginia Plan proposed a national legislature with two chambers and representation determined by the number of free inhabitants of the state or else by the state's financial contribution to the national government. Madison had been consistently frustrated by the fact that delegations from small states, representing but a few people, had such a disproportionate weight in the Confederation Congress compared to his own state, the most populous. An American living in Delaware, he believed, had no more right to representation in the national legislature than one living in Virginia.

The theory of "checks and balances" pervades the Virginia Plan. Madison divided the legislative power, the repository of most national responsibilities, into two branches. Madison's Virginia experience convinced him that the two chambers should be more or less equal. The Virginia Senate was mostly limited to voting bills up or down or amending legislation. They could not initiate bills or amend bills that related to revenue. As a result, the Virginia Senate was too weak an obstacle in the way of unwise legislation.

Members of the first chamber (later known as the House of Representatives) would be elected directly by the people and would choose members of the second chamber (later known as the Senate) from a pool nominated by state legislatures. Madison envisioned some role for the states in the selection of the second chamber's members, but he acted to make senators not so wholly reliant on the states as members of Congress under the Articles were.

Each chamber would have the power to originate laws. They would have the same powers as the Congress of the Confederation, as well as new authority in those areas where individual states were incompetent to act separately. The new Congress would have a veto over the laws of state legislatures, and it was empowered to call forth the armed forces of the union against any state that failed in its obligations. These new powers proposed by Madison were the primary cause of and purpose for the meeting.

The veto over state legislatures was not for the purpose of allowing Congress to meddle in internal state affairs, but to keep the states from infringing on the national interest. From Chester County's adventures in P.O.W. policy to New York's treating with the Indians and Georgia's negotiations with Spain, the states had a history of creating anarchy and paralysis in clearly national issues. Madison's proposed congressional veto over state legislation was a mechanism for preventing further abuses. And the power to use force against the states for noncompliance with federal legislation had long been, in Madison's mind, the only solution to the chronic impotence of the national government. He lamented that for want of authority to send a single frigate into the port of a recalcitrant state, the nation was perpetually bankrupt. Only federal authority backed by force, Madison believed, would have caused states to comply with requisitions.

Madison's plan also envisioned a national executive, chosen by the legislature, empowered to execute the laws of the country, and possessed of all the executive authority of the government. Together with members of the judiciary, the executive would form a Council of Revision with the power to veto bills proposed by the national and state legislatures, subject to some ability of Congress to override that decision.[6] What Madison was proposing was similar to New York's Council of Revision, made up of the governor and certain members of the judiciary, which could, by majority vote, veto a bill; the veto could be overridden by a two-thirds majority of the legislature.*[7]

He also proposed a national judiciary, which had not existed under the Articles of Confederation. A federal judiciary could settle conflicts between states. In one instance, two states had spent years arguing over where the tribunal should meet to hear their dispute. And a permanent and independent judiciary would be necessary for enforcing federal laws. Besides, even while the Convention was meeting at Philadelphia, the British were still refusing to vacate their posts in American states, ostensibly because states like Virginia had closed their courts to British creditors in defiance of the Treaty of Paris. The federal judiciary would consist of one or more supreme tribunals, with inferior courts established by the national legislature. Judges would hold office during good behavior.

---

* Veto power was a rarity in 1787. Presidents of the Continental Congress and Congress of the Confederation had no such authority, nor did the governors of most states. Americans, including Madison, feared the veto power that Royal Governors had had over colonial legislatures. The South Carolina Constitution of 1776 was the first to give the governor veto power, but when the executive finally used it, the backlash forced him to resign. The veto was then eliminated from the South Carolina Constitution in 1778.[7] The Virginia Governor had no role in legislation. But Madison believed that the Virginia governor, like most of his counterparts in other states, was too weak and that the executive should play some role in the legislative process.

The Virginia Plan also included provisions for admitting new states to the union, for amending the new articles of union without the involvement of the national legislature, and for ratifying the results of the Constitutional Convention by state conventions elected directly by the people, instead of by state legislatures.

This last provision was crucial. The same state legislatures that had resisted the national impost and trade authority for Congress would surely reject the Constitution. Ratification by convention would provide a chance for passage—and the legitimacy of the people's assent.

Madison's Virginia Plan was ambitious—and unlike anything that had been tried before anywhere in the world. It was an attempt to form a new government in light of the best and worst of mankind's previous endeavors, from the recent experiments in the states to the ancient experiences of governments gone by. It was a delicate balance of competing interests poised against one another in order to protect the rights of all.

For example, while Madison favored a House of Representatives that reflected the will of the people, he wanted a Senate that had some autonomy and could act as a check on the House. The division of power that he proposed was developed in light of the fact that power corrupts; those in power are always tempted to act in self-interest. While Madison feared trampling of minority rights, such as those of the Baptists and other religious dissenters in Virginia, he was equally worried about the development of an oligarchy in which a few would use their power to oppress the multitudes.

Madison also feared attempts to redistribute wealth using the government. In the Convention he made the case that the Senate would serve as a bulwark against the redistribution of wealth: "In framing a system which we wish to last for ages, we should not lose sight of the changes which ages will produce. An increase of population will of necessity increase the proportion of those who will labor under all the hardships of life, and secretly sigh for a more equal distribution of its blessings. These may in time outnumber those who are placed above the feelings of indigence."[8]

Madison noted that "symptoms, of a leveling spirit, have sufficiently appeared in certain quarters to give notice of future danger." He went on, "How is this danger to be guarded against on Republican principles? Among other means by the establishment of a body in the government sufficiently respectable for its wisdom and virtue, to aid on such emergencies, the preponderance of justice by throwing its weight into that scale." Such was the intent of the Senate.

More than three months of debate, amendments, proposals, counterproposals, and compromise followed the introduction of the Virginia Plan. The delegates were creating a new national government on a blank canvas. Nothing was truly settled until the last day of the Convention. But having successfully introduced such a detailed plan first, Madison had ensured that his ideas would govern the discussion that followed. Ultimately this plan, with some notable alterations, became the basis for the United States Constitution. In Philadelphia, Madison would earn the sobriquet, "Father of the Constitution."

On Sunday, June 10, Madison finally had a chance to write Monroe. With "great mortification in the disappointment it obliges me to throw on the curiosity of my friends," Madison told Monroe of the gag rule the delegates had agreed to, preventing him from revealing anything of the proceedings. Madison thought the rule, which would allow for open and free debate, a wise one. Eleven states were present, and Virginia's delegates had perfect attendance records with the exception of George Wythe, whose wife was not well (she would die on August 18).

Monroe was cheering the Philadelphia Convention on from afar. To Elbridge Gerry, a good friend in Congress whose best man he had been, Monroe wrote of his "great anxiety as to the success of the business in which you are engaged. To bind the states together by the strongest ties, and to commit their interests to the direction of one common head is the first of my wishes; and I hope will be the event of this meeting."[9]

By June 13, the Virginia Plan had been digested through the body of the Convention, emerging in essentially the same form as crafted by Madison. But meanwhile, the smaller states had been working on a competing proposal of their own. William Paterson of New Jersey took the floor to ask for a recess until the next day, when the opposition plan would be presented. The New Jersey Plan agreed with Madison's Virginia Plan in granting the new Congress powers to tax and regulate trade. But otherwise, the two plans had very little in common. Aside from those two new powers, the New Jersey plan closely followed the Articles of Confederation.

But when Madison was finished deconstructing Paterson's proposal in Convention, delegates chose to stick with the Virginia Plan. Virginia, North Carolina, South Carolina, Pennsylvania, Massachusetts, and Georgia voted for the Virginia Plan, while New York, New Jersey, and Delaware voted against it. The delegation from Maryland, the quintessential border state, was divided.

It is noteworthy that the Southern states were such strong defenders of national power at the Constitutional Convention. Having recently been conquered by the British, living in constant tension with various Indian tribes, and sharing a substantial border with hostile European powers, the South chose the plan that would best serve its interests. Only a strong, well-financed government could deter and repel hostile enemies.

But how could the smaller states be persuaded to agree to the Virginia plan?

To illustrate the issues at stake, it is helpful to look at the population differentials from the census of 1790.[10] (The populations of the new states formed between 1787 and 1790 are included in population figures for the states from whose territory they were primarily formed.)

State:	Total population:	Slave population:
Virginia (includes Kentucky)	821,287	305,057
Massachusetts (includes Maine)	475,327	None
Pennsylvania	434,373	3,737
New York (includes Vermont)	425,659	21,324
North Carolina	393,751	100,572
Maryland	319,728	103,036
South Carolina	249,073	107,094
Connecticut	237,946	2,764
New Jersey	184,139	11,423
New Hampshire	141,885	158
Georgia	82,548	29,264
Rhode Island	68,825	948
Delaware	59,094	8,887

Virginia had almost fourteen times the population of Delaware, and yet both states had the same power in the Confederation Congress.** Madison fought hard for representation based on population in the Senate as well as the House. He could never be convinced, he said, that the present equality among the states in Congress was just, "nor necessary for the safety of the small states against the large states." He pointed to concessions by Paterson himself and another member of the New Jersey delegation on this very issue.

** It is worth noting that Virginia, the most populous state, had only around fourteen residents for every one in Delaware. Today, California has over sixty-three residents for each resident of Wyoming. Philadelphia Convention delegates seem to have believed that population gaps would diminish, not increase enormously in the future. But over 220 years after the Convention, the residents of the smallest state have sixty-three times the senatorial representation of those who live in the largest.

Madison did not believe the largest states would ever pose a threat to the smaller ones. There were significant economic, religious, and cultural differences among Virginia, Pennsylvania, and Massachusetts; and the history of the Confederation demonstrated that they were not typically prone to vote together. But Madison's logic could not convince the small states to give up their disproportionate power. The problem seemed intractable.

It was then that Franklin rose to speak, noting the "small progress we have made after four or five weeks," the "different sentiments on almost every question," and the high number of dissenting states on recent votes. Franklin went on, "We have gone back to ancient history for models of government, examined the different forms of those republics which having been formed with the seeds of their own dissolution no longer exist. And we have viewed modern states all round Europe, but find none of their Constitutions suitable to our circumstances."

Considering the impasse the delegates had reached, Franklin wanted to know why they had not appealed to God. He asked why the delegates had not "once thought of humbly applying to the Father of lights to illuminate our understandings?" He continued,

> In the beginning of the contest with Great Britain, when we were sensible of danger, we had daily prayer in this room for the divine protection. Our prayers, sir, were *heard*, and they were *graciously answered*. All of us who were engaged in the struggle must have observed frequent instances of a SUPERINTENDING Providence in our favor. To that kind Providence we owe this happy opportunity of consulting in peace on the means of establishing our future national felicity. And have we now forgotten that powerful friend? Or do we imagine that we no longer need his assistance?
>
> I have lived, sir, a long time, and the longer I live the more convincing proofs I see of this truth—that God governs in the affairs of men. And if a sparrow cannot fall to the ground

> without his notice, is it probable that an empire can rise without his aid?[11]

Franklin believed that the delegates risked becoming builders of a modern-day Tower of Babel, an ugly byword for human failure in future generations. He wanted God's aid in this great project, and to that end he proposed a chaplain be appointed to conduct daily prayer at the start of each session of the Convention.

Alexander Hamilton agreed with Franklin, but wondered about the effect on public perception should the delegates send for a pastor. The discussion continued, and Franklin's proposal was not given a vote before adjournment. But this sincere appeal from their senior member could not pass without having a profound effect on the delegates.

The delegates began working toward compromise. "When a broad table is to be made," Franklin said, "and the edges of planks do not fit, the artist takes a little from both, and makes a good joint...both sides must part with some of their demands." He proposed that each state elect an equal number of senators, who would have equal suffrage on issues of state sovereignty. But on issues of taxing and spending Franklin suggested the states should vote in proportion to their contribution to the national treasury.

James Wilson of Pennsylvania suggested that every state have at least one senator and that when the smallest state had at least one hundred thousand residents, the other states would be awarded an additional senator for every additional hundred thousand residents. Madison was willing to accept this proposal, but it went nowhere.

Gunning Bedford of Delaware suggested that if the large states went their own way, the small would "find some foreign ally of more honor and good faith, who will take them by the hand and do them justice." He did not offer this prediction as a threat, he said, but he felt that it would be the natural result if the large states ignored the rights of the small states.

Slavery would also plague the Constitutional Convention, as it did the Congress and country for most of the early history of the republic.

In the debate over representation, there was argument over what population would be counted for purposes of awarding House members to the states. Southern delegates insisted on counting slaves as full persons for representation, in sharp contradiction to the legal and moral arguments they used to defend slavery. This argument was made for the benefit of the master, not the slave. Northern delegates resisted; slaves could not be counted as property for one purpose and persons for another, whichever suited the whims of the slaveholder at the moment. Debate over popular representation had strained the Convention to its breaking point; this fight over slavery threatened to push beyond it.

Ultimately, it was settled that "other persons" would be counted as three-fifths of a person.

And the Convention reached a compromise in the conflict between small and large states as well. At the end of the debate, the proponents of equal representation of the states in the Senate prevailed by a single vote.

But this compromise, though settled upon in Convention, would still need to be approved by the public. And the chance of public ratification was small considering only half the delegates plus one supported the compromise. Randolph warned, "It will probably be in vain to come to any final decision with a bare majority on either side." He suggested an adjournment for further consideration and conciliation. But Paterson argued that the small states could in no way cede further ground to the larger states, and that if Randolph wanted to adjourn the session permanently, he ought to move to do so, and he, Paterson, would second the motion "with all his heart." Randolph declined.

When the delegates reconvened, they turned their attention to other issues. As they continued to hammer out the finer points of what the government should be, the members of the Philadelphia Convention knew that the final product would have to be presented to the general public in coherent form. A Committee of Detail was appointed to draft a document setting forth all points that had been settled so far. The Convention adjourned from July 26 through August 6 for the committee to prepare its report.

Meanwhile back in Virginia, James Monroe was active in the private practice of law. Elizabeth had given birth to a daughter, a new member of the family "who though noisy, contributes greatly to its amusement," he wrote to Jefferson. Monroe was increasingly confident in his abilities as a lawyer, but also frustrated with his sabbatical from public life. Monroe continued his letter to Jefferson, "I consider my residence here as temporary, merely to serve the purpose of the time." He was still hoping to move closer to Monticello. As always, Monroe became wistful when he was removed from the theatre of action. "With the political world I have had little to do since I left Congress. My anxiety however for the general welfare hath not been diminished."[12]

In this letter to Jefferson, Monroe—frustrated at being left out of the deliberations in Philadelphia—made an extraordinary claim. His exclusion from the Constitutional Convention, he said, was intentional. Monroe claimed that he had been relegated to private life as part of a conspiracy involving one of his closest friends. Monroe wrote, "The Governor [Edmund Randolph] I have reason to believe is unfriendly to me and hath shown (if I am well informed) a disposition to thwart me; and Madison, upon whose friendship I have calculated, whose views I have favored, and with whom I have held the most confidential correspondence since you left the continent, is in strict league with him and hath I have reason to believe concurred in arrangements unfavorable to me; a suspicion supported by some strong circumstances, that this is the case, hath given me much uneasiness."[13]

Jefferson never responded to Monroe's accusation, and we have no evidence that Monroe aired his complaint to anyone else.

Monroe was quick to perceive slights where none were intended. He tended to take things personally, regardless of whether they were meant that way. There is no doubt that Monroe would have been an exceptionally well-qualified delegate to Philadelphia. But an examination of the qualifications of those selected in his stead makes Monroe's claims that he was unfairly excluded implausible.

Representing Virginia at Philadelphia were George Washington, James Madison, Edmund Randolph, George Mason, George Wythe, John Blair, and James McClurg. The reasons for Washington's inclusion are so patently obvious they need not be explored. Madison's long and distinguished tenure at the state and national level and his work in calling the Convention made his presence there inevitable. Randolph was the governor as well as a former member of Congress. Mason's career in Virginia stretched back to the House of Burgesses and included authorship of Virginia's Constitution and the Declaration of Rights. George Wythe, the nation's preeminent legal scholar, had been a signer of the Declaration of Independence, a member of the Continental Congress, Speaker of the Virginia House of Delegates, and a member of the Court of Appeals. John Blair was one of the most senior Virginia judges, a former Burgess and member of the Council of State, and a drafter of Virginia's Constitution and Declaration of Rights.

It is unlikely that Monroe could have considered himself more entitled to a place in the delegation than any of these men. The only delegate he could reasonably have considered himself more qualified than was Dr. James McClurg. McClurg was selected by Governor Randolph to fill the vacancy created when Patrick Henry, and then Richard Henry Lee, declined to attend. Henry was a former Burgess, two-time governor, and consistently the most powerful member of the House of Delegates. And Lee was a former Burgess, an influential member of the House of Delegates, and a long-standing member of Congress who had introduced the motion in favor of American independence. Monroe could not have entertained the presumption that he should have been chosen in the stead of any of these men.

McClurg's must have been the place Monroe thought should have been his. Monroe, though eleven years McClurg's junior, easily outdistanced him in political experience—which is not to say that McClurg had none. A college classmate of Jefferson, McClurg was the foremost physician in Virginia and one of its wealthiest residents. He was serving on the governor's Council of State when Randolph chose him for Philadelphia. After Henry and Lee passed, Randolph chose a colleague he knew well and respected. Monroe, unlike McClurg, did not have a friendship or working relationship with Governor Randolph. Monroe had been away from Virginia in Congress for three years and was nowhere near Richmond when the appointment was made.

And there is no evidence that Madison was consulted about the choice of McClurg. Monroe, living in Fredericksburg after his time in Congress, appears to have done nothing to indicate his interest in being selected for the Convention. He was passed over for five people with substantially better credentials than his, and one very esteemed and successful professional who worked with the governor who made the appointments.

But in July of 1787, as the Constitutional Convention met in Philadelphia, Monroe evinced a belief that Madison had violated their friendship and did not have his best interests at heart. Monroe stewed in Fredericksburg, feeling a new distance from his mentor, political ally, partner, and friend.

As things stood in Philadelphia, delegates had come to the hard-won decision that the number of representatives in the House would be based on the population of each state while the number of representatives in the Senate would be equal for each state, regardless of population. The delegates moved quickly through the remaining issues.

On August 15, Madison proposed that all acts, prior to becoming laws, should be submitted to the president and Supreme Court; if either should object, a two-thirds majority in Congress could override the veto, or if both objected, a three-fourths majority would be necessary to override. While a two-thirds legislative override was adopted for presidential vetoes, the override for judicial decisions failed. The idea of such an override is one that deserved more consideration at the time and, in light of the evolution of our national institutions, one that deserves our attention today.[14]

Madison had originally wanted Congress to have general powers with specific limitations in only certain areas. But the consensus in Convention was that congressional powers should be clearly enumerated.

As the delegates neared the end of their labors, Randolph was becoming increasingly dissatisfied with the new constitution that was emerging from the Philadelphia Convention. He cited "features so odious…that he doubted whether he should be able to agree to it." Randolph had originally proposed Madison's Virginia Plan to the Convention, but he could not accept the final product of the compromise that emerged from that Plan. After months of debate, what did the dissatisfaction of so prominent a member of the Virginia delegation portend for the Constitution's passage, both in Philadelphia and in the states?

Chapter Ten

A RISING OR A SETTING SUN?

"The political concerns of this country are, in a manner, suspended by a thread."
—George Washington

"I am a very incompetent prophet of the Constitution."
—James Madison

During the last hours of the Philadelphia Convention, things started to fall apart.

On September 12, 1787, the Committee of Style, on which Madison sat, produced a draft of the new constitution. Here Madison and the other delegates who had worked so long and hard for an energetic national government made a disastrous error that nearly cost them everything.

George Mason suggested that the Constitution should be prefaced by a bill of rights, which he argued would "give great quiet to the people." With the state constitutions as their models, Mason thought, such a bill of rights could be prepared within a few hours. Certain rights were considered inviolate throughout the continent, as was evidenced by their protections in several state constitutions. These rights, he thought, should also be made explicit in the Constitution of the United States. Elbridge Gerry agreed with Mason and moved to form a committee to prepare a bill of rights. But the measure did not receive the sanction of a single state.

Some of the hesitation to pass the measure should be attributed to the delegates' eagerness to leave. The Constitutional Convention had started in May, and delegates had met nearly all day for six days a week, with only two short adjournments, during which committee members had met. Delegates to Philadelphia had probably not expected to meet for so great a length of time—participants in the Annapolis Convention had convened only three times over the course of one week.

A bill of rights was also seen by many as superfluous. The Constitution already restricted governmental incursion on the people's rights, some argued, by strictly enumerating the government's powers in the text of the Constitution. Individual rights were thereby implicitly reserved. There was even a possibility that enumerating some rights might mean implicitly ceding others.

Looking back, it is clear that Mason had real foresight. The absence of a bill of rights would become the rallying point for opponents to the Constitution, while the Federalists in their campaign for ratification would scramble to promise amendments in the new Congress. The whole controversy over a bill of rights—which nearly sunk the Constitution—could easily have been preempted during the Philadelphia Convention.

Edmund Randolph had serious reservations about the new Constitution. Not only did he object to the lack of a bill of rights; Randolph was also deeply concerned about the consolidated executive power. He argued for two sets of state conventions: one in which states could choose whether to ratify the document, and another in which they could propose potential amendments. He also wanted to "keep himself free, in case he should be honored with a seat at the convention of his state, to act according to the dictates of his conscience." On Saturday, September 15, Randolph refused to sign the Constitution in Philadelphia, but he remained undecided whether to support its ratification in Virginia.

George Mason agreed with Randolph, seeing dangerous new powers in a government that would "end either in monarchy, or in a tyrannical aristocracy."[1] He could not sign the Constitution. And he would vote against it in Virginia. Charles Pinckney observed, "These declarations from members so respectable at the close of this important scene, give a peculiar solemnity to the present moment."

That present moment brought with it the crucial question: would the Constitution even be sent to the people for ratification?

The Clerk called the roll: "On the question to agree to the Constitution, as amended. All the States ay."

On Monday, September 17, 1787, the Constitution of the United States was read aloud. Benjamin Franklin had written a speech, which James Wilson delivered on his behalf:

> I confess that there are several parts of the Constitution which I do not at present approve, but I am not sure I shall never approve them. For, having lived long, I have experienced many instances of being obliged, by better information or fuller consideration, to change opinions, even on important subjects, which I once thought right, but found to be otherwise. It is therefore that, the older I grow, the more apt I am to doubt my own judgment, and to pay more respect to the judgment of others....
>
> In these sentiments, sir, I agree to this Constitution, with all its faults, if they are such; because I think a general government necessary for us....
>
> I doubt, too, whether any other Convention we can obtain may be able to make a better Constitution. For, when you assemble a number of men to have the advantage of their joint wisdom, you inevitably assemble with those men, all their prejudices, their passions, their errors of opinion, their local interests, and their selfish views. From such an assembly can a perfect production be expected? It therefore astonishes me,

> sir, to find this system approaching so near to perfection as it does; and I think it will astonish our enemies, who are waiting with confidence to hear that our councils are confounded. . . .[2]

After Franklin's speech, according to Madison, "The members then proceeded to sign the instrument." He continued: "While the last members were signing it, Franklin looking towards the President's Chair, at the back of which a rising sun happened to be painted, observed to a few members near him, that painters had found it difficult to distinguish in their art a rising from a setting sun." Throughout the Philadelphia Convention, Franklin said, he had looked at the sun on the President's Chair without being able to tell whether it was rising or setting. "But now," Franklin said, "at length I have the happiness to know that it is a rising and not a setting sun."

Franklin, who had signed his name to the Declaration of Independence in that same room eleven years earlier, capped off over fifty years of public service by putting his signature on the Constitution. It was his last act on behalf of the people he loved.

By the end of the Convention, thirty-nine of the fifty-five appointed delegates had signed the Constitution. Only three delegates—Mason, Randolph, and Gerry—refused. Though these three were the only men present to refuse to sign the document, they were not the only ones who disagreed with the measures being taken at Philadelphia. Many delegates had chosen to leave the Convention rather than stay and argue their position. That is not to say, however, that all of those who left were against the Constitution. Oliver Ellsworth, the great conciliator, along with several others, left early to attend to business obligations. A few delegates left early for personal reasons such as their health or that of their spouses.

William Jackson, the secretary of the Convention, took a copy of the Constitution to the city of New York to be presented to Congress. After months of secrecy, the delegates would finally see the fruit of their labor presented to the anxious public.

Virginia nervously awaited news from Philadelphia. Newspapers throughout the state, such as the *Winchester Gazette* and *Virginia Independent Chronicle*, published the entire Constitution. Many weekly newspapers rushed out special editions to meet the public demand. The Virginia House of Delegates paid for the printing and distribution of five thousand copies.

Washington sent copies to Patrick Henry, Benjamin Harrison, and Thomas Nelson, three former Virginia governors, offering his belief that "it is the best that could be obtained at this time," and drawing their attention to the mechanism for obtaining amendments to satisfy whatever objections they might have. Washington made clear that he favored ratification and observed that "the political concerns of this country are, in a manner, suspended by a thread."

As the Constitution was unveiled, James Monroe was busy with the proceedings in *Lewis v. Dixon*, winning an appeal for John Lewis who had lost a case at trial over an uncollected debt.[3] While Madison had been caught up in the momentous events in Philadelphia, Monroe had been slogging away at the mundane affairs of his legal practice. At least for a time, he had felt sidelined and betrayed by Madison, his friend and close political ally. But now the Constitution drafted in Philadelphia was public knowledge, and Monroe would be taking a position on whether it should be ratified by the people, or not.

On September 20, still in Philadelphia, Madison sent a copy of the Constitution to Edmund Pendleton. Madison wrote, "The double object of blending a proper stability and energy in the government with the essential characteristics of the Republican form, and of tracing a proper line of demarcation between national and state authorities, was necessarily found to be as difficult as it was desirable, and to admit of an infinite diversity concerning the means among those who were unanimously agreed concerning the end."

On September 23, Virginia Congressman Edward Carrington warned Madison that Richard Henry Lee was already preparing amendments. Indeed, Lee was furiously writing to rally opposition to the Constitution. He hoped to encourage Randolph, whose opposition would be decisive in Virginia, to join his cause. Lee recognized the dangers the Constitution was designed to address but believed that adopting what he saw as a bad form of government to avoid anarchy was like committing suicide to avoid dying.[4]

On September 24, Madison returned to Congress in New York and found that the opposition had already been stirred up. "I found," he wrote Washington, "on my arrival here, that certain ideas, unfavorable to the act of the convention, which had created difficulties in that body, had made their way into Congress."[5] Opponents in Congress attempted to have the report from Philadelphia invalidated, because it had not "amended" the Articles of Confederation, but had instead replaced them.

Madison pointed out in response that the purpose of the Philadelphia Convention had been to create "a firm, national government."[6] By replacing the Articles with the Constitution, he argued, the delegates at Philadelphia had fulfilled that mandate.

Monroe's Spotsylvania County colleague John Dawson wrote Madison that the Constitution was "the subject of general conversation in every part of the town and will be soon in every quarter of the state.... Although there are many warm friends to the plan, be assured that the opposition will be powerful."[7]

The champions of the Constitution took the gathering opposition seriously and moved swiftly to meet it. In October of 1787 there began to appear in the newspapers of New York a series of articles under the pen name "Publius," arguing for the ratification of the Constitution. These would become known as the "Federalist Papers," a comprehensive exposition of the nature of the proposed government. The eighty-five essays, written principally by Madison or Hamilton, with several written by Jay, would continue to appear until New York ratified the Constitution.

If Madison was entertaining doubts about the Constitution's chances for ratification in Virginia, Monroe confirmed them. Former governors Henry, Nelson, and Harrison were all rumored to be opposed. On October 13 Monroe wrote, "This ensures it a powerful opposition, more especially when associated with that of the two dissenting deputies [Randolph and Mason]." Monroe was back in his old role of confidential correspondent to Madison. He seemed to have reconsidered his suspicions that the more experienced politician had played some role in keeping him away from Philadelphia, or perhaps he had decided to overlook the slight. Monroe continued, "The report from Philadelphia has presented an interesting subject to their consideration. It will perhaps agitate the minds of the people of this state, more than any subject they have had in contemplation since the commencement of the late revolution. For there will be a greater division among the people of character than then took place, provided we are well informed as to the sentiments of many of them."

Though he did acknowledge some misgivings, Monroe's first reaction was to support the Constitution: "There are in my opinion some strong objections against the project; which I will not weary you with a detail of. But under the predicament in which the union now stands and this state in particular with respect to this business, they are overbalanced by the arguments in favor." Monroe wrote a similar letter to Lambert Cadwalader two days later. He ended that letter with a more emphatic statement of support for the Constitution, "My wishes are of course for its success."

A town meeting in Fredericksburg, like others being held across the state, discussed the Constitution. The document was read aloud and unanimously approved. Attendees then sent a resolution to their legislators, Monroe and John Dawson, extolling the virtues of the Constitution and recommending an immediate ratification convention.[8]

On October 25, the House of Delegates passed a resolution calling for a state convention to consider ratification. Some supporters of the

Constitution had feared that hostile legislatures would simply refuse to act. But Monroe had previously told Madison that this was not cause for concern, at least not in Virginia. Those who stood in the way of even holding a ratification convention were likely to lose favor with the public and could face opposition from challengers who favored giving the Constitution a fair hearing.

On December 6, Monroe resumed his legislative updates to Madison. Henry had introduced a bill to ban imports of alcohol, but it was likely to fail. Nothing would be done respecting the British debt. Monroe's wife Elizabeth and sister-in-law were with him in Richmond, and he was considering leaving before the end of session.[9]

When Monroe returned to Fredericksburg in February of 1788, he informed Madison of the sentiments taking hold in their native state: "The new Constitution still engages the minds of people with some zeal among the partisans on either side. It is impossible to say which preponderates. The northern part of the state is more generally for it than the southern. In this county (except in the town) they are against it I believe universally."

Monroe continued, explaining why the legislature had scheduled the convention for June: "The object in postponement of the meeting of our convention to so late a day was to furnish an evidence of the disposition of the other states to that body when it should be assembled. If they or many of them were against it our state might mediate between contending parties and lead the way to a union more palatable to all."[10]

Monroe had run to be a delegate for King George County for the forthcoming Virginia ratification convention, but had been defeated by an opponent who had Washington's support. Monroe would succeed on his second attempt, winning a place at the convention on a snowy Spotsylvania Court Day.

The arrival of the Constitution in the Commonwealth had awakened a sleeping giant. Patrick Henry had retired to Prince Edward County just over a year before, after a long career in the Burgesses, the House of Delegates, and Congress, as well as five terms as governor.[11] But by the third Monday of March, 1788, Henry had been lured out of retirement and was campaigning to be elected Prince Edward County's delegate to Virginia's convention to consider ratifying the Constitution. An observer said that Henry, who had never been a man of fashion, looked "like a common planter, who cared very little for his personal appearance."[12] Henry carefully tended his image as a man of the people. On Election Day he climbed the brick steps of the courthouse and addressed perhaps five hundred people, proclaiming the republic to be in a state of "extreme danger."[13]

Henry defended the Confederation under the Articles, indicted the Constitution's authors for exceeding their mandate, and painted a bleak picture of what the new government—distant and powerful—would mean for his audience.[14] Referring to the Constitution as "that paper," he called it "the most fatal plan that could possibly be conceived to enslave a free people."[15] The Prince Edward County Sheriff, responsible for conducting the election, saw the euphoric crowd and decided that no vote would be necessary. He declared Henry elected by acclamation.[16]

Madison's fellow congressman Cyrus Griffin in New York wrote him in March, after Madison's departure for Virginia: "A prospect of the new Constitution seems to deaden the activity of the human mind as to all other matters; and yet I greatly fear the Constitution may never take place." New Hampshire's ratification convention had met and adjourned without taking a vote. Rhode Island, which had played no part in drafting the Constitution, had rejected it outright. (Contrarian as always, Rhode Island held a public referendum instead of the prescribed convention.) Griffin was concerned by "formidable opposition" in New York, as well as the "antipathy of Virginia."[17]

Back in November Archibald Stuart had written Madison from Virginia, pleading with him to hurry home and stand in the upcoming election to the ratification convention. The Federalists believed Madison's abilities would be crucial in winning Virginia's support for the new Constitution. But for his part, Madison had not intended to be a delegate. He sensed an impropriety in the authors of the Constitution serving as its final judges. It seemed like a party to a lawsuit serving on his own jury.

"Light Horse" Henry Lee had written in December, warning that Orange County was bitterly divided and that there were many opposed to Madison and the Constitution. James Madison Sr. wrote a month later, warning of Baptist opposition to the Constitution and of many others who were undecided or hostile.

In light of the confusion and opposition, Madison decided that he would do as he had been asked and run for delegate to the ratification convention, despite his scruples and the fact that running might endanger relationships he valued. "I sacrifice every private inclination to considerations not of a selfish nature," he wrote to Washington on February 20. "I foresee that the undertaking will involve me in very laborious and irksome discussions; that public opposition to several very respectable characters whose esteem and friendship I greatly prize may unintentionally endanger the subsisting connection."[18]

Madison left New York on March 4 and arrived in Orange the day before the election. "I had the satisfaction to find all my friends well on my arrival; and the chagrin to find the county filled with the most absurd and groundless prejudices against the Federal Constitution," he wrote to Eliza Trist in Philadelphia.

On Court Day, when the elections were held, Madison mounted a "rostrum before a large body of the people," and launched "into a harangue of some length in the open air and on a very windy day." Though he had won several elections, James Madison—like other eighteenth-century candidates who "stood" rather than "ran" for office—had never before made a campaign speech. Madison's debut on the stump can be viewed as a success. He won by a four-to-one majority and brought fellow Federalist James Gordon to victory with him.[19] Francis Taylor, his cousin, noted 202 votes for Madison, 187 for Gordon, 56 for Thomas Barbour, and 34 for Charles Porter. Madison, not prone to pettiness or personal grievances, may still have enjoyed trouncing Porter, who had defeated him for the House in 1777.

Madison would be at the June convention to fight for the Constitution. But he had no idea who would be joining him there and felt the outcome of the convention was very much in doubt.

The only way forward, the only way the experiment could succeed, Madison believed, was unconditional ratification of the Constitution. But the Anti-Federalists were increasingly discussing other options—ratifying with preconditions such as the adoption of particular amendments, or else having another convention. "Conditional amendments or a second general convention will be fatal," Madison flatly declared.[20]

Madison believed that the 1787 Convention had succeeded because of the temperament of its participants. Statesmen who put the national interest ahead of regional concerns and selfish personal ambition had come together in Philadelphia with the honest intention of repairing the flaws in the general government of the United States. If a second convention should meet, even if it were wiser than the first, "the game would be easy as it would be obvious," Madison thought. Opponents to the union were sure to be elected. They would propose ideas unacceptable to other regions of the country with the express purpose of causing the convention to fall apart.[21]

Intelligence continued to trickle in to Madison on the state of the elections to the Virginia ratification convention. Carrington wrote, "Most of the elections in the upper and middle parts of the south side of the James River, have been made in frenzy, and terminated in deputations of weak and bad men, who have bound themselves to vote in the negative, and will in all cases be the tools of Mr. H."[22]

Missing from the puzzle were the sentiments of some notable delegates. "I say nothing of the Governor," Madison wrote, referring to Randolph, "because it is not yet certain which party will have most of his aid; nor of Monroe whose precise sentiments are not generally known. If I mistake not, he will be found not an enemy to the Constitution."[23]

Madison lobbied Governor Randolph, knowing that his opposition could be fatal. He appealed to Randolph's desire for union and pointed out how improbable it was that a second convention would produce a constitution any closer to his ideal.

On April 10, 1788, Madison wrote to Washington of his uncertainty about the prospects for ratification: "I am a very incompetent prophet of the fate of the Constitution."[24] The Kentucky region, inching toward statehood but still part of Virginia, was at first supportive, but "the torch of discord has been thrown in and has found the materials but too inflammable."[25]

Madison continued to do what was in his power, writing letters in support of the Constitution. He did not limit his correspondence to Virginia. In the Maryland convention, which was in doubt, Madison wrote a delegate, "The difference between even a postponement and adoption in Maryland, may in the nice balance of parties here, possibly give a fatal advantage to that which opposes the Constitution."[26] Thankfully, Maryland ratified the Constitution, 63–11, with no amendments proposed.[27]

With the ratification convention just two months away, Monroe wrote to Jefferson, apparently as a friend of the Constitution. Rather than displaying a gradual movement toward the Anti-Federalist camp, Monroe seemed even more favorable toward the Constitution in this April 1788 letter than in his October 1787 missives to Madison and Cadwalader: "The people seem much agitated with this subject in every part of the state. The principal partisans on both sides are elected. Few men of any distinction have failed taking their part.... That it will be nowhere rejected admits of little doubt, and that it will ultimately, perhaps in two or three years terminate, in some wise and happy establishment for our country, is what we have good reason to expect."[28] When Monroe had expressed his first impressions of the Constitution in October, he had at least mentioned reservations. Now, the next spring, he seemed not to have any. Madison wrote Jefferson in April, saying, "Monroe is considered by some as an enemy; but I believe him to be a friend though a cool one."[29] But Monroe would shortly reveal himself to be cooler toward the Constitution than Madison realized.

Jefferson's next letter included a pedometer, a device for counting steps, along with instructions. "To the loop at bottom of it you must sew a tape, and at the other end of a tape, a small hook...cut a little hole in the bottom of your left watchpocket. Pass the hook and tape through it, and down between the breeches and drawers, and fix the hook on the edge of your kneeband, an inch from the kneebuckle. Then hook the instrument itself by its swivel hook on the upper edge of the watch-pocket."[30] One wonders if Madison used Jefferson's pedometer as he nervously paced Montpelier in the days counting down to June—with his entire life's work in the balance.

Hamilton, writing from New York, was distraught about the elections to his state convention. He believed that only news of prior ratification by Virginia could ensure victory in New York: "The moment any decisive question is taken, if favorable, I request you to dispatch an express to me with pointed orders to make all possible diligence, by changing horses etc. All expenses shall be thankfully and liberally paid."[31]

In the immediate approach to the convention, Monroe completed the straightforwardly titled "Some Observations on the Constitution." Before the election for convention delegates he had intended to publish it for distribution in Spotsylvania County. Delays at the printer and the low quality of the final product prevented him from distributing it there. But Monroe did send his "Observations" to people he respected, including George Washington. Monroe was revealing himself to be an opponent of the Constitution drafted in Philadelphia.

In the letter that accompanied Washington's copy of his "Observations," Monroe attempted to explain away his earlier support for the Constitution: "I had not at that time examined it with that attention its importance required, and of course could give you no decided opinion respecting it."[32] Whether he had truly not formed an opinion before, Monroe inarguably had one now. His "Observations" included his concerns about the vast, sweeping powers of the new government. Monroe had become convinced that the Constitution would lead to the destruction of the states. Then the national legislature would be left to manage the enormous "territory between the Mississippi, the St. Lawrence, the Lakes, and the Atlantic ocean" too large for it to govern.

Monroe was also concerned that the Constitution failed to protect fundamental liberties. "How are we secured in the trial by jury?" he asked. If the national government is given powers, "unless we qualified their exercise by securing this, might they not regulate it otherwise?...As it is with the trial by jury so with the liberty of conscience, that of the press and many others."

And Monroe was flatly against the direct taxation allowed for in the Constitution, believing that it must end in either anarchy or the suppression of liberty. He believed the government would use tyrannical collection tactics and that these coupled with oppressive taxes would inflame the people to rebellion.

In his "Observations," Monroe acknowledged the great defects of the Confederation, but cautioned against hastening into the proposed replacement: "Political institutions, we are taught by melancholy experience, have their commencement, maturity, and decline; and why should we not in early life, take those precautions that are calculated to prolong our days, and guard against the diseases of age? Or shall we rather follow the example of the strong, active, and confident young man, who in the pride of health, regardless of the admonition of his friends, pursues the gratification of unbridled appetites, and falls a victim to his own indiscretion, even in the morn of life and before his race had fairly begun."

Monroe had determined that he could not support the new Constitution: "Although I am for a change, and a radical one, of the Confederation, yet I have some strong and invincible objections to that proposed to be substituted in its stead." What is the hurry, he asked? "Is it to be supposed that unless we immediately adopt this plan, in its fullest extent, we shall forever lose the opportunity of forming for ourselves a good government?"

Monroe concluded his "Observations" with an appeal: "To the people of America, to you it belongs to correct the opposite extremes. To form a government that shall shield you from dangers from abroad, promote your general and local interests, protect in safety the life, liberty, and property, of the peaceful, the virtuous, and the weak." Monroe knew that his position would place him at odds with some of his oldest and dearest and friends and political allies: "To differ in any respect from these men is no pleasant thing to me; but being called upon an awful stage upon which I must now bear a part, I have thought it my duty to explain to you the principles on which my opinions were founded."[33]

While Monroe was getting his thoughts about the Constitution on paper, Madison was getting ready for the ratification convention. He studied the debates in South Carolina, which had ratified by a 149–73 vote on May 23, as well as the "Address of the Minority," produced by the Anti-Federalists in the Maryland ratifying convention. Madison was mastering the very best arguments on both sides, in expectation of the battle to come.

Chapter Eleven

THE BATTLE OF SHOCKHOE HILL

"From the first moment that my mind was capable of contemplating political subjects, I never, till this moment, ceased wishing success to a well regulated republican government."

—James Madison

When the Constitution was being considered in the ratification convention at Richmond, there was no more scope for negotiation or compromise. All the complex political issues had been reduced to one up-or-down question: Yes or No on the Constitution drafted at Philadelphia. Supporters and opponents were equally certain of the righteousness of their cause, and equally certain of the dire consequences should the other party prevail.

The date was June 2, 1788.

The delegates to the Virginia Ratification Convention met in the state capitol, chose a chaplain to say morning prayers, and elected Edmund Pendleton as chairman.

Pendleton was sixty-seven years old, asthmatic, and unable to walk without crutches. He had been thrown from a horse, his health was deteriorating quickly, and he was permitted to sit instead of stand while chairing the Convention. Pendleton began his chairmanship with a warning to the delegates:

> We are met together on this Solemn Occasion as Trustees for a Great people, the Citizens of Virginia, to deliberate & decide upon a Plan proposed for the Government of the United States, of which they are a *Member*.
>
> The trust is sacred and important, and requires our most serious attention. Let us calmly reason with each other, as friends, having all the same end in view, the real happiness of our constituents, avoiding all heats, intemperance and personal altercations, which always impede, but never assist fair investigation. Let us probe the plan to the bottom, but let us do it with candor, temper, and mutual forbearance: and finally decide as our judgment shall direct.[1]

The capitol at Richmond could barely accommodate the 168 delegates and spectators, so George Mason moved to adjourn and reconvene the following day at the New Academy building on Shockhoe Hill.

Madison arrived in Richmond later that evening to find a "very full house," much to his surprise. Delays before a quorum could be reached typified meetings of the time, but the delegates to the 1788 Virginia Convention were there on the first day and prepared for a fight. Madison observed to Washington that "the federal party are apparently in the best spirits. There is reason to believe nevertheless that the majority will be but small, and may possibly yet be defeated."[2]

The truth was that both sides were unsure of their numbers. By the time of the elections for the Virginia Ratification Convention, during the spring of 1788, candidates had already had more than six months to study the Constitution and form their opinions. Nearly all of the hopeful candidates had staked out their positions on the Constitution. But the number of supporters and opponents seemed to be about even, and there were a number of wild cards. The outcome appeared to depend on the votes of a few delegates who had yet to announce how they would vote—

including especially Governor Edmund Randolph, who had refused to sign the Constitution in Philadelphia.

The New Academy had been built for the Chevalier Quesnay de Beurepaire, the grandson of King Louis XV's court physician. De Beurepaire had dreamed of founding the first American institution of higher education that would be competitive with European universities, bringing over the finest instructors from throughout the world, and offering students the broadest curriculum available in America.[3] Unfortunately, financial problems and the French political situation prevented the launch of the New Academy, but the building remained intact and at the time of the Convention was serving as the home of Richmond's finest theater.[4]

When the Ratification Convention reconvened in the New Academy, perhaps Madison was reminded of his first days in public office, as a delegate to the Virginia Convention of 1776. Pendleton had chaired that meeting as well and authored the resolutions declaring Virginia independent. Madison had been twenty-five, unsure of himself and his place in the world, serving with the strongest leaders in Virginia. By the time of Virginia's convention to consider ratification of the Constitution, Madison was thirty-seven years old, an experienced congressman and Virginia Delegate, and the primary author of the document that the Convention delegates were to vote on.

Before delegates rushed into debate about the Constitution, Governor Randolph successfully moved to adopt the rules of the House of Delegates. By taking this measure Randolph was able to forestall what could have been days of bickering over which procedure to use.

George Mason then urged a clause-by-clause review of the proposed Constitution, with unlimited debate, before a final vote be taken: "The curse denounced by the divine vengeance will be small compared to what will justly fall upon us if, from any sinister views we obstruct the fullest inquiry."[5]

Madison surprised Mason and the other Anti-Federalists by standing up to agree to Mason's proposal. The truth was, both sides were afraid to test their strength, and each was terrified that the other party would force an immediate vote. Neither friends nor enemies of the Constitution feared debate, though there was some concern about its length. The Virginia legislature was scheduled to begin a special session June 23, and delegates felt that that the Convention should end before that date. Madison, who felt that attacks on the Constitution up to this point had been unfounded and emotional, believed that a clause-by-clause consideration of the document would only help his cause.

The Convention adopted Mason's proposal and adjourned until 11:00 a.m. the following day. It would be their last act of consensus for some time.

On the morning of June 4, Patrick Henry wasted no time in making mischief. In his first Convention speech, he moved that the Virginia resolutions for appointing delegates to Annapolis and Philadelphia be read aloud. Henry's not-so-subtle intimation was that the far-reaching changes that the Constitution made to the federal government were outside the mandate of the delegates.[6] If Henry could make the process by which it had been drafted look tainted, perhaps he could cast a shadow on the Constitution itself.

Pendleton answered Henry from the floor. "Although those gentlemen were only directed to consider the defects of the old system, and not devise a new one," Pendleton argued, "if they found it so thoroughly defective as not to admit a revision, and submitted a new system to our consideration, which the people have deputed us to investigate, I cannot find any degree of propriety in reading those papers." After all, Congress had transmitted the Constitution to the legislatures, the people had elected delegates to conventions, and eight state conventions had already voted for ratification.

Henry backed down; picking a public fight with the well-respected Pendleton was not in his interest. Besides, undecided members who were eager to get to work might not have appreciated wasting time sitting through readings of old resolutions. So the Convention proceeded to debate the Constitution line by line, beginning with the preamble and the first two clauses of Article I.

One can imagine the otherwise silent room, with many of the greatest men in American history present, as those now familiar introductory words to our Constitution were read aloud by the clerk:

> We the People of the United States, in Order to form a more perfect Union, establish justice, insure domestic Tranquility, provide for the common defense, promote the general Welfare, and secure the Blessings of Liberty to ourselves and our Posterity, do ordain and establish this Constitution for the United States of America.[7]

Henry would contest every inch of the battlefield. Not even the flowery preamble would be considered without his condemnation. "I consider myself as the servant of the people of this Commonwealth," he announced, "as a sentinel over their rights, liberty, and happiness." He believed the people were opposed to the Constitution, and that he was there to speak on their behalf. He argued that the delegates at Philadelphia had needlessly divided a country where all had been well. "I conceive our Republic to be in extreme danger," he said, and "If a wrong step be now made, the Republic may be lost forever." "What right had [the delegates]...to say, 'we the people?'" Henry wondered, "...instead of 'we, the states?' The people gave them no power to use their name. That they exceeded their power is perfectly clear."[8]

Then Randolph rose to speak. Federalists and Anti-Federalists alike waited anxiously to hear what he would say. Randolph's vote was the most important variable of the Convention. As governor, he had enormous influence. It was well known that Randolph had refused to sign the Constitution in Philadelphia. If he opposed it in Richmond, he would likely end its chances of ratification in Virginia. "I refused to sign, and if the same were to return, again I would refuse," he said. But Randolph, who had introduced the Virginia Plan in Philadelphia, believed in "a firm, energetic government," and declared that he would never "assent to any scheme that will operate a dissolution of the Union, or any measure which may lead to it." Because eight other states had already ratified the Constitution (and only nine were required to put it into effect), rejecting the Constitution would likely cut Virginia off from the new union of the states under that Constitution's authority.

One gambit by Anti-Federalist legislators had backfired. In October of 1787 they had called for such a late convention in the hope that rejection by other states would slow momentum for ratification in Virginia and possibly create an opening for a new try at amending the Articles. But the delay had inadvertently created a party of delegates who were willing to vote for the Constitution despite their reservations. There were both supporters and opponents of the Constitution in the Convention, but there was now also a third party, who had serious reservations, but—with eight other states already on board—would vote to ratify for the sake of union. That faction would be led by none other than Governor Randolph. If the Anti-Federalists had scheduled an early convention, Madison might not have been able to attend, or might not have appreciated the danger that necessitated his return. And Randolph, opposed to the Constitution and desirous of a second convention, would almost certainly have voted to reject, not to ratify.

But by the June Convention, Randolph was willing to argue for ratification for the sake of union. He took on Henry directly, mocking the Confederation, calling it Henry's "favorite system."[9]

George Mason, who like Randolph had withheld his signature in Philadelphia, continued to oppose the Constitution because it lacked guarantees of "the great essential rights of the people." However, Mason said, he would be willing to sign the document if his concerns about the people's rights could be dealt with in due fashion. He claimed that if a set of amendments to ensure basic rights could be added to the Constitution, he would "most gladly put [his] hand to it."

Madison tried to rein in the speakers and keep their focus on the clause-by-clause discussion. After all, the only part of the document yet under consideration was the preamble and the first two clauses.

But as the day ended and another began, it was clear that neither side would adhere to the rules. Clause-by-clause consideration of the

Constitution would give way to wide-ranging debate. Pendleton began by condemning the "totally inadequate" Articles, whose weaknesses had resulted in "our commerce decayed, our finances deranged, public and private credit destroyed." He simply could not accept Henry's vision of a bountiful America at peace, safe in the arms of the magnificent Articles of Confederation. If the public mind was at ease, Pendleton said, it was not from a clear understanding of the real state of affairs, rather "it must have been an inactive unaccountable stupor."

Pendleton was also incensed by Henry's assertion that the Articles of Confederation had won the Revolution: "Union and unanimity, and not that insignificant paper, carried us through that dangerous war. 'United, we stand—divided, we fail,' echoed and re-echoed through America, from Congress to the drunken carpenter.... The moment of peace showed the imbecility of the Federal Government."[10]

Henry oscillated between extolling the Articles and the America they governed and attacking the Constitution: "The rights of conscience, trial by jury, liberty of the press, all your immunities and franchises, all pretensions to human rights and privileges, are rendered insecure." Was abandoning these rights essential for liberty? Henry next returned to the theme of his most famous speech, "Give me liberty, or give me death": "Liberty, the greatest of all earthly blessings—give us that precious jewel, and you may take every thing else: but I am fearful I have lived long enough to become an old fashioned fellow: perhaps an invincible attachment to the dearest rights of man, may, in these refined enlightened days, be deemed old fashioned: if so, I am contented to be so."

Henry defended the Articles, which "rendered us victorious in that bloody conflict with a powerful nation...secured us a territory greater than any European Monarch.... [S]hall a government which has been this strong and vigorous, be accused of imbecility and abandoned for want of energy?"[11]

Henry rejected the possibility of improving the Constitution with amendments: "A trifling minority may reject the most salutary amendments," he argued. Two-thirds of Congress and three-fourths of the states would never agree to anything. He believed that even if the union were in the balance, liberty was still to be preferred. Henry claimed that government under the

Constitution would be "replete with such insupportable evils" that he would rather be ruled by "a King, Lords, and Commons."

But Henry was not ready to concede that disunion would necessarily be the price of rejection. If nine other states formed a government without us, "May not they still continue in friendship and union with her [Virginia]?" The disunion argument, advanced by Randolph and others, "'Tis a bugbear, Sir."

Henry concluded his epic speech against the Constitution by saying, "No matter whether a people be great, splendid, and powerful, if they enjoy freedom.... I speak as one poor individual—but when I speak, I speak the language of thousands."[12]

On June 6, Madison followed Henry's grand exposition with one of his own. He spoke so quietly that the stenographer would sometimes fail to record his words. But Madison was not Henry. What his arguments lacked in drama, force, and bombast, they compensated for with a steady drip of well-informed logic.

Madison asked for the Constitution to be examined on its merits, "whether it will promote the public happiness." He asked the delegates to rely not on "feelings and passions," but to undertake "a calm and rational investigation."

Opponents to the Constitution were relying on "general assertions" about its supposed "dangers." If the new Congress would have dangerous powers, "let them be plainly demonstrated," Madison said. "Since the general civilization of mankind, I believe there are more instances of the abridgment of the freedom of the people, by gradual and silent encroachments of those in power, than by violent and sudden usurpations."

Addressing Henry's arguments head on, he confessed "I have not been able to find his usual consistency.... He informs us that the people of this country are in perfect repose; that every man enjoys the fruits of his labor, peaceably and securely, and that every thing is in perfect tranquility and safety. I wish sincerely, sir, this were true." If America was secure, why did the states convene in Philadelphia, and why were the delegates here today?

Madison knew that ratification conditioned on specific amendments to the Constitution would be worse than a rejection: "If one state demands amendments, other states will do the same. Some will be different than others, and many will be contradictory." Madison believed that the enumerated powers of the Constitution sufficiently protected the rights of the people. The Federal Government, he said, "can only operate in certain cases: it has legislative powers on defined and limited objects, beyond which it cannot extend its jurisdiction."

Madison closed his speech by addressing the issue of taxation, which was a matter of great concern to Anti-Federalists and skeptics of the Constitution. "It can be of little advantage to those in power to raise money in a manner oppressive to the people," he argued. And the next morning, Madison picked up where he had left off the day before. He said that the power to lay and collect taxes was "indispensible and essential to the existence of any efficient, or well organized system of government." The system of requisitions had proven itself unreliable.

With that, Henry retook the floor, to turn on its head the argument that Virginia must stay in the union. If Virginia joined the eight states that had moved to ratify, he asked, would it disassociate from the other four as a result? He also revived the issue of the Mississippi River. Ironically, Henry argued that the Constitution would make it easier to cede the river to Spain—despite the fact that a slim majority in the Confederation Congress had nearly succeeded in abandoning the Mississippi. His argument about the Mississippi was utterly specious, but Henry rode it hard and to great effect.

Henry refused to concede the failures of the Confederation. He defended even the disastrous mechanism for funding the federal government with requisitions from the states: "I never will give up that darling word 'requisitions'—my country may give it up—a majority may wrest it from me, but I will never give it up till my grave."

On Sunday the delegates, increasingly divided, attended church together, praying to the same God with equal fervor for the opposite results that each side respectively believed necessary to avert disaster.

Meanwhile, Hamilton realized that the elections for delegates to New York's convention on ratification—scheduled for even later than

Virginia's—were even worse than he had initially realized. At least two-thirds of the delegates, he found "beyond expectation, favorable to the Anti-Federal party." Hamilton had succeeded in winning a resolution similar to the one in Virginia, so that the Constitution would also be debated clause by clause in New York—buying Hamilton desperately needed time. If the New York delegates voted before Virginia ratified, they would almost certainly reject the Constitution. "God grant that Virginia may accede," he wrote Madison.[13] If New York, a populous state and important commercial center, rejected the Constitution, the new national government could be doomed. Both Virginia and New York had to ratify to guarantee the success of the Constitution, and there was no hope in New York without a prompt and favorable result in Virginia.

If Madison had been well enough to attend the ratification convention on Monday, June 9, he would have seen Henry produce a new and surprising argument against ratification. No less an "illustrious citizen" than Thomas Jefferson, Henry told the delegates, "advises you to reject this government, till it be amended."[14]

His source was a February 7, 1788, letter from Jefferson to Alexander Donald. It was a private letter, not intended for publication, but Henry was using it in this very public debate. The letter itself was confusing; in it, Jefferson said he wanted the first nine states to ratify, with the other five holding out until a bill of rights was adopted. This was an obvious numerical error on Jefferson's part, the equivalent of a typo. There were thirteen states in all, not fourteen. And Jefferson later made his intention clear; he had meant to say that he desired nine states to ratify, and the remaining *four* to hold out until a bill of rights was passed. In June, with eight states having ratified, this would have been an argument for Virginia to ratify and become the ninth state.

But in any case Jefferson had changed his mind since he wrote the February letter. Jefferson had already repudiated his earlier thoughts in a May 27 letter to Edward Carrington. He now supported the model used by the Massachusetts Convention, which had unconditionally ratified the Constitution but recommended amendments for the first Congress to consider. Jefferson believed that Virginia, as well as all the remaining states, should do the same—ratifying unconditionally, but recommending a bill of rights, as well as term limits for the Senate and the presidency.

But here was Henry, arguing that Jefferson wanted Virginia to reject the Constitution. Jefferson, far away in Paris, had no idea how his name was being used and could not appear to explain his true feelings about the Constitution.

Henry used scattershot tactics, raising every conceivable argument against ratification. He came very close to accusing Edmund Randolph of dishonesty. Henry asked Randolph where the dangers he had recognized when he refused to sign the Constitution were: "The internal difference between right and wrong does not fluctuate. It is immutable." Henry also argued that the president would become a dictator, that the government would cost too much, and that no government could reign over so large a territory as the United States. He believed that the new government could do nothing to raise revenue, and that in any case the financial straits of the government were due to a lack of "thrift and industry." Incredibly, Henry charged that the proposed government lacked checks and balances. In fact, it was the dominance of Virginia government by the House of Delegates over the impotent Senate, governor, and judiciary, and the dominance of that House by one man—Patrick Henry—that had convinced Madison of the need for the separation of powers and the strong checks and balances that he had written into the Constitution.

Henry argued that any amendments to the Constitution to alleviate his concerns could never be hoped for from the new government. "Does it not insult your judgments to tell you—adopt first, and then amend? [I shall] take that man to be a lunatic, who should tell me to run into the adoption of a government, avowedly defective, in hopes of having it amended afterwards."

A tense moment followed during which Randolph, who had likely seethed with growing anger through the previous speech, stood up to address Henry's attack on his consistency. Henry also stood up, saying that he had not meant offense, but that he was entitled to his opinion. But for this concession, Randolph claimed, "he would have made some men's hair stand on end, by the disclosure of certain facts." Henry said that if Randolph had something to say, he ought to say it. Randolph produced a letter that he had written to his constituents prior to his election as a delegate to the Ratification Convention, explaining his opposition to the Constitution but declaring his intention to ratify it for the sake of union. He placed the letter on the clerk's table, "for the inspection of the curious and the malicious." Randolph then pointed out that six or seven states had no bill of rights, and pledged to "join any man in endeavoring to get amendments," but only after the original document had been ratified.

From his sickbed, Madison, suffering from the hot weather and one of his frequent bilious attacks, wrote, "[T]he chance at present seems to be in our favor. But it is possible things may take another turn." He was concerned to learn that Eleazer Oswald, the Anti-Federalist leader from Philadelphia, was in Richmond working with the opposition.[15]

James Monroe had hitherto been quiet on the question of ratification in the Convention. On Tuesday, June 10, his silence would end. Early that day, he arose from his seat and declared himself an Anti-Federalist. Monroe began with measured language very different from Henry's emotional rhetoric: "For my own part, sir, I come forward here not as the partisan of this or that side of the question, but to commend where the subject appears to me to deserve commendation; to suggest my doubts where I have any; to hear with candor the explication of others; and, in the ultimate result, to act as shall appear for the best advantage of our common country."[16]

There is nothing to record how Madison first learned about Monroe's opposition to the Constitution. Madison may have been aware of Monroe's "Observations." And surely the two friends would have had time to talk prior to the speech of June 10. It seems likely that Madison must by this point have known his friend's sentiments. The news came no doubt as a disappointment in light of all that they had worked on together. But by what means it came, what was said, and how the two reacted, remains between Madison and Monroe.

In his June 10 speech, Monroe dismissed the arguments in which Madison had compared and contrasted the current and proposed American governments with those of other confederacies. Those other governments, Monroe argued, were too different from that of the United States to provide any sort of guidance. Unlike Henry, Monroe was no apologist for the current government under the Articles of Confederation. "Is the Confederation a band of union sufficiently strong to bind the states together? Is it possessed of sufficient power to enable it to manage the affairs of the Union? Is it well organized, safe, and proper? I confess that, in all of these instances, I consider it as defective; I consider it to be void of energy, and badly organized."[17]

Monroe still believed that a national government should control national affairs, with local interests entrusted to the states. He maintained his long-held position that the federal government should have absolute control over commerce. Monroe was also consistent in his view of the impost, agreeing that the national government should have the power to impose tariffs on trade. He believed the impost would be nearly sufficient to fund the operations of government. The impost, along with requisitions, sales of Western lands, and increased economic activity once the Federal government regulated trade, would be enough to fund the national government.

But the new Constitution gave the new national government more power than it needed—and more power than was consistent with the liberty of the people, Monroe thought. To improve the Constitution, Monroe said, "I would take from it one power only," the power to tax individuals directly. He believed that this taxing power was a threat to liberty. Monroe was also concerned about double taxation by the state and national governments, which he believed would lead to the annihilation of the states, as people sought to throw off the yoke of one master of the two.

Monroe would have stripped from the Constitution the power to tax individuals, and he would have added a bill of rights. The lack of protections for individual rights was at the heart of Monroe's opposition to the Constitution: "I am a decided and warm friend to a bill of rights," to guard and check against the general powers of the government.

Monroe remained unconvinced by the Federalist argument that it was unnecessary or even dangerous to enumerate rights. "Permit me," he said, "to examine the reasoning...that all powers not given up are reserved." Monroe believed there was ample scope within the government's enumerated powers for it to infringe on the people's rights. Congress had the power to lay direct taxes, he pointed out, and also the authority to make all laws "necessary and proper" for the execution of their enumerated powers. If Congress were to determine that eliminating trial by jury was necessary and proper to collect taxes, there would be nothing to stop them. "I conceive that such general powers are very dangerous," he said. "Our great unalienable rights ought to be secured from being destroyed by such unlimited powers, either by a bill of rights, or by an express provision in the body of the Constitution."

Monroe agreed with Henry that the checks and balances in the proposed Constitution were too weak: "The branches will join together against the states, tighter by conflict.... I have never yet heard or read, in the history of mankind, of a concurrent exercise of power by two parties, without producing a struggle between them. Consult the human heart. Does it not prove that, where two parties, or bodies, seek the same object, there must be a struggle?"[18] Monroe also believed that, were the Constitution ratified, American rights to the Mississippi would rest on a less secure footing—though less than two years before, Monroe had led the fight to protect the river against an attempt to bargain it away by a bare majority in the Confederation Congress.

Monroe also aired a scattering of other objections. He was concerned that members of Congress were not impeachable, and also that the president commanded the army during impeachment proceedings, which were conducted in part by the Senate. (Monroe, like others, thought that the Senate would function as the president's council of advisors.) Monroe believed the Electoral College would be too easy to corrupt, and he was particularly concerned about foreign influence. He thought the president ought to depend directly on the people for his election and re-election and should be subject to term limits, lest he abuse the powers of his office to maintain control indefinitely. "Upon reviewing this government, I must say, under my present impression, I think it a dangerous government, and calculated to secure neither the interests nor the rights of our countrymen. Under such a one, I shall be adverse to embark the best hopes and prospects of a free people. We have struggled long to bring about this revolution, by which we enjoy our present freedom and security. Why, then, this haste—this wild precipitation?"[19]

The political evolution of James Monroe—from leader of the nationalists in the Congress and longtime friend to the cause for energetic federal government, to a full-blown opponent of the Constitution—has been little considered by history.

Monroe would become the only President of the United States who had once opposed the Constitution.

The consequences of this shift are critical, both for the history of the country and for a proper understanding of the man. This change in Monroe's position deserves a thorough examination.

In August of 1786, as a member of the Confederation Congress, Monroe had written to Patrick Henry, "I am thoroughly persuaded the government [under the Articles] is practicable and with a few alterations, the best that can be devised." At the time he wrote to Henry, Monroe had been in Congress a full three years. He had been able to observe the manifold weaknesses and failures of the Confederation government at close quarters. And yet Monroe did not support a wholesale rewrite of the Articles. The Constitution that was drafted in Philadelphia was a much more radical change than Monroe had ever supported. Amending the Articles of Confederation to allow an impost and federal power to regulate trade would likely have fully satisfied Monroe.

In the same letter to Henry in which he praised the Articles, Monroe shared his belief that the deficiencies of the government had arisen from the election of certain people, not from flaws inherent in the structure of the government.[20] If right-minded people were elected to the legislatures, he reasoned, requisitions would be complied with and revisions to the Articles would be made as necessary.

Monroe had been an enthusiastic supporter of both the Annapolis and Philadelphia Conventions—because he believed those conventions would procure the remedies he believed necessary: the impost and authority for Congress to regulate trade. But naturally the Monroe who wrote to Henry in 1786, before Annapolis and Philadelphia, would have opposed a new Constitution.

The real mystery about Monroe's thinking is the change—or changes—in his position that occurred in the eight months between the revelation of the Constitution and the Richmond Convention.

In his later years, Monroe wrote in his memoirs,

> From the time that the Constitution was reported from Philadelphia … the citizens throughout the country became much divided respecting its merits, those opposed to it contending that it would lead to consolidation and monarchy; those who supported it, that its adoption was indispensible to the preservation of the union and free government. By degrees the parties became violent, each imputing to the other selfish and improper motives. Those in favor of it were called Federalists; those against it, Anti-Federalists.
>
> Although Mr. Monroe was a member of the party called Anti-Federal, yet his conduct was moderate. He had been an advocate for an essential change of the system, and in the convention of the state, by whom the Constitution was adopted, he had declared that sentiment in decided terms.[21]

This recollection is true on nearly every count. Monroe had been a leader in Congress on establishing an impost as an independent revenue source for the government. He had strongly favored an amendment to the Articles to allow Congress to regulate trade. He had chaired a committee on the nation's finances and knew as well as anyone the ruinous condition they were in. Monroe had traveled to a number of recalcitrant legislatures to plead on behalf of Congress for the powers necessary to do their job.

It is questionable, however, whether Monroe can be considered a "moderate" Anti-Federalist. His first floor speech in Convention was not limited to one or two specific objections. Instead, he marshaled a host of attacks against the Constitution, some in regard to the most minute details of that document. As the Convention went on, his objections became more and more trifling, to the exasperation of attendees, including the usually unflappable Madison.

One Convention delegate wrote to another that Monroe was "desirous of exciting alarms on every subject which might get them a few votes." It is most accurately the case, then, that while Monroe's objections hung on several key provisions of the Constitution, once he had resolved to kill it, or to stop it by conditional ratification, he fought against it fiercely. Late in coming to the Anti-Federalist cause as he was, and a reluctant partisan for rejection though he may have been, Monroe pulled no punches in his attempt to defeat the Constitution. In his memoirs, Monroe explained what his thinking on the Constitution had been during this crucial period:

> Its powers transcended the limit which he had contemplated, but still he entertained doubts whether it would contribute most to the interest of the union to adopt it, in the hope of amending any of its defects afterward, or to suspend a decision on it until those amendments should be previously obtained.
>
> We find that he was decidedly for a change and a very important one in the existing system, but that the Constitution reported had, in his opinion, defects which required amendment and which he thought had better be made before it was adopted.[22]

These recollections are mostly supported by the record. Monroe's journey from October 1787 to June 1788 was long and not without complications.

On May 23, 1787, he had written Madison at the Convention in Philadelphia with enthusiasm for the project on which he believed the rest of American history would turn. It is tempting to attribute Monroe's opposition to the Constitution, once it emerged from the Philadelphia Convention, to that imagined nefarious conspiracy between Randolph and Madison excluding Monroe from Philadelphia. But Monroe was too patriotic and conscientious to decide a question of such national importance on the basis of a personal slight. Monroe would never have acted contrary to the best interests of his country as he saw them. In the same July 27 letter in which he complained to Jefferson of his exclusion, he was still solidly behind the Philadelphia Convention, writing that its failure "would complete our ruin." He concluded that letter by saying, "I shall, I think, be strongly in favor of and inclined to vote for whatever they recommend."

In October, after Monroe had a chance to read the Constitution drafted at Philadelphia, he wrote to Madison and Cadwalader that his objections, while serious, "were overbalanced in favor" of maintaining the union and ending the current calamitous state of affairs. He explicitly called for the adoption of the Constitution. Monroe was still a supporter of the Constitution in his April 10, 1788, letter to Jefferson, in which he claimed he believed the Constitution would nowhere be rejected (its rejection in Rhode Island was unknown to him at the time) and would result in a "wise and happy" establishment.

Monroe's support for the Constitution from October 1787 to June 1788 seems to contradict the position he had held before, and the best arguments that can be made in his defense are that he recognized the defects of the Confederation and the exigencies of the time; that certain measures he had long championed were included in the Constitution; and that it was associated with people who had long been his political allies and heroes, such as Madison and especially Washington. Those considerations delayed but did not defeat Monroe's joining the Anti-Federalist camp.

The Virginia Anti-Federalists, well organized and led by great Virginians such as Patrick Henry and George Mason, gave Monroe cover to do what he increasingly thought was right. Without such a well-developed faction in opposition, it is unlikely that Monroe would have stood alone. But he could draw strength knowing that he was in good company.

Not the least of the party opposed to ratifying the Constitution was Joseph Jones, whose heroic efforts in the national interest made him another unlikely Anti-Federalist. Jones, like his nephew and surrogate son Monroe, opposed ratifying the Constitution without a bill of rights.

Monroe can be taken at his word; his serious concern about the need for a guarantee of rights was genuine. And history has demonstrated that he clearly had the better argument than Madison and the Federalists on this issue substantively if not procedurally. Even after the adoption of the Bill of Rights, the federal government has continually violated fundamental liberties. Less than ten years after the adoption of the First Amendment, for example, the Congress passed the Alien and Sedition Acts, which made criticism of the government punishable as a crime. How much more would the Congress have tread on free speech rights were they not explicitly protected in the Constitution?

The Constitution had polarized Virginia's leaders, creating allies of enemies and enemies of old friends. For now, the political partnership of James Monroe and James Madison was at an end.

Chapter Twelve

THE RACE FOR NINTH

"Loving his country as he does, he would not surely wish to trust its happiness to an experiment, from which much harm, but no good may result."

—Patrick Henry

The question of the Mississippi had the power to swing the entire Constitutional debate. The undecideds at the Virginia Ratification Convention largely hailed from the Kentucky district, which was bordered on the west by the great river. If they could be convinced that the new government posed a threat to American rights to the Mississippi, they would vote against the Constitution.

On June 11, Madison argued in Convention that the weakness of the current government posed the greatest threat to the Mississippi. The new government, he claimed, with power to bring the combined resources of the union together for common defense, was its best protection. The constitutional power to implement a direct tax would guarantee the United States the revenue it needed for the common defense and ensure that "none would be willing to add us to the number of their enemies."

Next, Madison addressed Monroe's arguments against direct taxation head on. In a time of war, Madison claimed, trade would be hurt, and imposts would decrease. "I hope we are considering government for a perpetual duration," he said, and "we ought to provide for every future contingency." Madison saw very little difference between the direct tax and requisitions—except that the direct tax could actually be collected in an emergency, whereas the requisitions never were. Instead of the national government taxing states, which passed the expense on to the people, it could more effectively and efficiently tax the people directly. Madison also pointed out the opportunity cost of requisitions, considering how much of every legislative session was spent debating how or whether to pay them, with as many as twenty-five hundred state legislators unable to discuss other important business.

Madison pointed to the unsettled national debt as a danger to the nation's liberty. Direct taxation would free America from onerous obligations to creditors. In one of the most lively and entertaining speeches of the Ratification Convention, William Grayson argued that the national debt was not a serious concern. "I believe that the money which the Dutch borrowed of Henry IV is not yet paid," he said. A loan involving Queen Elizabeth was repaid "at a very considerable discount." Loans between nations, Grayson argued, were not like loans from private individuals. Nations lend money and assistance to one another in the furtherance of their national interest. France did no more for us, he argued, than "pluck the fairest feather from the British crown."[1]

Grayson also ridiculed Governor Randolph's alarmism about the current state of affairs in America under the Articles of Confederation:

> ... we shall have wars and rumors of wars; that every calamity is to attend us, and that we shall be ruined and disunited forever, unless we adopt the Constitution. Pennsylvania and Maryland are to fall upon us from the north, like the Goths and Vandals of old; the Algerines, whose flat-sided vessels never came farther than Madeira, are to fill the Chesapeake with mighty fleets, and to attack us on our front; The Indians are to invade us with numerous armies on our rear, in order to convert our cleared lands into hunting-grounds; and the

> Carolinas, from the south, (mounted on alligators, I presume,) are to come and destroy our cornfields, and eat up our little children![2]

Henry Lee, thinking that argument absurd, asked whether Grayson imagined "that he that can raise the loudest laugh is the soundest reasoner?" Henry Lee and the Federalists did not find Grayson's speech funny at the time, but this would not always be the case. When the volumes of the debates of the Virginia Convention were finally published, Madison and Grayson, as members of the new Congress, would share a laugh over this comedic diatribe.

By June 12, Pendleton had obtained the letter from Thomas Jefferson that Henry had used two days earlier in support of his contention that Thomas Jefferson "advises you to reject this government, till it be amended." Pendleton read the letter aloud to the delegates, making it clear that Jefferson had wanted the first nine states to ratify, and only four to hold out until certain amendments were passed. Jefferson's letter was actually a strong argument for the position taken by Randolph and other delegates who supported ratification on the grounds of unity despite their reservations about the Constitution: "We must take care, however," Pendleton read, "that neither this, nor any other objection to the form, produce a schism in our union. That would be an incurable evil; because friends falling out never cordially re-unite."

In light of events during Madison's election for the House of Representatives, which would take place in just over six months, his next argument is worth noting. "Is a bill of rights a security for religion?" he asked. "Would the bill of rights of this state exempt people from paying for the support of one particular sect, if such sect were exclusively established by law?" Madison argued that true religious freedom came from a multiplicity of sects, where no denomination could form a majority to "oppress and persecute the rest." He believed that the diverse patchwork of religious denominations across the American states was a better guarantee of religious freedom than any explicit constitutional language would be. Madison then reverted to his enumerated powers argument, saying, "There is not a shadow of right in the general government to intermeddle with religion. Its least interference with it would be a most flagrant usurpation." Madison held up his "uniform conduct on this subject" as a champion of freedom of religion as proof that he argued against the need for a constitutional guarantee as a true friend of religious liberty, not an enemy.

On June 13, Patrick Henry reverted to bold and unpredictable maneuvers. He called on anyone with personal knowledge to disclose what he knew about the issue of the Mississippi in Congress. Henry Lee argued that Jay had never been directed to give up the Mississippi and that the Confederation Congress had "earnestly wished to adopt the best possible plan of securing it."

This inaccuracy prompted Monroe to answer Henry's call. "There was a time, it is true, Sir, when even this state, in some measure, abandoned the object, by authorizing its cession to the Court of Spain." At that time, however, the South had been in the hands of the enemy. South Carolina and Georgia had been defeated, and North Carolina was offering feeble resistance to the British. Virginia was invaded, and the enemy moved freely and caused much carnage throughout the commonwealth. But after the peace, Monroe recalled, Gardoqui was sent to treat on the issue of the river, and Jay was instructed to enter into no treaty that did not acknowledge America's rights to the Mississippi. Monroe then brought the convention up to speed on what had happened when seven Northern states had voted to repeal Jay's instructions.

Madison announced that he was reluctant to engage on the subject, veering as it did from the question at hand. But Monroe's argument was so thin that Madison could not fail to respond. Madison pointed out that under the new Constitution, the president and two-thirds of senators present would have to agree on every treaty. The Anti-Federalist argument was that the president and two-thirds of the Senate could give the river away more easily than nine states in the Confederation Congress. Madison asked the obvious question: Couldn't the Northern senators be absent just as easily as those from the South? The root of the problem of the Mississippi, Madison argued, was that the present system of government in the United States was weak. American weakness induced countries like Spain to make extraordinary demands. A strong system, like the one for which he was advocating, would deter this and future threats.

Grayson doubled down on the argument that American rights to the river would be more vulnerable under the Constitution, pointing out that the new Senate would have at most twenty-six members. A quorum would be fourteen, and two-thirds of a quorum would be ten. That meant that ten senators could ratify a treaty to give away the Mississippi.

George Nicholas had heard enough of this argument. He jabbed at Henry, pointing out that the Mississippi was already almost given away, and "By whom?—by Congress, under the existing system, the worthy member's favorite confederation." Nicholas pointed out what would need to happen for the Anti-Federalists' proposed scenario to play out: "First, that on the important occasion of treaties, ten Senators will neglect to attend; and in the next place, that the Senators whose states are most interested in being fully represented, will be those who fail to attend."

Even as they met there, Nicholas pointed out, Congress was preparing a bill for Kentucky statehood. This would mean two new senators in favor of keeping the Mississippi, as well as an increase in the number needed for a two-thirds majority. He also explained a glaring problem with the current system: under the Articles, nine states were needed to make a treaty. Therefore, even if the Congress of the Confederation grew from thirteen states to one hundred states, the number needed to ratify treaties would still be nine, unless the states unanimously agreed to amend it.

Randolph was also aghast. "I have seen so many attempts made," he said, "and so many wrong inducements offered, to influence the delegation from Kentucky, I must, from a regard to justice and truth, give my opinion on the subject." He argued that the new government had no power to give away the territory of a state. He appealed to the statesmanship of the Kentucky delegates, "Let me entreat those gentlemen, whose votes will be scuffled for, to consider in what character they are here. For what have they come hither? To deliberate on a Constitution, which some have said will secure the liberty and happiness of America...Will they, as honest men, not disdain all applications made to them from local interests? Have they not far more valuable rights to secure?"

As the storm of words raged inside the New Academy, a rainstorm raged outside, growing in intensity until the Convention had to be adjourned for the day.

Back in his room, Madison was more pessimistic than ever. The delegates from the Kentucky district were unlikely to look past the river issue. For what would it profit a man to gain the best new government in the world, only to lose his property, watch his friends and family lose theirs, or see the economy of his homeland decimated? With the rain pounding the walls and windows of his room, Madison wrote to Rufus King, who had served with him at the Constitutional Convention, "The issue of it is more doubtful than was apprehended when I last wrote... the vote of Kentucky will turn the scale, and there is perhaps more to fear than to hope from that quarter. The majority on either side will be very small and at present the event [result] is as ticklish as can be conceived."[3] It is worth noting that King, as a congressman from Massachusetts, was the chief proponent of Jay bargaining away the Mississippi. It is interesting to consider whether King regretted this, especially in light of how his actions now jeopardized the Constitution that he so strongly supported.

The following day, as the storm outside abated, the tempest in the New Academy proceeded apace. The debate from here on out would be more focused on the Constitution itself. The third section of Article I, which concerns the powers of the Senate, was read aloud. As delegates leveled a trickle of minor criticisms, we can almost see Madison throwing his hands up. He pointed out that "it was not possible to form any system to which objections might not be made." By the time Article I, Sections 4 and 5 were read, the Convention had considered only the preamble and five sections of one article in the eleven days since they first met. On day twelve, the pace picked up, and delegates began to move quickly through the rest of the Constitution. But Madison's frustration with trifling objections from the Anti-Federalists, including his former ally Monroe, was still palpable.

Monroe challenged Madison on state control of the time, place, and manner of elections. Under the new Constitution, elections for Congress would be regulated by the state legislatures, but Congress had power to alter their regulations. Madison responded, "The power appears to me satisfactory, and as unlikely to be abused as any part of the Constitution." The states, Madison explained, would have the opportunity to conduct elections, but if that power were abused, the federal government could step in. (He gave the case of Charleston, South Carolina, which had thirty representatives in the state legislature, far out of proportion to its share of the population, as an example of the kind of abuse that would justify federal intervention.) Monroe pressed further, asking for an explanation of why the House or Senate could not adjourn for more than three days without the consent of the other. Couldn't this increase the influence of one body over the other? Madison wondered how this clause could possibly "meet with a shadow of objection."

Clauses 6 and 7 of Article I were reviewed in a similar fashion, with the Anti-Federalists attempting to raise whatever objections they could. During the debate over Clause 8, Madison and Henry engaged in an interesting dialogue that reveals the increasing tension in the room.

"From the first moment that my mind was capable of contemplating political subjects," Madison said, "I never, till this moment, ceased wishing success to a well regulated republican government. The establishment of such in America was my most ardent desire."

Henry responded, "Loving his country as he does, he would not surely wish to trust its happiness to an experiment, from which much harm, but no good may result."

Madison answered, "The honorable member expresses surprise that I wished to see an experiment made of a republican government, or, that I would risk the happiness of my country on an experiment. What is the situation of this country at this moment? Is it not rapidly approaching to anarchy? Are not the bands of the union so absolutely relaxed as almost to amount to a dissolution?" Madison was convinced that the flaws in the current federal government were so fundamental that it was failing. The only realistic hope that republican government could succeed was the new Constitution.

The delegates adjourned until Monday at 9:00 a.m., a new and earlier start time that would stand throughout the Convention. They had covered a lot of ground, and a lot of ground was still left to be covered.

"The necessity of a bill of rights," Henry argued, "appears to me to be greater in this government, than ever it was in any government before." Unless a bill of rights was attached to the Constitution, "Excisemen may come in multitudes...go into your cellars and rooms, and search, ransack, and measure, every thing you eat, drink, and wear."

As Section 9 was read and debate began over titles of nobility and *habeas corpus*, Madison began to believe a deliberate strategy was under way to delay Virginia's decision until New York had the chance to reject. Delaying the vote would prevent a favorable outcome in Virginia from influencing New York to ratify, and if news of rejection in New York reached Richmond in time, it would dramatically undercut the argument for union and likely spell defeat for the Federalists.

The remainder of Article I was quickly debated, and Article II, which lays out the executive powers, was on deck. Monroe announced his opposition to the Electoral College. The president, he believed, "ought to depend on the people of America for his appointment and continuance in offices." Monroe was concerned that small states would conspire to deadlock the Electoral College in order to force the race into the House. When the House decides the presidency, each state has a single vote. Monroe argued for presidential term limits, believing that the powers of the office would guarantee the holder life tenure, if he so desired. He would not be the last to complain that the "Vice President is an unnecessary office." Monroe also argued that the vice president's tie-breaking vote in the Senate gave one state three votes in that body.

The Electoral College had been the subject of extensive debate in Philadelphia and was the product of hard work and compromise. Madison stood up, frustrated that nobody had "pointed out the right mode of election." It was easy for Anti-Federalists to criticize what the delegates to the Constitutional Convention had drafted; in most cases, they had not proposed alternatives.

By the following day, the Convention was debating Article III, which deals with the judiciary. During the second day of debate on this Article, Madison argued for one Supreme Court to create uniformity in the law. He believed, "This power cannot be abused, without raising the indignation of all the people of the states." Madison also believed that good government without virtuous people "is a chimerical idea. If there be sufficient virtue and intelligence in the community, it will be exercised in the selection of these men."

Monroe's old schoolmate John Marshall joined the debate on the Federalist side, asking what makes us trust our judges, and then answering his own question: "their independence in office, and manner of appointment." If Congress "were to make a law not warranted by any of the powers enumerated, it would be considered by the judges as an infringement of the Constitution which they are to guard.... They would declare it void." Marshall, who would be the first Supreme Court Justice to use judicial review to invalidate an unconstitutional law,* asked, "To what quarter will you look for protection from an infringement on the Constitution, if you will not give the power to the judiciary?" Madison added that the lack of impartial courts has "prevented many wealthy gentlemen from trading or residing among us," as well as permitting many debtors to avoid payment.

Article IV was quickly read and considered, and the remainder of the Constitution was read through on June 23. The Convention was hurtling toward a vote.

With the Constitution now thoroughly debated and examined, each side advanced closing arguments.

George Wythe argued that while some amendments might be necessary, nobody could deny how excellent much of the Constitution was, nor how important the union, nor how weak the Confederation. He urged ratification with recommendation of amendments.

Patrick Henry presented a list of amendments and rights he wanted forwarded to the other states prior to ratification. He argued that "previous amendments"—that is, amendments that would have to be added

* One party to the case in question was none other than James Madison. In *Marbury v. Madison*, Chief Justice Marshall ruled part of the Judiciary Act unconstitutional, in the first exercise of federal judicial review.

to the Constitution before Virginia would ratify—would provide "union, firm and solid."

Governor Randolph reviewed all of the rights Henry proposed enumerating, explaining either where they were already guaranteed in the Constitution, or where Congress had no power to trample them. Randolph claimed that if he could "bring [his] mind to believe that there were peace and tranquility in this land, and that there was no storm gathering which would burst, and that previous amendments could be obtained, I would concur.... For nothing but the fear of inevitable destruction would lead me to vote for the Constitution in spite of the objections I have to it." He was willing to vote for an imperfect Constitution only because the alternative was worse.

Madison then made his closing argument in favor of the document whose principle author he was: "Nothing has excited more admiration in the world, than the manner in which free governments have been established in America. For it was the first instance from the creation of the world to the American Revolution, that free inhabitants have been seen deliberating on a form of government, and selecting such of their citizens as possessed their confidence, to determine upon, and give effect to it." Every state could never be totally happy, Madison explained. How much less could every individual be satisfied? "It has never been denied by the friends of the paper on the table, that it has defects." It would later be argued by Anti-Federalists that Madison said in Convention that not a letter of the Constitution could be spared. But he was not claiming it was perfect. He conceded that it had been a product of "mutual deference and concession." The Constitution was not perfect, but it was the best that would be drafted. It had been conceived before the creation of parties, when "men's minds were calm and dispassionate." "Everyone has their objections," Madison said, "but if Virginia will agree to ratify this system, I shall look upon it as one of the most fortunate events that ever happened, for human nature."

Henry, among the greatest courtroom lawyers of his generation, began his own closing argument with a storm gathering outside the hall. Where Madison saw the blessings of the proposed government, Henry saw the threat:

> I see the awful immensity of the dangers with which it is pregnant. I see it. I feel it. I see beings of a higher order anxious concerning our decision. When I see beyond the horizon that binds human eyes, and look at the final consummation of all human things, and see those intelligent beings which inhabit the ethereal mansions, reviewing the political decisions and revolutions which in the progress of time will happen in America, and the consequent happiness or misery of mankind, I am led to believe that much of the account on one side or the other, will depend on what we now decide. Our own happiness alone is not affected by the event. All nations are interested in the determination. We have it in our power to secure the happiness of one half of the human race. Its adoption may involve the misery of the other hemispheres.[4]

With lighting flashing outside and casting a light into the chamber, and rain and thunder drowning out his words, Henry was forced to stop.

On June 25, George Nicholas made a motion to ratify the Constitution.

Monroe spoke in opposition. He "could not conceive that previous amendments would endanger the union. Adopt it now unconditionally and it will never be amended, not even when experience shall have proved its defects." And "What are the amendments brought forth by my friends? Do they not contemplate the great interests of the people, and of the union at large?" Monroe believed that by holding out, Virginia could dictate more favorable terms at a second convention, or pressure those states that had ratified to meet again and adopt changes.

At the Convention's close, a number of first-time speakers rose, men who had previously been content to let others carry the debate but now wanted to explain their decision—the most important most of them would ever make in public life. Randolph was clearly mindful of his place in history as he delivered his last remarks:

> The suffrage which I shall give in favor of the Constitution, will be ascribed, by malice, to motives unknown to my breast. But although for every other act of my life, I shall seek refuge in the mercy of God—for this I request his *justice* only. Lest, however, some future analyst should, in the spirit of party vengeance, deign to mention my name, let him recite these truths—*that I went to the Federal convention*, with the strongest affection for the union; that I acted there, in full conformity with this affection: that I refused to subscribe, because I had as I still have objections to the constitution, and wished a free enquiry into its merits, and that the accession of eight states reduced our *deliberations* to the single question of *union or no union*.[5]

Patrick Henry then made a substitutionary motion, that prior to ratification, "a declaration of rights" together with proposed amendments be referred to the other states for their consideration. It was a desperate last-ditch attempt to delay the process in Virginia. But if it worked, it would almost certainly achieve the defeat of the Constitution. New York would vote to reject, the states would not agree on amendments, and the argument from union would have lost much of its strength when and if Virginia considered ratification again.

Henry's motion was the first test of the strength of the parties in Convention. If Henry's proposal passed, the Convention would end without ratification. The roll call must have been agonizing. At times the "ayes" were winning, at times the "nays" pulled ahead. When the results were in, there were eighty votes in favor and eighty-eight opposed to Henry's motion.

The main question was then put back on the floor: Should the Constitution be ratified and amendments be recommended to the first Congress?

By the ever so slender margin of eighty-nine to seventy-nine, Virginia ratified the Constitution of the United States. Two committees were then formed: one to draft a form of ratification, and the second with members from both parties to recommend amendments.

Oblivious to New Hampshire's ratification earlier in the week, the delegates in Richmond believed Virginia had been the ninth state to ratify, and thus had launched the new government under the Constitution. But though they had not truly witnessed what they thought, they had seen something no less historic. Virginia had not been the state whose ratification brought the new government into existence. But the Virginia delegates were certainly, more than those of any other state, the ones that ensured the Constitution—and perhaps even the Union—would live into the future. A nine-state union without either Virginia or New York could not have survived long, and if it did would have utterly failed in its objectives. What value would the power to regulate trade be when Virginia, New York, North Carolina, and Rhode Island were free to set their own rules, adopt their own currency, create their own regulations?

Madison wasted little time writing to Hamilton to tell him of the results. And on the same very day in Poughkeepsie, New York, Hamilton wrote Madison to tell him, "Our chance of success here is infinitely slender, and none at all if you go wrong."[6]

On June 26, the Virginia Ratification Convention sent a copy of their ratification to the President of Congress and arranged to pay their own officers, president, secretary, chaplain, sergeant, and doorkeepers. They also appropriated funds to pay for any damage they might have done to the building.

The next and final day of the Convention produced a committee report that recommended a bill of rights with twenty provisions, plus twenty structural amendments to the Constitution.

As the delegates in Richmond parted, nobody could feel truly at peace. Ratification had been far too closely won for rejoicing. The victory at the expense of old friendships and alliances came with drawbacks even for the Federalists. And the Anti-Federalists believed that they had come agonizingly close to saving their country from monarchy or anarchy, and had failed.

Late that evening, Patrick Henry received a strange summons. He was asked to appear in the chamber of the Virginia Senate, at a meeting of the Anti-Federalist delegates, apparently led by William Cabell and David Meade Randolph. Their sinister purpose was to resist the new government by any means possible. But Henry would have nothing to do with any plans for extralegal resistance. He had "strenuously" worked to defeat the Constitution, done everything he could, as they all had. Now, "[t]he question had been fully discussed and settled," he said, and "as true and faithful republicans, they had all better go home!"[7] Henry was not surrendering, but he would confine his formidable opposition to legal avenues. His statesmanship prevailed, and the secret meeting scattered.

On July 2, a messenger appeared in Poughkeepsie, New York, with a letter for Hamilton. His stomach must have been tight with anticipation. If Virginia had ratified, New York might follow suit. If they had rejected, the Constitution was doomed in his home state.[8]

Hamilton read Madison's letter to the delegates of the ratification convention in Poughkeepsie, New York. Already aware of New Hampshire's ratification as the ninth state, New York would now have to choose between union with ten states or separation with Rhode Island and North Carolina only. It would take twenty-four more days of pushing by Hamilton, but on July 26, 1788, the leader of the Anti-Federalists and twelve of his party voted for the Constitution. New York approved the Constitution by a vote of thirty to twenty-seven—making Madison's ten-vote victory in Virginia look like a landslide.[9]

As the Anti-Federalist monster lay dying in New York, it fired off one powerful closing salvo. The "New York Circular Letter" was produced by New York's ratifying convention and agreed to unanimously (Hamilton and the other Federalists had been forced to agree as a concession to achieve ratification). The Circular called for all the states to join in a second constitutional convention to repair the defects of the first. It would take two-thirds of the states to trigger such a convention, but with New York and likely Virginia leading the charge, that might easily be possible. If the Anti-Federalists' concerns about the Constitution were not addressed in the First Congress, a new convention was the likely result. And, Madison foresaw, it would be fatally easy for Anti-Federalists to use a second constitutional convention to bring down the Constitution and split the Union.

In 1857, a man in his ninetieth year and undoubtedly the last living witness to the Virginia Ratification Convention, recalled that remarkable event: "I was a stripling, and clerk in one of public offices, and could of course only attend the debates at intervals snatched from the duties of the office. But the impressions made by the powerful arguments of Madison and the overwhelming eloquence of Henry can never fade from my mind. I thought them almost supernatural. They seemed raised up by Providence, each in his way, to produce great results: the one, by his grave, dignified, and irresistible arguments to convince and enlighten mankind; the other, by his brilliant and enrapturing eloquence to lead whithersoever he would."[10]

This little known epoch, when the Constitution itself hung in the balance, has faded from memory, obscured by the great events that preceded and followed it. Filling the void is the myth that America's Founders were all-knowing, and therefore always agreeing—a band of demigods who always recognized and always chose the right.

Perhaps modern esteem for these figures serves as a reminder that, though statesmen may have to struggle mightily to advance their cause, and though they may lose on an issue or come out on the wrong side in the judgment of history, their principled determination is sufficient to win them a place in people's hearts, long after they are gone.

Chapter Thirteen

THE TERRIBLE SESSION

"Something is surely meditated against the new Constitution, something more animated, forceful and violent, than a simple application for calling a convention."

—EDMUND RANDOLPH

In July Madison returned to New York, where the Confederation Congress was busy planning the start date and location of the First Congress under the Constitution.[1]

It was determined that members of the Electoral College would be chosen in January and meet the following month to choose the president and vice president. The new Congress would meet in March of 1789, in New York. Though Madison had his heart set on a site near the Potomac River for the Capitol, tensions were high, and he yielded the point.

Madison knew that the Constitution was nowhere close to being out of the woods. Virginia Federalists had saved the Constitution in New York. But Virginia Anti-Federalists were working hard to influence the convention considering ratification in North Carolina. And in August, Anti-Federalists triumphed there. North Carolina refused to ratify the Constitution. The Jefferson letter that Patrick Henry had made use of to such dramatic effect in the Virginia Ratification Convention once again made an appearance, and once again influenced the deliberations. In the end, North Carolina adopted a list of amendments that must first be passed by the new Congress before the state would ratify.

North Carolina, the fifth-largest state, was home to nearly four hundred thousand people. North Carolina's absence from the Union separated South Carolina and Georgia from the rest of the ratifying states and left a significant part of the country outside the new government.

The New York Circular had a major impact on Virginia, Madison wrote Randolph, as "a signal of concord and hope to the enemies of the Constitution every where, and will I fear prove extremely dangerous."[2] Madison confessed to Washington that New York's ratification of the Constitution along with the Circular was perhaps more dangerous than a rejection would have been. He wrote, "If an early general convention cannot be parried, it is seriously to be feared, that the system, which has resisted so many direct attacks, may at least be undermined by its enemies."[3] Washington did not need convincing. He too was in terror of a second constitutional convention. Such an event, he believed, would "set every thing afloat again."[4] Meanwhile, Anti-Federalists in Pennsylvania were meeting to plot their next steps and organizing for the upcoming state and national elections.[5]

The recent opposition between Madison and Monroe in the Virginia Ratification Convention did not seem to have affected their relationship. Madison resumed their friendly correspondence where he had left off, and Monroe promptly replied. Monroe had bought lottery tickets for his family and friends, including Madison. His friends had all won, Monroe informed Madison, and the only losing tickets he'd bought were for himself and his own family.[6]

Madison now had to consider what role he wanted to play in the new government. James Gordon, his Orange County seatmate from the ratification convention now serving in the House of Delegates, was eager to know. "It will be a matter of satisfaction to your friends in this state," he wrote, "to know whether you wish to be in the Senate or House of Representatives so soon as the districts are laid out."[7]

On September 16, 1788, Madison succeeded in passing a congressional resolution declaring the navigation of the River Mississippi a "clear and essential right of the United States," and forbidding any further negotiations. Gardoqui departed for Spain without the prize he had so eagerly sought and had almost won. Monroe was thrilled with the result and congratulated Madison on his success. The business of the Mississippi would be passed on to the new government.[8]

In fact, nearly everything would be passed on to the new government. On October 17, Madison wrote to Jefferson that Congress had been unable to reach a quorum, and that he did not expect nine states, or even seven states, to be in attendance ever again. In the clarity of the post-ratification period, Madison shared his thoughts on amendments with his friend, still in France: "My own opinion has always been in favor of a bill of rights; provided it be so framed as not to imply powers not meant to be included in the enumeration. At the same time I have never thought the omission a material defect, nor been anxious to supply it even by subsequent amendment, for any other reason than that it is anxiously desired by others. I have favored it because I supposed it might be of use, and if properly executed could not be of disservice."[9]

The Virginia House of Delegates attained a quorum on October 21, 1788.[10] They had previously met for a week in June after the Convention, but that special session was called only for the House to act on a decision by the Court of Appeals. During the regular October session, the Anti-Federalists would make their first legislative moves against the new Constitution and its supporters.

Patrick Henry stood astride the House like a colossus. He was surrounded by a loyal pack of followers, and those who could not be led by other means were bullied, threatened, and intimidated. Members who still stood in his way were trampled underfoot. Defeat was as unfamiliar to Henry as it was unwelcome, and the victory of the Federalist party at the ratification convention had been a severe blow. But here on the floor of the House of Delegates, his natural habitat, Patrick Henry was without equal.

The evidence for Henry's standing and abilities is abundant. While praise from friends must be weighed skeptically, praise from adversaries is almost always reliable. In the House of Delegates, James Gordon testified, Henry was "greatly an overmatch for any Federalist I know in the same." The Federalists were "generally temperate and inactive," Randolph noted, while their opponents "furious and active." Washington observed that "the edicts of Mr. Henry are enregistered with less opposition by the majority of that body than those of the grand monarch are in the parliaments of France. He has only to say let this be law—and it is law." Henry Lee believed that "Mr. Henry is absolute and every measure succeeds."

In the House, Henry would not face the worthy opponents he had faced in Virginia's Ratification Convention. Most Federalist leaders were not members of the legislature. Those who were, such as Marshall and Nicholas, were absent on business at the beginning of the October 1788 session. Francis Corbin was the only Federalist member of the House of Delegates present who had spoken in the Convention.

Henry wasted no time fulfilling his promise to oppose the Constitution by every legal avenue. If he had disappointed his followers in the Senate chamber meeting, he would now exceed their wildest hopes. For the friends of Federalism, this would be a legislative session of terror.

When Henry arrived in Richmond for the opening of the session, Randolph observed that "he appears to be involved in a gloomy mystery." Randolph feared some attack on the Constitution "more animated, forceful and violent, than a simple application for calling a convention."[11] The first shot across the Federalists' bow came as the New York Circular was presented to the House for its consideration. The task of writing a response was sent to a committee.

Edward Carrington, for years a friend and supporter of Madison, had been a member of Congress when he was elected to House of Delegates.

He had resigned from Congress shortly before taking his seat, as one could not simultaneously hold both offices. This procedure was not without precedent; no one had made an issue of it in the past. But after arriving in Richmond, Carrington began to hear rumors that his right to serve in the House of Delegates was in doubt. Before a series of contentious votes should divide and inflame the members, Carrington thought it best to force the immediate consideration of the issue.

On October 23, Benjamin Harrison reported from the Committee on Privileges and Elections. Carrington had become a congressman in November of 1787. In April of 1788 he had been elected in Powhatan County to the House of Delegates. On October 20 he had resigned his seat in Congress. Since he did not hold both offices simultaneously, the committee determined he was eligible to serve.[12] Harrison had been a determined Anti-Federalist, but he never contemplated abusing his power to punish those who were at odds with him.

Normally, such allegations would never have been taken seriously. If they had been investigated at all, the initial committee report would have ended the matter. But in the toxic atmosphere of Patrick Henry's House of Delegates, a motion was made to recommit the issue to committee. The following day, the committee issued a more extensive report, citing the various applicable laws in support of Carrington's right to serve. They resolved that "Edward Carrington, Esq., was capable of being elected a Delegate to represent the said county of Powhatan in this present General Assembly."

But this straightforward issue was politicized on the House floor. Patrick Henry gave a speech denouncing the evils of the Constitution—not especially germane to the validity of Carrington's election. A motion was made to strike the word "capable" and replace it with "incapable." It passed by a wide majority, and the House of Delegates issued a writ for a new election from Powhatan.[13]

The Carrington incident demonstrates how Henry's beliefs about the Constitution and his enormous power in the legislature manifested themselves in intensely petty and personal ways. Carrington was re-elected in Powhatan only days later.

Monroe, delayed by some unfinished business in his law practice, took his seat on October 26. Though Monroe had served with Carrington when they were young delegates and their families had planned to live together in Richmond, the fight over the Constitution had hardened hearts. Monroe evinced no sympathy for his friend, the victim of unnecessary, obviously politically motivated harassment: "The merits of the case I know not and only judge from external circumstances," Monroe said.[14]

On October 30, a resolution was offered "for quieting the minds of the good citizens of this commonwealth, and securing their dearest rights and liberties, and preventing those disorders which must arise under a government not founded in the confidence of the people, application be made to the Congress of the United States, so soon as they shall assemble under the said Constitution, to call a convention for proposing amendments to the same."

The Federalists offered a substitute resolution, calling for the Constitution to be examined by the new Congress, with proper amendments to be recommended by them. The Federalists were defeated by a vote of eighty-five to thirty-nine. Monroe was appointed to the committee to respond to the New York Circular, along with French Strother and William Cabell.

Strother had represented Culpeper County in the legislature for many years. He had served in the Virginia Conventions of 1776 and 1788, where he voted against ratification. Cabell, who represented Amherst, was born in 1730, and had served in the Burgesses before independence. He too had served in the Conventions of 1776 and 1788, and had also voted against ratification. Both Strother and Cabell were considered possible candidates for the First Congress, but would later support their younger colleague.

Their committee report surprised no one. It stated, "The slow forms of Congressional discussion and recommendation, if indeed they should ever agree to any change, would we fear be less certain of success. Happily for their wishes, the Constitution has presented an alternative, by admitting the submission to a convention of the states. To this therefore, we resort, as the source from whence they are to derive relief from their present apprehensions."[15]

As the Anti-Federalists began their offensive, Madison began to make his intentions for his own future clear. "I mean not to decline an agency in the new government," Madison wrote Randolph on October 17, indicating his preference for the House of Representatives, "chiefly because if I can render any service there, it can only be to the public, and not even in imputation, to myself."

In the modern era it is unthinkable that anyone with a realistic chance of serving in the House or Senate would prefer the former. Each election cycle brings with it hordes of representatives seeking membership to the upper chamber. No incumbent senator has vied for a place in the House of Representatives in modern memory, while even powerful members of the House have run for the Senate when the opportunity presented itself.

In 1789, however, the House of Representatives would enjoy a heightened legitimacy because its members were directly elected by the people. Members of the Senate were indebted to the state legislatures that chose them, and while the length of their terms offered a degree of independence, members who strayed too far from the instructions of their legislatures would find themselves ousted in favor of more complaisant candidates.*

The Senate was also initially less exclusive than it is today. The current House is over four times as large as the Senate, but during the First Congress the Senate was actually over twice the size of the House.

The House of Representatives also had the power to originate all revenue bills. Today this power exists in a more diminished form. The Senate simply writes its own bills dealing with revenue issues, waits for the House to deliver House revenue bills, and then amends them to conform to the Senate's wishes. But in the First Congress, the House would have the first crack at creating a national revenue system and establishing the executive departments.

Though Madison preferred the House, his supporters would try to put him in the Senate. Carrington, no doubt speaking for many Federalists,

---

* Senators would not be directly elected until 1913, with the adoption of the Seventeenth Amendment.

believed that Madison was the only Federalist who had the remotest chance of winning one of the two seats. But Alexander White, a Federalist Delegate, believed a "strong party" existed "against Mr. Madison. It is a doubt notwithstanding his great abilities, his virtue, and his respectful polite behavior to all men of all parties whether he will be elected as one."[16] Richard Henry Lee and Richard Grayson would be the Anti-Federalist candidates.

On October 31 Madison was chosen by the legislature to serve in the final Congress of the Confederation. Their choice has been interpreted by some as a maneuver by Henry to keep his greatest adversary far from Virginia so that he could continue to work his mischief against the Constitution undisturbed. That explanation certainly cannot be ruled out. Similarly, it is possible that Madison had, years earlier, helped Henry become governor to remove him from the debate over religious freedom. But it is just as likely that Madison's reelection was nearly automatic, so long as he wanted to serve in Congress. There is surprise among some historians that Madison accepted the seat, but his acceptance makes sense. It was too late for Madison to join the legislature, so his choice was between serving in Congress or sitting at home in Orange. During the few intervals in his public service after 1776, Madison had found himself bored and unsatisfied. In addition, there was always the possibility that Anti-Federalists in Congress might make decisions that would hamstring the new government. And the Mississippi issue, while it appeared settled, had the potential to flare up again. Plus, Madison was already in New York. He anticipated winning a seat in the new House of Representatives without returning to Virginia and was already where he needed to be when Congress reconvened.

On November 8, the day set for Senate elections, Patrick Henry took the floor and personally nominated Richard Grayson and Richard Henry Lee. Madison's was the only name offered by the Federalists in the House.

Henry engaged in a "pointed attack" on Madison for his "attachment to the federal government."[17] He called Madison "unworthy of the confidence of the people" and warned that his election "would terminate in producing rivulets of blood throughout the land."[18] One disappointed observer declared, "Hereafter, when a gentleman is nominated to a public office, it is not his virtue, his abilities, or his patriotism we are to regard, but whether he is a Federalist or Anti-Federalist."[19]

Henry's diatribe was not without effect. Lee and Grayson won with ninety-eight and eighty-six votes, respectively. Madison trailed at seventy-seven. Delegates had two votes each, and of the 162 legislators, sixty-two voted for Madison alone. Carrington encouragingly pointed out to Madison that many members had ignored their Anti-Federalist principles to support him, in a testament to his personal worth. The ballot was secret, so we do not know whether Monroe voted for his old friend and political ally or if Anti-Federalist partisanship prevented him from supporting Madison.

On November 14, the bill for the election of representatives pursuant to the Constitution came before the House for a vote. Monroe was one of fifteen members on the committee to draft the statute. The committee decided to choose Virginia's ten members from districts rather than using the at-large system planned in some other states.[20] Anyone eligible to vote for the legislature could vote for Congress.

In 1789, eligibility to vote for the legislature was limited to male freeholders older than twenty-five who owned either twenty-five acres with a house or fifty unimproved acres. In the cities of Williamsburg and Norfolk, the only towns represented in the assembly, freemen with six months residency could vote if they owned a "visible estate" worth fifty pounds or had served an apprenticeship to some trade within the town for five years.

For the 1789 Virginia elections for Congress, boundaries followed county lines.** The 5th Congressional District created by the election bill included the counties of Albemarle, Amherst, Fluvanna, Goochland, Louisa, Spotsylvania, Orange, and Culpeper. This was a transparent act of what would later be known as "Gerrymandering." The strategy is

** In the 1960s, the Supreme Court ruled that districts for the House of Representatives must adhere to the "one man, one vote" principle, and each must be equal in population.

simple: create as many safe seats for your political party as possible and draw district lines that will make it as difficult as possible for your opponents to win. In this case, the 5th Congressional District was designed to exclude a single man: James Madison. The committee Monroe was serving on had squeezed Madison's home county into a district with overwhelmingly Anti-Federalist counties.

One historian has noted Henry's "rare bit of luck...that the wits of Virginia did not" think to describe "this trick as 'Henrymandering;' and that he thus narrowly escaped the ugly immortality of having his name handed down from age to age in the coinage of a base word which should designate a base thing—one of the favorite, shabby maneuvers of less scrupulous American politicians."[21] Today, the decennial redistricting process has become a million-dollar battle for both political parties, a bare-knuckled fight to create the most favorable playing field for elections over the next decade. Modern technology allows politicians to determine the effects of moving a boundary line a few feet in any direction.

Patrick Henry and his allies had only one tool at their disposal, but it was a powerful one. The elections to the Virginia Ratification Convention had been held less than a year before, and most candidates had been open about their positions on the Constitution. Thus it was fairly easy to gauge the predispositions of the voters of each county. In the 5th Congressional District, Anti-Federalist candidates had won both seats in Amherst, Fluvanna, Goochland, Spotsylvania, and Culpeper. In Louisa, the two delegates were split. Only in Madison's home county of Orange and Albermarle were two Federalists elected. And if Henry's forces could have figured out a way to keep Madison in the 5th District but exclude Orange, they might well have done so.

The 1790 census, conducted by the U.S. Marshals,[22] broke down the county population of white men above the age of sixteen. Although the requirements for voting were more restrictive, a look at the population of each county will give a general sense of what Madison was up against. The margin of victory in the delegate elections was closer in some places than others. Still, it is clear that Madison had his work cut out for him.

Population for the counties voting for two Anti-Federalist delegates:

Amherst	2,056
Culpeper	3,372
Fluvanna	589
Goochland	1,028
Spotsylvania	1,361
Total	8,406

Population for the counties voting for two Federalist delegates:

Albemarle	1,703
Orange	1,317
Total	3,020

Louisa, where one Federalist and one Anti-Federalist delegate had been elected, had 957 white males older than sixteen. Madison would be facing an electorate nearly three times more Anti-Federalist than Federalist.

Madison's supporters offered an amendment to the election bill to add Fauquier County, which had voted for two Federalist delegates, to the 5th District. This amendment has been held up by Henry apologists as proof that Federalists were playing the same game as the Anti-Federalists but were simply outvoted. Fauquier, according to the 1790 census, had 2,674 white males older than sixteen. Using the same formula as before, if Fauquier had been added to the 5th District, it would have meant an Anti-Federalist majority of 2,712, instead of 5,386. Rather than "Henrymander" the district in their favor, the Federalists were only trying to make it slightly more competitive. With Henry leading the charge against Madison, the amendment was defeated handily. "We wished to get Fauquier but the powers of the Antis were too strong for us," Carrington lamented.

The election law of November 19 further required that voters would "assemble at their respective county courthouses on the second day of February next and then and there vote for some discrete and proper person being a freeholder and who shall have been a bona fide resident for twelve months within such a district." This was an outrageous provision, designed for no other reason than to force Madison to run in the district the Anti-Federalists had created deliberately to defeat him.

Monroe, who helped draft this election statute, had gotten a seat in the Virginia Ratification Convention only by running in Spotsylvania after being defeated in King George. Other prominent Anti-Federalists including George Mason had done the same.

An amendment to strike out the residency provision was defeated eighty to thirty-two, by a margin that indicates some Federalists voted against it. Perhaps they were prevailed upon by their opponents to be "non-partisan" and "reasonable." The Anti-Federalists definitely had the advantage in this battle. They were atop a hill, fortified, with the wind at their backs, while the Federalists were trudging upward, outnumbered, with the sun in their faces.

Patrick Henry had, "within four weeks from the opening of the session ... succeeded in pressing through the legislature, in the exact form he wished, all these measures for giving effect to Virginia's demand upon Congress for amendments."[23] He had won the election of two Anti-Federalist senators, an achievement that was probably less sweet to him than having excluded Madison. The latter would now have to fight in a most unfavorable district for a seat in the House of Representatives. Madison appeared to have been shut out of Congress altogether.

The November 19 *Virginia Centinel* published a letter from one of the Delegates, a cry for help: "You may expect every evil from this assembly which Anti-Federalism can produce." The anonymous author bemoaned the recent U.S. Senate elections, the defeat of Madison, and the ad hominem attacks pushed by Henry.[24]

Madison's supporters urged him not to take the bait. His cousin, the Reverend James Madison, encouraged him to run in a different district, as his "election appears certain in the lower part of the country. If a freehold be required in the district, lots in this town may be had at a very low rate." Along with Madison's other supporters, his cousin was pessimistic about his chances in the 5th District. "I should not have written you upon this subject had it not been reported that the views of some or of a party were to endeavor to exclude you altogether from a share in the new government."

Randolph was of a similar mind and suggested that Madison move to Henrico County. It is a testament to Madison's popularity and esteem that perhaps the only congressional district where he might lose was the one configured by his enemies for that very purpose.

As for the residency requirement created to anchor Madison in the district, many of his supporters believed it was unconstitutional. The measure blatantly defied Article I, Section 2 of the Constitution, which sets forth the requirements for members of the House. A member must be twenty-five years old, a citizen for seven years, and a resident of the state where he is running. Throughout history and in the present day, members of Congress have represented districts in which they are not residents. The Virginia legislature had acted in an area where they had no authority, and their residency requirement directly conflicted with the Constitution.

Some noted that the new representatives were judges of their own membership. It was unthinkable that the new House would expel Madison from Congress for violating the residency requirement. The vote to invalidate his election would take a two-thirds majority. But if the House failed to invalidate Madison's election, the Virginia Anti-Federalists would certainly file complaints with Congress, and an embarrassing investigation would be sure to follow.

Not all of Madison's supporters agreed with the carpetbagger approach. Alexander White poured cold water on the idea of running in a different district. He believed that flagrantly breaking the law for any reason would cause a public uproar and could endanger Madison's chances in any district. The House of Delegates was still the most respected and powerful institution in Virginia, drawn from the ranks of the best-regarded members of every community. It enjoyed greater legitimacy among the voters than the new national government. Pointing out the unconstitutional nature of the residency requirement would do little to quiet the uproar. It would be also be a most unwelcome distraction from the issues in the election and Madison's record of public service.

Madison's position on adhering to the rules of the game, particularly residency rules, was already on record. In 1777 Madison had accepted defeat rather than bribe voters as his opponent and so many other Delegates had done. And in 1786 Madison had written to Washington about Benjamin Harrison, who had been defeated for the legislature—"baffled in his own county," as Madison put it. Elections were held on different days in different counties, and it was rumored that Harrison would run in Surry, "and in case of a rebuff there to throw another die for the borough of Norfolk. I do not know how he construes the doctrine of residence." Madison's amusement and disapproval of Harrison's wanderings reveal his scorn for this sort of gamesmanship.[25] There had been a humiliating inquiry into Harrison's election.[26]

Madison's supporters did agree that he must return as soon as possible to campaign in person. Madison expected to stay in New York, preferring election by "the spontaneous suffrage of his constituents." But his friends were telling him that his presence in the district was absolutely necessary.

Meanwhile, the Anti-Federalists were looking to field their most viable candidate. They seem to have considered a handful of men, including French Strother. But James Monroe, a youthful war hero with considerable experience, was the strongest possible candidate—if they could persuade him to run. There was little doubt, particularly after the Senate elections, that Madison would run for Congress from the district including Orange. Monroe was reluctant to run against his friend, and even with the built-in advantage of such a heavily Anti-Federalist district, Madison would be no pushover.

Joseph Jones discouraged Monroe from running. Jones consistently advised Monroe to focus more on law and less on politics, but he had another reason for advising his nephew to stay out of this race. It seems that Jones, though he had opposed the Constitution, thought Madison would be the better congressman. While Monroe was the closest thing he'd ever had to a son, Jones took the extraordinary step of staying neutral in the race that followed.[27]

But Monroe was encouraged to run by people he respected—likely Mason, Strother, Joel Early, and even Patrick Henry himself. Monroe seems to have protested, citing his friendship with Madison and his reluctance to deny him a place in the House.[28] The Anti-Federalists persisted—and prevailed by appealing to Monroe's feeling that he had a duty to represent their shared beliefs in the upcoming election. The Anti-Federalists would have their preferred candidate.

On December 8, Madison informed Thomas Jefferson that he would return to Virginia and personally fight for the seat. Burgess Ball, an ally with a good understanding of the district and its important players, handicapped the race for Madison: "The counties annexed to ours are arranged so, as to render your election, I fear, extremely doubtful, the greater number being Anti-Federal."[29] Culpeper, the most populous county in the district, "you know is much at the disposal of one man, and it is pretty certain he means to exert himself in favor of your opponent, Colonel Monroe." This was French Strother, the longtime Delegate for that county.

"This county," Ball said of his home of Spotsylvania, "I'm in hopes, will be at least as much for you as against you, the principal men having declared themselves for you." If Madison could post a respectable number in Monroe's home county, it would go a long way toward his success. If Madison could meet voters in person, Ball had "no doubt that you would frustrate the designs of that great man [Henry]."

In Albemarle, Ball believed that Madison would lose only a few votes, while in Amherst he would receive only a few. Louisa was likely to split down the middle again, as it had in the election for the Ratification Convention. "Thus, sir, on Culpeper it is generally thought the decision will depend." Ball felt that Orange would be secure, but he worried that Strother's influence would extend to Charles Porter, the man who had defeated Madison for the legislature in 1776. Porter, as a former Delegate, could be a beachhead for the Anti-Federalists in Madison's backyard.

Ball also knew that the road to Congress led through the critical community of the Baptists. "Upon the whole, the Baptist interest seems everywhere to prevail...I think upon such an occasion, I would even solicit their interest through some friends in a proper manner."

Ball closed the letter with more sad news. Madison's devoted friend James Gordon had fallen victim to a mental breakdown, though there were hopes of a speedy recovery. The cause was thought to be the ferocious combat of the previous legislative session.

Chapter Fourteen

THE FIRST ELECTION

"The present crisis is the most important that will probably ever happen in this country... on the choice of these persons depends our future well-being and prosperity."

—The Virginia Centinel

These were the very first elections for Congress under the new Constitution. And no residents of a U.S. congressional district have ever had a better selection of candidates since the 5th District of Virginia in the election of 1789.

Both candidates had long records of public service—each had served with great distinction in the House of Delegates, the Council of State, the Congress of the Confederation, and the Virginia Ratification Convention. Madison was the more prominent public figure, the chief architect of the Constitution, and perhaps the greatest political thinker in American history. But he was running as a Federalist in an overwhelmingly Anti-Federalist district that had been drawn deliberately to exclude him from Congress. Monroe was also a prominent, popular, and respected Virginia statesman; a lawyer with a successful private practice; and a Revolutionary War hero.

Both candidates were highly motivated to win the election. James Madison's shining career of public service had not been interrupted since Charles Porter's bribery of the voters with meat and drink had cost Madison a place in the first Virginia House of Delegates. And James Monroe much preferred public service to the law practice he had had to resort to when he failed to return to Virginia to campaign in person for the 1786 House of Delegates election—and lost it by four votes. But each man believed, and they were right in so believing, that much more was at stake than their personal careers. The future of the Constitution and the new government it established hung in the balance.

Both candidates bore the scars of their previous electoral losses.

Madison had been defeated in the election to hold his seat when the 1776 Virginia Convention became the first House of Delegates. He surely did not regret complying with the law, which forbade bribing the voters with food and drink. But Madison may have regretted not making an issue of his opponent's breaking that law. He had relied on the voters to prioritize his public service over full bellies, and they had disappointed him. This time, Madison would brave long distance, rough roads, and frigid temperatures to confront his opposition directly. The Anti-Federalists were claiming that Madison believed the Constitution was perfect as written; he would spare no pains to answer this distortion of his words and beliefs.

Monroe had been defeated in King George's County in the legislative elections of 1786. His manager had pleaded with him to campaign in person, predicting that an in-person campaign would prevail, while an absentee candidate would go down to defeat. This prophecy proved correct, by four votes. Monroe, occupied with business in Congress and newly married, did not travel to Virginia for the canvass. This defeat meant nearly a year without the opportunity to serve. If this weren't bad enough for a man who chafed whenever he found himself not engaged in public service, it meant a life practicing law, something Monroe dreaded.

Monroe was resolved never to lose again, certainly not for lack of hard work. Despite his initial hesitancy to run, Monroe poured himself into the campaign with frenetic energy, determined to campaign everywhere, to personally engage voters, and to make liberal use of his pen to correspond with community leaders. From the first days of the race, Monroe wrote letter after letter to voters and mailed them to a county's prominent Anti-Federalists, who would then distribute them personally to the intended recipients.

In this crucial race, both Madison and Monroe would engage in a style of retail campaigning that was rare in the eighteenth century.

George Lee Turberville, a young supporter of Madison from Amherst and a former member of the House of Delegates and the Virginia's ratification convention, had also served with Monroe in the Revolution. Turberville witnessed the Anti-Federalist machine in action and was alarmed.[1] Monroe's letters addressed to William Cabell were filling the Amherst post office. Cabell was as powerful as any one man could be in a county. The county seat, Cabellsville, was named for his family. Cabell would soon run as a presidential elector, receiving 270 votes in Amherst for himself to absolutely zero for his opponent. Cabell was taking Monroe's letters and distributing them to other men of influence.

Tuberville heard first hand the relentless message of the opposition: Madison was a friend to direct taxation and a believer that "not a letter of the Constitution could be spared." The first charge was misleading; the second, flatly false. The Constitution did give Congress the power to lay direct taxes on individuals. Madison argued that the power of direct taxation was necessary. His defense of this power did not mean, however, that he intended to support its exercise. Madison believed that simply having the power to raise money for defense would deter nations such as Spain from acts of hostility. If war could not be avoided, Madison believed the tax would be essential. Madison was not running for Congress in order to raise taxes on individuals. As to the second charge, it is simply counterfactual to suggest that Madison believed the Constitution to be perfect. He had always said otherwise.

Monroe did not have—and would never have had—anything to do with dishonest campaigning, especially against his friend. Monroe was an honest person who would campaign on his political differences with Madison. His surrogates and allies, however—Cabell, Strother, Henry, and others—did not feel similarly constrained.

Tuberville was not the only Federalist concerned about the state of the campaign. With their candidate still in New York, Madison's anxious supporters began the race without him. In December, a pamphlet written by "A True Federalist" was distributed and published throughout the district, and even picked up by newspapers in New York and Philadelphia. This essay defined the message of the Federalists for the rest of the campaign. According to "A True Federalist," this election for Congress was not about whether the Constitution should be amended, but how and by whom.

The writer of the pamphlet took exception to the negative campaigning of the other side and asked the public to consider "whose conduct has been the most temperate, consistent, and dignified, and best adapted to the attainment of the great end—the amendments which we all think necessary."[2] James Madison possessed "the most patriotic and unblemished character, whose life had been an uninterrupted series of great and useful services; whose virtues stand only equaled by his talents, which to the last ages will be the boast of his native land, as they are at present the admiration of America and the world."

The essay complained of Madison's exclusion from the Senate, because, it said, "he had appeared the firm and able advocate of the new system and because one man [Henry] thought this...a crime so black, as to obliterate the remembrance of his former services, to make him the victim of his country's censure; and above all, to banish his virtues and talents from that council where they would have been most signally useful."[3] "Show yourself the generous protectors of personal virtue," the essayist exhorted in his closing. These false allegations were the "last effort of a disappointed party, which attempted to clog the operations of a government, the establishment of which it could not prevent."

It was summer when Madison had last traveled from Virginia to New York. He had come from the successful Ratification Convention, buoyed on the wave of his native state's support for the Constitution. Virginia had agreed to join with her sister states in the new government.

It was winter when Madison took the same road again, returning to Virginia. The Anti-Federalists' resolve had not been broken by their initial defeat; they had dug in and redoubled their efforts. New York, later joined by Virginia, had called for a second constitutional convention.

Madison expected defeat at the hands of Monroe, but he wasn't giving up yet. By December 18, he had arrived in Alexandria and written to request that his father send a carriage to take him and his belongings to Montpelier. His decision to return, he noted, was "rather of a recent date."

Perhaps the greatest enemy of any political campaign is time—a finite but critical resource. Madison had a lot of ground to cover before the February 2 election, and not a minute to spare. His supporters offered suggestions to help him fill his schedule.

George Nicholas was particularly helpful with scheduling, as well as with campaign strategy: "Every art has been used to prejudice the minds of people against you," he warned. Nicholas advised Madison to publish his address in newspapers that would be delivered to "every freeholder's fireside." Because freezing temperatures and snow would limit attendance at January "Court Days," during which legal proceedings and other events important to the community were held, newspaper publicity would become especially important. Still, Nicholas encouraged Madison to attend every Court Day he could. No opportunity to meet even a few voters could be ignored.[4]

Nicholas also suggested campaigning at polling places on January 7, the day set for the election of the Electoral College—even though the presidential election, he believed, would be poorly attended, too, not only because of the weather but because the election of George Washington as president was a foregone conclusion.

Nicholas pointed out that Fluvanna and Amherst Counties would not have another Court Day before the election and suggested specific influential people in those places and others that Madison should write to personally. Like Burgess Ball, Nicholas suggested Baptist Minister John Leland, whose reach extended into Louisa and Goochland Counties.[5]

Nicholas also impressed upon Madison that he was so intrinsically tied to the Constitution in public opinion that his defeat would be perceived across the continent as a rejection of his great work. For Madison, the stakes—both political and professional—could not have been higher.

Newspapers were a significant source of information for voters during the election of 1789; both sides made use of them. An "Appeal for the Election of James Monroe" ran in January.[6] The Constitution, the author of the "Appeal" argued, "in its present form has not the hearts and affections of the people: their fears and apprehensions are greatly alarmed and in my opinion very justly." If "proper men are elected...the amendments will take place and thereby the minds of people quieted and I hope peace and happiness secured." James Monroe, the author pointed out, is a man of character, integrity, and experience, having served as a member of Congress, House of Delegates, and Council of State.

The "Appeal" painted Monroe as a defender of the liberty America had been blessed with: "Nine tenths of the habitable globe are immersed in and groaning under the most dreadful oppressions of tyranny, and that never was the design of providence ... it is only by a strange and unaccountable perversion of His benevolent intention to mankind that they were ever deprived of liberty."

Monroe, the essayist argued, was the only choice for voters who wanted to amend the Constitution to make their liberty secure. While "A True Federalist" had conceded that amendments were necessary but claimed that Madison was the best man for the job, the author of the

"Appeal" could point out that his candidate had been a leading proponent of amending the Constitution at a time when Madison was its chief defender. The choice, he argued, was between one candidate who had been "uniformly in favor of [amendments], or one who has been uniformly against them...the object of amendments can alone be promoted by one who feels a desire for their introduction."

The Anti-Federalists were determined to make this race a referendum on amendments—to convince voters that a vote for Monroe was a vote for amendments; a vote for Madison, against them.

American politicos today obsess over electoral results, believing they can use them to divine the future. Things were no different on January 7, 1789, when Virginia held its first elections for the Electoral College. Since both candidates were pledged to Washington, the race became a test between the candidates' positions on the Constitution. General Edward Stevens, a Revolutionary War hero who supported the Constitution, faced off against William Cabell, the Anti-Federalist.

The electoral districts and congressional districts were not exactly coextensive, there being twelve of the former and only ten of the latter. But six of the counties in the 5th Congressional District were in the same electoral district, and the vote in them held out some hope to Madison.[7]

	Stevens	**Cabell**
Albemarle	109	71
Amherst	0	270
Culpeper	177	26
Fluvanna	15	66
Orange	113	4
Spotsylvania	268	10

The Federalist Stevens had beaten the Anti-Federalist Cabell by 682 to 447 in those counties which were in the 5th Congressional District.

Monroe's residence in Spotsylvania, however, meant that he would probably fare better there than Cabell had, and perhaps even do as well as Stevens. Also, Stevens hailed from Culpeper, the population center of the district. Louisa and Goochland were part of a different Electoral College district, where the exact tallies are unknown. The results of this election meant only that the race between Madison and Monroe was close; either side could take the win.

On January 12, Jefferson sent Madison copies of various declarations of rights circulating in Europe, which everyone seemed to be "trying their hands at forming." He also thanked Madison for a previous letter including samples of the Mohican language. Jefferson was comparing Mohican to the languages of Asia and trying to detect a common ancestry. While Madison much preferred natural science and political theory to a winter of difficult campaigning, he preferred public service to both. And he knew that he would have nothing but time to study were he to lose.

Both candidates courted critical constituency groups. No group of this kind was more numerous, or more politically motivated, than Virginia's religious dissenters. Baptists and other dissenters had been motivated by something experienced by such minority sub-groups throughout history—political intolerance and abuse by their government.

Monroe was planning to attend a meeting of Baptist preachers in Louisa. Ben Johnson, a Madison supporter, caught wind of this meeting and told Monroe that he would find out where and when the meeting was to be held and forward the information on by special messenger at his own expense. It is likely that even this message was delivered by special messenger while Madison was campaigning in Louisa.

Though Madison had supported their rights to religious liberty in the past, the Baptists were not an easy sell. Back on March 7, 1788, in the run-up to Virginia's ratification convention, the Baptist General Committee had had its regular meeting in Goochland County. There they had unanimously resolved that the Constitution did not "make sufficient provision for the secure enjoyment of religious liberty." This resolution was an easy decision for them. (A more contentious issue—whether to call for the "yoke of slavery to be made more tolerable"—was a topic they held over until the next session.)

The Baptists were the most consequential voting bloc in the 5th District, and they probably had no leader more important than George Eve. Born in 1748, Eve was raised in Culpeper County. He first professed faith and joined the Baptists at the age of twenty-four when an itinerant preacher visited the community. At thirty years old, Eve became a minister, creating the "Ragged Mountain Baptist Society" in his home county. In order to avoid religious persecution, the group met secretly in an orchard of beech trees.[8]

Because there were few Baptist ministers at the time, it was not uncommon for a man like Eve to serve multiple congregations. In addition to his duties to Ragged Mountain, he was the pastor of Blue Run and Rapidan Churches. Eve himself may have been present in the latter church when its pastor, Elijah Craig, was arrested at the pulpit. Adam Banks, another member of Rapidan, was arrested in a private residence simply because of the content of a prayer. The owner of the home, who was not a Baptist, was jailed as well for permitting such an offense.[9] Between Ragged Mountain, Rapidan, and Blue Run, Eve had hundreds of congregants in the 5th Congressional District and was recognized as a leader in the broader Baptist community.

It was to George Eve, then, that Madison, much to the relief of his supporters, began to explain his true beliefs. And Madison's letter didn't arrive in Eve's hands a moment too soon.

On January 17, 1789, Eve presided over a worship service at Rapidan Church, in Culpeper. Adam Banks, the same man who had been jailed for worship in a private home, made a motion that the congregation should debate the upcoming election for Congress. He further moved that the church unite its formidable voting bloc behind a single candidate.[10]

Joel Early, an Anti-Federalist member of Virginia's late ratification convention, seconded the motion. In the debate that followed, Early alleged that while in convention Madison had called the Constitution flawless, "the nearest to perfection of any thing that could be obtained." Early said that proof could be found in the second volume of the debates, which he insinuated were being held back for sinister reasons. Early had been repeating these allegations throughout Culpeper County to anyone who would listen.

Madison had always freely conceded that the Constitution was imperfect, the product of compromise. The Anti-Federalists were twisting his argument that the Constitution was the best actually viable alternative into an absurd claim he had never made—that the Constitution was beyond criticism or amendment. The Anti-Federalists were by now accustomed to making these allegations without challenge, as they had done for months in meetings, at taverns, and by firesides throughout the district. Having made the same claim in the House of God, Early must have convinced himself of its veracity. On this cold Culpeper night, the Anti-Federalists would finally be confronted with the truth.

Eve held a letter from Madison, dated January 2, explaining his real position regarding amendments. Madison's brother William had told him that Eve was skeptical of the Anti-Federalists' accusations against him and stood ready to defend him if Madison would only provide the necessary ammunition. With Madison's letter in hand, Eve was able to relay Madison's real sentiments to the Baptist congregation at Rapidan.

In the letter Eve held, Madison confronted the accusations against him—that he was "opposed to any amendments whatever to the new Federal Constitution" and that he had "ceased to be a friend to the rights of conscience." As a candidate for Congress, Madison wrote, he felt it important "that my principles and views should be rightly understood." He freely admitted that he did not see the same dangers in the new Constitution as some others did. Madison also admitted to having opposed amendments before the ratification process was complete. He had believed a second convention or conditional ratification to be dangerous.

But Virginia had ratified the Constitution, and "*Circumstances are now changed*," Madison wrote. Amendments, he said, "*if [they are] pursued with a proper moderation and in a proper mode, will be not only safe, but may serve the double purpose of satisfying the minds of well meaning opponents, and of providing additional guards in favour* [sic] *of liberty.*" Now, he explained, "it is my sincere opinion that the Constitution ought to be revised, and that the first Congress meeting under it, ought to prepare and recommend to the States for ratification, the most satisfactory provisions for all essential rights, particularly the rights of conscience in the fullest latitude, the freedom of the press, trials by jury, security against general warrants, &c...."[11]

Madison was introducing the First Amendment and the Bill of Rights as a campaign promise to the most influential constituency in his district in the midst of a contentious election. With this written guarantee in hand, Eve was a powerful advocate for Madison. In addition to these promises, Eve reminded his flock that it was Madison who had shepherded the Virginia Statute of Religious Freedom through the House of Delegates and who had been the prime opponent of the dreaded general assessment that would have taxed all Virginians to support the Episcopal Church.

It is a common campaign practice for opponents of candidates with long legislative records to take particular votes out of context to use as ammunition. One member of Rapidan Baptist pointed out that Madison had voted in favor of establishing the Episcopal Church as the official state religion. Madison regretted this vote perhaps as much as anything he'd ever done, but it had been only tactical. Madison had voted for establishment to keep proponents of state-established religion from going even further—actually taxing the people, including dissenters, to support the Episcopal Church. And Madison had passed a repeal of religious establishment in the very next session (a fact his critic ignored entirely). Eve explained this compromise and also pointed out that Monroe had voted for state establishment of Anglicanism, too—despite having promised the Baptists not to.

Ben Johnson was one Virginian present in Rapidan the night that Eve turned the tables on the opponents of Madison. After the meeting, he traveled with some of the attendees to the river. Church meetings were some of the few social outlets for rural Virginians in the 1700s. The isolating nature of farm life prompted them to brave the weather to enjoy the company of friends for a little while longer. In talking with the Rapidan Baptist congregants, Johnson learned that Eve had "greatly damaged Early's cause"—by answering the Anti-Federalist case against Madison and reminding Baptists of the very good reasons they had for trusting him.

While both candidates were seeking support among the Baptists in Louisa, Madison also wrote a letter to Thomas Mann Randolph, a prominent citizen of Goochland County.[12] He admitted and defended his opposition to amendments before the ratification process was completed. Madison also freely admitted that he did not see amendments as the panacea that others did, but acknowledged they could make the Constitution "better in itself; or without making it worse, will make it appear better to those who now dislike it." Winning the honest critics of the Constitution was the goal. Madison pledged to Thomas Mann Randolph that his "sincere opinion and wish" was that "Congress, which is to meet in March, should undertake the salutary work," of the "clearest and strongest provision...for all those essential rights which have been thought in danger," with specific promises to protect the "rights of conscience, freedom of the press, trials by jury," and "exemption from public warrants." This letter was published in the January 28 edition of the *Virginia Independent Chronicle*, just six days before the election.

Meanwhile, on January 14, Madison discussed the heated contest in a letter to the anxious General Washington. He wrote, "The field is left entirely to Monroe and myself. The outcome of our competition will probably depend on the part to be taken by two or three descriptions of people, whose decision is not known, if not yet to be ultimately formed." Madison told Washington that he was campaigning in Culpeper and Louisa, personally asking for votes and pushing back against falsehoods that he saw as the "most likely to affect the election, and the most difficult to be combated with success within the limited period." Madison lamented the active campaigning he was now engaging in, telling Washington, "I have pursued my pretensions much farther than I had premeditated."

Monroe and Madison were engaging in a personal campaign that was a dramatic break with tradition. The new congressional districts were the largest that Virginia—which at the time had no statewide elected officials—had ever seen. Madison and Monroe were used to elections in one county; there were eight counties in the 5th District. Previously, the limited number of voters in any district had meant that candidates could (and according to the dictates of the time, should) rely on their reputations in any bid for public office. More active campaigning for votes was regarded as unseemly. It is telling that Madison did not make a public address until eleven years after first being elected to office. But if the voters in the 5th District of Virginia in 1789 were disgusted with undisguised ambition in a candidate for office, they had no alternative—despite misgivings, Madison and Monroe were both campaigning hard to win.

After a bitterly cold and snowy period of campaigning, Madison's friend David Jameson asked him to come back to Culpeper. Monday would be Court Day, and Monroe would be in attendance. Jameson appreciated and acknowledged his friend's reluctance to engage in retail campaigning, but prodded him, "When we find there are evil minds using every measure which envy or malice can suggest to our prejudice, it frees us from the restraint we otherwise should feel."

On January 15, the *New York Daily Advertiser* printed a letter from "a gentleman in Virginia to his friend in New York City." He wrote, "In this district Mr. Madison and Mr. Monroe are competitors and I am told will spare no pains to forward their election. In whose favor it will terminate is very doubtful." The author predicted an Anti-Federalist victory in a close race. The letter was reprinted widely in other newspapers in other states, suggesting the national importance of this Virginia congressional race.

On January 17, Henry Lee offered Madison his own update about the campaign. Madison was quickly making up lost ground, building a network of powerful and active supporters throughout the district, and his personal appearances were yielding dividends. But Lee did not dare to make a final prediction, the outcome being shrouded in "much doubt and difficulty."[13] Madison was gaining ground, but were the efforts of the Federalists too little, too late for victory?

While the candidates traveled the district, met with voters, and wrote letters asking for support, the war by proxy continued in the newspapers. A Federalist using the name "Candidus" launched the next salvo against the opposition. He urged his readers to remember that the old government had been far too weak. The Anti-Federalists, he claimed, "would imprudently pull down an edifice of which we all stand in need, and which hath been constructed by able artists, without trying its advantages, because they have dreamed they can improve upon it." The Constitution was the final product of America's greatest minds. Could the Anti-Federalists really do better? Candidus urged his countrymen to "elect friends to the union as our representatives in Congress."

The two candidates made numerous appearances together in front of different audiences. "We used to meet in days of considerable excitement," Madison later remembered, "and addressed the people on our respective sides. . . ."[14] Madison and Monroe rode together, lodged together, and dined together, keeping each other company on the lonely campaign trail. Since it had begun in November of 1784, Madison and Monroe's relationship had been conducted almost entirely through the mail. Ironically, the most time the men had ever spent together was on the campaign trail against each other. The conversation was friendly, and unlikely to have included the great issues that had brought them there. Each was intimately familiar with the other's position. And soon enough the decision between them would be in the hands of the voters. Madison knew very well that Monroe had neither started nor encouraged the dishonest attacks on him. "There was not an atom of ill-will between us," Madison remembered.[15]

But there were significant political differences. Since Madison now agreed that the Constitution should be amended with a bill of rights, the chief issue that still divided him from Monroe was the new federal government's power to impose a direct tax on citizens of the United States. Their opposing arguments shed light on what was really at stake in the battle over the Constitution. Monroe made an honest Anti-Federalist's case that the new national government had powers that it did not need and that were dangerous to the people's liberty. And from the Federalist side of the debate Madison, the chief author of the Constitution, made the strongest possible case for the document, and for the absolute necessity of the new government's powers for the peace and liberty of the United States.

Monroe believed the Constitution's power for direct taxation was unnecessary. He had written, "The demands and necessities of government are now greater than they ever will be hereafter, because of the expense of the war in which we were engaged, which cost us the blood of our best citizens, and which ended so gloriously."[16] The United States was at peace, with no war on the horizon. Monroe believed that the impost on imported goods could fully fund all legitimate activities of the new government and that if it didn't, there were several other methods of raising revenue besides resorting to a direct tax. The sale of the great lands to the west, with their navigable rivers and rich, fertile soil, would provide a steady stream of income for the new government. If the impost and the sale of Western lands were insufficient, the government could always secure a loan using those lands as collateral. If funds were still insufficient, Congress could requisition the states.

Monroe believed that direct taxation by the federal government was unnecessary. But he also thought it unjust—and dangerous to Americans' liberty. He had argued, "Consider the territory lying between the Atlantic Ocean and the Mississippi. Its extent far exceeds that of the German Empire. It is larger than any territory that ever was under any one free government. It is too extensive to be governed but by a despotic monarchy. Taxes cannot be laid justly and equally in such a territory."[17] Would the direct tax be on land? If so, landholders would suffer, while people engaged in commerce and the arts would be free of paying any tax at all. Should each person be taxed the same amount? If so, large landholders would not be paying their fair share.

In America in 1789, the different regions of the country had very different economies. In the cities of the North, people worked as shopkeepers, tradesmen, artisans, and manufacturers and lived in towns, while the Southern economy was anchored in agriculture conducted on large estates. In eighteenth-century America, it was very easy to imagine that the representatives of some other region might dominate the national government and use direct taxation to impose the costs of that government disproportionately on your own region. Monroe believed that direct taxation, by giving the federal government a power that ran exactly parallel to state power, would ultimate undermine the states' authority. Virginians could end up being ruled by a distant, alien, and even monarchical government instead of by their own Delegates. In short, they risked losing all they had just won in the Revolution.

Madison knew that fear of the direct tax threatened to destroy his candidacy. His January 29 letter to George Thompson—the longest surviving letter he wrote during the campaign, and the one written closest to the election itself—is entirely devoted to that issue. Along with Madison's defense of the direct taxation power in Virginia's ratifying convention, this letter provides a clear picture of what Madison was thinking on this important question.[18]

Madison, so used to calling others to the national interest, in this instance also argued that the direct tax was in Virginians' self-interest. If the power of direct taxation were denied to the federal government, he pointed out to Thompson, the impost alone would be used to fund the government. As revenue demands increased, the impost tax would increase. "Now who is it that pays duties on imports? Those... who consume them. What parts of the continent manufacture least and consume imported manufactures most? The Southern parts." Since the Constitution required the direct tax to be laid by population, it would distribute the burdens more equally than the impost.

> Not only would Virginians pay more taxes under the impost than under direct taxation, but If war ever breaks out against America where will it fall? On the weakest parts. Which are

> the weakest parts? The Southern parts; particularly Virginia, whose long navigable rivers open a great part of her Country to surprise and devastation whenever an enemy powerful at Sea chuses to invade her. Strike out direct taxation from the list of federal authorities and what will be our situation. The revenue from commerce must in great measure fail along with the security of Commerce. The invaded and plundered part of the Union will be unable to raise money for its defence. And no resource will be left; but under the name of Requisitions to solicit benefactions from the Legislatures of other States, who being not witnesses of our distresses cannot properly feel for us; and being remote from the scene of danger cannot feel for themselves....[19]

If the North opposed direct taxation it would make sense, as "a local interest is not always postponed to the general interest. But that a southern state should hearken to the measure, and be ready to sacrifice its local interest as well as the general interest, admits of no rational explanation to which I am competent."

But the real thrust of Madison's argument for direct taxation was not from regional interests—quite the opposite. Madison wrote, "I approve of this part of the Constitution because I think it an essential provision for securing the benefits of the Union: the principal of which are the prevention of contests among the states themselves: secondly, security against danger from foreign nations."

Contests between the states could not be prevented so long as each does not "bear its just share of public burdens," Madison wrote:

> If some States contribute their quotas and others do not, justice is violated.... The question to be considered then is which of the two systems, that of requisitions or that of direct taxes, will best answer the essential purpose of making every State bear equitable share of the common burdens. Shall we put our trust in the system of requisitions, by which each State

> will furnish or not furnish its share as it may like? Reason tells us this can never succeed. Some states will be more just than others... some will be more patriotic; others less patriotic; some will be more some less immediately concerned in the evil to be guarded against or in the good to be obtained.... Those who furnish most will complain of those who furnish least. From complaints on one side will spring ill-will on both sides; from ill will, quarrels; from quarrels, wars; and from wars a long catalog of evils including the dreadful evils of disunion.... Such is the lesson which reason teaches us.[20]

Holland was struggling to defend against Spain with two of its seven provinces failing to pay their quotas. "A government which relies on 13 individual sovereigns for the means of its existence is a solecism in theory and a mere nullity in practice," Madison wrote to Thompson. What would be the outcome if every county in Virginia were free and independent to pay their due as they saw fit, when they saw fit? Shall the Commonwealth "depend upon their generosity?" Look to the Dominion of New England, Madison argued, in which colonies including Massachusetts, Connecticut, and New Hampshire had confederated for mutual defense against the Indian tribes and the French. The requisition was "violated with impunity and only regarded when it coincided perfectly with the views and immediate interests of the respective parties." Massachusetts was less exposed than the others and better armed, and thus refused to render contributions for the protection of its neighbors.

"Such had been the experience on this continent of requisitions, from the time of the Peace Stamps through the war." Such experience, Madison pointed out, "proclaims the necessity of resorting for safety to the other system; the system of direct taxes which the Constitution has substituted."

Some had argued that requisitions "ought first to be tried" in the new government, "and if they fail, that direct taxes are then to enforce them." This argument, Madison pointed out, "admits that requisitions are not likely to be complied with voluntarily." Favoring the power to levy direct taxes was not the same as advocating a levy of direct taxes, he pointed out. "If extraordinary aids for the public safety be not necessary," Madison argued, "direct taxes will not be necessary."

Without a reliable source of revenue, Madison wrote,

> They must invite foreign attacks by showing the inability of the Union to repel them: and when attacks are made, must leave the Union to defend itself, if it be defended at all, as was done during the late war, by a waste of blood, a destruction of property, and outrages on private rights, unknown in any country which has credit or money to employ regular means of defense. Whilst the late war was carried on by means of impress'd property, &c., the annual expense was estimated at about twenty millions of Dollars; at the same time that thousands of our brave Citizens were perishing from the scarcity or quality of the supplies provided in that irregular way: to say nothing of the encouragement given by such a situation to the prolongation of the war. Whereas after the General Government was enabled by pecuniary aids of France to provide supplies in a regular way, the annual expense was reduced to about eight millions of dollars, the army was well fed, the military operations went on with vigor & the blessings of peace were visibly and happily accelerated. Should another war unfortunately be our lot (and the less our ability to repel it, the more likely it is to happen), what would be the condition of the union if obliged to depend on Requisition?...[But who] could be expected to lend to a Government which depended on the punctuality of a dozen or more Governments for the means of discharging even the annual interest of the loan? No man who will candidly make the case his own, will say that he would chuse to become a creditor of a Government under such circumstances....Or if loans could be attained at all, it could only be from usurers who would make the public pay threefold for the risk and disappointment apprehended.[21]

In "any period since the peace... if Great Britain had renewed the war, or an attack had come from any other quarter, and money had become essential for the public safety... how was it to have been obtained?" Requisitions from the states? "There is not a man acquainted with our affairs who will pretend it."

Direct taxation, Madison believed, was not the threat to liberty that Monroe feared. It was a necessary support of the union under an effective government. And that union, and that government, were the necessary guarantees of the freedom that Americans enjoyed, that had been under constant threat in the recent war, and that had been held only precariously under the fragile Confederation government.

Perhaps the most significant debate of the race took place at the Hebron Lutheran Church in Culpeper. Like the Baptists, the Lutherans had suffered mistreatment from the state as well as in the private realm—persecution that had made them, like the Baptists, intensely interested in the political process. The Lutherans were eager to hear what their candidates for Congress had to say and usually voted as a bloc to maximize their influence. Their "vote might very probably turn the scale," Madison thought.[22] Both candidates' presence in the pivotal county of Culpeper, and the willingness of the congregation—now completely up for grabs in this election—to vote as one, made this a crucial night in the campaign.

The site of this great and little known event is the oldest Lutheran Church in the United States still in use. (It can be reached only by driving over two miles of unpaved road from what can only charitably be called a highway. The silence outside the white church makes imaging the night of the debate a bit easier. Miles of green hills, like the one the church is nestled on, roll out to the horizon, with only the rare silo or farmhouse in sight.) Before the debate, the candidates joined in the Lutheran Church service. Afterward, they were entertained by a musical performance with two fiddles. "They are remarkably fond of music," Madison wrote.[23]

The candidates and congregation then proceeded outside. Madison remembered, "When it was all over we addressed these people, and kept them standing in the snow listening to the discussion of Constitutional subjects. They stood it out very patiently—seemed to consider it a sort of fight of which they were required to be spectators."[24] Madison, the shortest man ever to serve as president, provided quite a contrast with the muscular Monroe, who stood six feet tall.

The debate probably lasted for hours, the two men who would in turn serve as President of the United States debating in the hills of Culpeper in a dark and snowy scene before an audience of rapt Lutherans and restless horses. The congregation stood silently huddled together for warmth, a great sea of black cloth coats and hats across the hill.

No notes or diary entries reflect what was said in that critical debate of the campaign. But not much imagination is necessary to fill in the dialogue for this scene. Debates in Virginia's ratifying convention and the contemporaneous letters of both Madison and Monroe establish the arguments and even the words that may have been used by the candidates.

Madison would have clarified his position in favor of amendments, particularly one guaranteeing religious liberty—the necessity for which was almost unquestioned in Virginia. With his unequivocal support for these measures, Madison may have blurred the line between himself and Monroe and robbed the Anti-Federalists of the most potent weapon in their arsenal. But on this important issue, Monroe may have made the claim that he had supported these measures more vocally—and when Madison had opposed them.

The district was heavily Anti-Federalist, but the Federalist candidate had the stronger record. Madison was one of the few people in America whose accomplishments could be said to trump Monroe's. Monroe needed to distinguish himself from his opponent with an issue on which voters agreed with him. Direct taxation would have provided just the vehicle he needed.

Vulnerability to being taxed by a national government made up of representatives from distant and alien places was potentially terrifying. After all, the Revolution had begun over this very issue. Religious minorities such as the Lutherans, who had paid taxes in the past to support the established denomination and in recent years had been threatened again by the prospect of the general assessment to support the Episcopal Church may have had a special fear of direct taxation by the new national government.

The Culpeper County citizens assembled at this dissenting place of worship were a key voting bloc in Virginia's 5th District. And the two candidates who faced these voters were ideally suited to put before them the best possible arguments for and against the new system of government that the U.S. Constitution had brought into effect. These swing voters had the power to decide which man would go to Congress. And the election of Madison or Monroe in that district could very well mean the difference between the survival of the United States under the Constitution, or its dissolution at the hands of a second, Anti-Federalist convention.

After the debate candidates and crowd dispersed into the cold darkness, considering carefully what had been said that evening. Madison, who probably made it to Montpelier to bed, but in any case had a long ride ahead of him after the debate, suffered frostbite on his nose that night. Even in old age he would remember this night to others, jokingly pointing to the left side of his nose, where he said he carried his only battle scars.[25]

After the hours riding to the event, greeting the congregants, attending the church service and the musical performance, and debating one another, Madison and Monroe must have been exhausted. After more hours traveling, a fire was surely a welcome relief from the deep chill, and a bed with blankets a greater one still.

Madison and Monroe had made a long and hard journey together to this point in the campaign. In a very few days, they would know which one of them would go on to Congress, leaving the other behind.

Chapter Fifteen

THE FEDERALIST ENDGAME

"It is an event which I am convinced would not have taken place a fortnight sooner, had it been then tried, and I am equally convinced, that had you stayed away, it would not have happened at all."[1]

—Edward Carrington

Court Days were some of the most important events on the campaign schedule for both Monroe and Madison. A Court Day was a set day of the month, different in each county, when lawyers and judges tried civil and criminal cases. "At a very early period, as far back as tradition or historical sketch carries us, country court day has been a day of interest to the people of Virginia."[2]

The historical antecedent to the primetime legal drama—appealing to Americans' fascination with trials and criminal justice—Court Days also "served the purposes of club, exchange, political assemblage, muster and social meeting time."[3] They were a "holiday for all the country side...from all directions came in people on horseback, in wagons, and afoot."[4] People gathered to see friends and acquaintances, "collect a note or give one, to make a contract or cancel one, to arrange a religious meeting or barbecue, to trade horses or to exchange views concerning the latest philosophy, to make speeches or to listen to them," or "find the people who were in any way related" to the exciting case at hand.[5]

Virginia county boundaries were drawn so that no courthouse was more than a half day's travel away for any resident of the county. People who lived farthest from the courthouse often left home the day before and stayed the night with friends to be sure to arrive no later than 9:00 a.m., when the festivities began. Court Days also included entertainments unrelated to the law, such as markets and county fairs. "Cheap John" vendors would sell soap, razors, cheap jewelry, clocks, and handkerchiefs, while patent medicine men would sell potions to "cure all the ills human flesh was heir to." Merchants set up tables on the courthouse lawn, selling every imaginable item, including livestock, tobacco, fruits, as well as "gingerbread, molasses, cakes, pies, apples, chestnuts." The alcohol flowed freely during Court Day, with taverns full of drunken revelers and owners of alcohol carts making a tidy profit. Fist fights were common, some spontaneous and some organized, with prizes to awarded to "winners" who ended the fight with fewer broken bones than their adversaries.[6]

On the important Orange County Court Day at which Madison and Monroe were to debate, Madison's cousin Francis Taylor was in attendance along with his father and brother. Like many of the other attendees, Taylor—having acquired a spyglass, keg of oysters, and ream of brown paper—was more occupied with his personal business than with the debate. He wrote that he "saw Col. Madison Jr. and Mr. Monroe, the candidates for Member of Congress." But he also loaned someone a dollar to settle a debt and arranged for a tailor to sew him a new pair of breeches.[7]

This was the circus atmosphere Madison and Monroe had to contend with. But the compensating advantage was that during Court Day in Orange and other counties, the two candidates had the opportunity to address hundreds—perhaps over a thousand voters. Their debates weren't limited to thirty-second or minute-long sound bites, as some debates today are; instead, they involved the two candidates explaining and justifying their views for hours.

The day after the Orange County debate, Madison wrote a widely read letter, later published in the Fredericksburg Virginia Herald as an "Extract of a letter from the Honorable James Madison Jr., to his friend in this county." The recipient, an unknown resident of Spotsylvania, must have been a good friend to Madison. He arranged for the letter to be printed in the Herald on January 29, two days after it was written. In the letter Madison continued to emphasize his support for amendments. He had no hope of actually winning Spotsylvania County, Monroe's home turf. But with the county carrying roughly 10 percent of the overall vote, Madison could not afford to lose there by too large a margin. Monroe had debated Madison at Court Day in Orange County, Madison's home, for the same reason.

The Philadelphia *Independent Gazetteer* picked up a hint that the Federalist efforts to neutralize the amendments issue had succeeded. A "gentleman from Virginia" wrote that the amendments controversy between the two parties had entirely subsided, "it being agreed, on all hands, that a *bill of rights*" was necessary "so as to fix the liberties of the people on the most safe and permanent foundation...."[8] The remaining issue between the parties, the Virginia gentleman noted, was the direct tax.

On Thursday, January 29, Monroe arrived in Culpeper County, where he would work tirelessly in the final days of the election.

In the final hours of the race, both candidates were exhausted from anxiety and overexertion. Madison and Monroe both knew that the stakes were high, and neither could be sure what the outcome of the election would be.

February 2 was Election Day. It had finally come.

The election was conducted by county sheriffs (ordinarily the most senior justices of the peace who had not yet served in that capacity). Sheriffs would in turn appoint clerks to assist them. Voters would enter the courthouse, approach the sheriff or one of his clerks, and announce their vote for Congress, which would be faithfully recorded in a poll book, under the tally for their preferred candidate.

Although law prevented the election from lasting more than one day, some sheriffs kept the polls open for as many as three. The weather had been miserable, with freezing winds and low temperatures. Traveling to vote was difficult, and the extended deadline for voters allowed many people to participate in the election who otherwise would not have been able to cast their votes.

The secret ballot seems so fundamental today that few can imagine voting in any other matter. If surveyed, most Americas would probably say that such a right is guaranteed by the Constitution. The secret ballot makes voter intimidation more difficult by allowing people the right to exercise their vote without the knowledge of their friends, family, employers, or their labor unions. It was not until Grover Cleveland's comeback in 1892, however, that all states guaranteed a secret ballot to general election voters. To this day the constitution of West Virginia allows voters the right, if they choose, to vote orally and openly. And that famous quadrennial exercise in American democracy known as the Iowa Caucuses still requires people to advocate publicly for their candidate of choice. So it was in this election.

Since his first defeat at the hands of Charles Porter, Madison had believed that a secret ballot was the only method of ensuring a fair election,[9] but voters had not yet secured this right. On February 2, 1789, until the polls closed, voters walked into the courthouse and announced their vote by calling out either "Madison" or "Monroe." Among those voting in other Virginia districts was George Washington, who traveled to his county courthouse and voted for Richard Bland Lee for Congress.

Then as now, Election Day was a punishing marathon for the candidates and their supporters. As today, volunteers went to the homes of voters identified as supporting their candidate, or perhaps those they thought were persuadable, and brought them to the polling place.

Some of Madison's supporters used wagons to offer voters a more comfortable ride to the polls, and perhaps Monroe's followed suit. At one polling place, the "get out the vote" efforts of Madison's team ran into an unexpected setback. An elderly voter was brought a great distance to cast his ballot for Madison. When the sheriff asked him his preference, the old man asked, "Who was Jemmy Monroe?" The sheriff indicated that someone else could better answer that question, pointing to Monroe himself, who was present campaigning for votes. This humorous happenstance excited the crowd in the courthouse, and the voter spoke for a moment with the candidate.

After speaking with Monroe, the old man announced his preference to the crowd, and the reason why. He had once been a young immigrant to Virginia, and while very poor, had been befriended and helped by the candidate's father, Spence Monroe. The old man turned to the sheriff and asked him to record his vote for "Jemmy Monroe."[10]

When the polls closed, each sheriff went to the courthouse door and proclaimed the candidate with the highest number of votes in the county. The clerks signed their names in the poll book and took an oath certifying accuracy. Election fraud was taken seriously, and officials who engaged in any sort of tampering were stiffly punished, with a fine of two hundred pounds per offense.

It would take some time before the final results of the election were known. The 5th was a district of eight counties, and communications were slow. The tallies trickled out, with various newspapers publishing incomplete results as the days went by.

The sheriffs took the poll books from their counties to the Albemarle Courthouse, as it was the first county named in the election statute. On February 10, the sheriffs met in Albemarle to certify the results. Edmund Randolph and Jesse Taylor, brother of Francis Taylor and cousin to James Madison, rode to Albemarle to be the first to learn who had won.

Just a few years before, the Albemarle Courthouse had been the Capitol of Virginia, as the British invaders pushed the government farther and farther west. It was here that Jefferson and the legislature had been minutes away from capture.

But in February of 1789 it seemed hardly imaginable that such an event had happened at this very place not eight years earlier. America was independent, and at peace. And the county sheriffs were certifying the results of the very first election to Congress in what would become the greatest republic in the history of the world.

The sheriffs were paid ten shillings for the day of travel and three pence per mile. Once together they would open their poll books and engage in "faithful addition and comparison." In the event of a tie vote, the sheriffs were obligated to vote among themselves to decide the winner. For the 5th Congressional District in 1789, no tie breaking would be necessary. The results would be announced from the steps and posted to the door.

	Madison	Monroe	Total	Margin of victory	Winner
Albemarle	174	105	279	69	Madison
Amherst	145	246	391	101	Monroe
Culpeper	256	103	359	153	Madison
Fluvanna	42	63	105	21	Monroe
Goochland	132	133	265	1	Monroe
Louisa	228	124	352	104	Madison
Orange	216	9	225	207	Madison
Spotsylvania	115	189	304	74	Monroe

James Madison of Orange had received 1,308 votes and won. James Monroe of Spotsylvania had received 972 votes and lost. At the end of the contest the candidates were separated by 336 votes, and a swing of only 169 voters from Madison to Monroe would have changed the outcome. The sheriffs sealed and certified the results and sent two duplicates to the Governor and Council of State.

The candidates had carried their home counties with varying degrees of decisiveness. The time Madison spent minimizing his losses in Spotsylvania had paid off. Monroe's margin was only 74 votes. Monroe, by contrast, had failed to make any sort of dent in Orange, where the favorite son won by 207, nearly two-thirds of his margin of victory.

It seems that Madison spent the day of the election in Orange, resisting entreaties to campaign in a county more populous or persuadable. The heavy Baptist influence in Orange, and its decisive support for Madison, led by fellow resident Baptist minister John Leland, likely played a role in his decisive margin.

Monroe's two best counties were Amherst and Spotsylvania, which turned out at 74 percent and 61 percent respectively. The next highest turnout came from Goochland, with only 51 percent participation, yielding a one-vote margin for Monroe. Madison won in Orange, Louisa, and Albemarle, which had turned out at 38 percent, 44 percent, and 33 percent. These figures are easy to explain: opponents of the new government released pent-up frustration while supporters, equating ratification with total victory, were lulled into complacency.[11]

Edward Carrington added his to the many voices now congratulating Madison on his election: "It is an event which I am convinced would not have taken place a fortnight sooner, had it been then tried, and I am equally convinced, that had you stayed away, it would not have happened at all." Carrington credited Madison's letters to Amherst voters with minimizing his losses in the hotbed of Anti-Federalism, won by Monroe 246 to 145.

Culpeper, which Madison had called "the critical county," provided a net gain to Madison of 153 votes, nearly half his margin of victory. Little Louisa, the only county in the district that had divided its vote at the Convention, had punched well above its weight. Its 44 percent turnout was the highest of all the counties won by Madison. Though its elections for the convention were the narrowest in the state, Louisa's votes for Congress went overwhelmingly for Madison, who bested Monroe there by a margin of 228 to 124. Louisa was home to one of the churches founded by John Leland. There as elsewhere, the Baptists and other dissenters were the key to Madison's triumph. Madison's promises to fight for amendments, particularly for the protection of freedom of conscience, had secured their support. His career-long advocacy of religious freedom had served as a powerful deposit on that promise, which might otherwise have been dismissed as an election-year conversion of convenience.

Washington, relieved to have such a capable and trustworthy ally headed for the new First Congress, praised Madison for his "respectable majority of the suffrages of the district for which you stood." Now it was time to get to work; Washington enclosed a draft of his first message to Congress; he was looking for Madison's assistance with his speech.

True to form, Madison did not entirely share in the general's enthusiasm. He wrote in response to Washington, "Whether I ought to be satisfied or displeased with my success, I shall hereafter be more able to judge. My present anticipations are not flattering. I see on the lists of representatives a very scanty proportion who will share in the drudgery of business. And I foresee contentions first between Federal and Anti-

Federal parties, and then between northern and southern parties, which give additional disagreeableness to the prospect."

On February 15, the defeated James Monroe wrote to Jefferson, expressing what may be his most complete thoughts on the election. The letter, a very late response to Jefferson's of August 9, had no doubt been delayed by Monroe's intense campaigning. Before addressing the campaign, he began by recapping the momentous and improbable events of the season. Eleven states had now ratified the Constitution, the New York Circular had called for a new constitutional convention, and Virginia had seconded New York's call for a second constitutional convention. On the subject of the election, Monroe wrote,

> The Commonwealth was divided into 10 districts from each of which a member was to be placed in the House of Representatives. A competition took place in many, and in this, consisting of Albemarle, Amherst, Fluvanna, Goochland, Louisa, Spotsylvania, Orange, and Culpeper, between Mr. Madison and myself. He prevailed by a majority of about 300. It would have given me concern to have excluded him, but those to whom my conduct in public life had been acceptable, pressed me to come forward in this government on its commencement, and that I might not lose an opportunity of contributing my feeble efforts, in forwarding an amendment of its defects or shrink from the station those who confided in would wish to place me, I yielded. As I had no private object to gratify, so a failure has given me no private concern.[12]

On March 29, Madison sent Jefferson his own election recap:

> It was my misfortune to be thrown into a contest with our friend, Colonel Monroe. The occasion produced considerable efforts among our respective friends. Between ourselves, I have no reason to doubt the distinction was duly kept in mind between political and personal views, and that it has saved our friendship from the smallest diminution. On one side I am sure it is the case.

It surely heartened Jefferson to know that his own dear friends were still friends, though they were no longer political allies.

Baptist minister John Leland offered his congratulations to Madison with characteristic modesty. He began by suggesting that his own efforts had earned at least one vote for Madison—his own.[13] Then Leland touched on religious liberty, where he trusted Madison to look out for the rights of dissenters. There was, he said "no danger to the destruction of liberty where the community is well informed. Ignorance always brings on, either mutiny or lethargy, which equally pave the way for tyranny.... One thing I shall expect; that if religious liberty is anywise threatened, that I shall receive the earliest intelligence."

The Reverend James Madison, who had been so concerned for his cousin's success, also joined the chorus of well wishers. He wrote,

> It afforded me great Satisfaction to hear of your Election.... I rejoice that you are in a Situation, which enables you to be extensively useful, & that, we who are to receive ye Law may at least be assured, one Voice will always utter what Wisdom & Virtue dictate.—I believe no People ever experienced a more important Crisis, than this at whc. Ama. is now arrived. For whatever may be said of the Perfection or Imperfection of ye general Plan upon whc. you are to proceed—certain it is, that the Prosperity of ye federal Govt. will depend in a great Measure upon the Wisdom of ye Laws & Arrangements first proposed.—If they shd fortunately, as I trust they will, bear the evident Stamp of Wisdom & Justice, they may gradually eradicate opposition, and thus in it's [sic] Stead establish in ye Affections of the People, ye strongest attachment to ye General Govt., and perhaps within ye Period of one Century, ye World may see a *Republic* composed of at least 60 millions of free Men,—for such will be the Population of America, within that Time, providing it continues nearly at ye Rate it hath hitherto observed.—The only Chain by which such a Multitude will be bound together is that of a wise & just law. May your Beginning promise such a Blessing....[14]

Meanwhile, William Jackson, Secretary of the Congress of the Confederation, was busy keeping up appearances. On October 10, 1788, the Confederation Congress had mustered seven states to reach a quorum for the last time. But New York, thrilled to be the first capital of the new government, happily went about refurbishing City Hall for the new Congress under the Constitution. The banging of hammers prevented those left in the old Congress from carrying on their business, adding insult to injury in the dying hours of a rejected government. So the Confederation Congress moved its temporary quarters to the Fraunces Tavern, the popular bar from which Washington had said farewell to his troops at the end of the war.

From February 19 until March 2, not one single delegate attended the "meetings."[15] On March 3, the day before the new Congress was to meet, Phillip Pell was walking down a bustling street when he was approached by Secretary Jackson. Jackson insisted that Pell accompany him to their temporary meeting space. The two of them sat in an otherwise empty chamber, the last remaining members of the old government. As one historian noted, "The faithful secretary had fought the good fight to preserve the 'visible head' of the union; he had persevered to the end, he had won the victory. The spark of life had been kept in the body of the dying Congress until its heir and successor was crossing the threshold."[16]

And the clock counted down the final minutes of the hapless first government of the free American people.

It was finished.

In the meantime Madison, who had left New York for Virginia burdened by the likely prospect of defeat at the polls, returned again triumphant along his well-worn path to the city of New York. He once again carried the weight of the nation on his shoulders.

Heading north to New York, Madison had time to consider the events that had brought him here. The Virginia Convention of 1776, the Revolutionary War, the tedious days of the Confederation Congress and the Virginia House of Delegates, Annapolis, Philadelphia, ratification, and his recent election to the House of Representatives.

It all seems so inevitable.

Chapter Sixteen

THE "FIRST MAN" OF THE HOUSE: PASSING THE BILL OF RIGHTS

"He is our first man."

—Fisher Ames

At the end of his life, Chief Justice John Marshall was asked to name the most eloquent orator of his age, for he had heard them all. "Eloquence has been defined to be the art of persuasion," he replied. "If it includes persuasion by convincing, Mr. Madison was the most eloquent man I ever heard." Jefferson agreed that Madison was unmatched as a speaker and debater, calling him "the first of every assembly of which he was a member."[1]

James Madison was the preeminent member of the first House of Representatives, leader of the dominant Federalist Party—a position he held because of his remarkable record of public service, but even more because of his remarkable powers of mind and unparalleled command of the issues facing the United States.[2]

Madison was soft-spoken; his audience sometimes had to strain to hear him. But in making his first official address to Congress,* he had every member's attention as he sounded the alarm on the perilous state of the nation's finances: "I take the liberty, Mr. Chairman, at this early stage of business to introduce...a subject, which appears to me to be of the greatest magnitude; a subject, Sir, that requires our first attention, and our united exertions."[3]

To raise revenue, Madison presented a plan to adopt the long-sought impost. It was essentially the same tax on imports that had been urged by the Confederation Congress for years but had repeatedly failed to gain the unanimous consent of the states required under the Articles of Confederation.[4]

The national debt was estimated to be a staggering 54 million dollars, 12 million of which was owed to foreign governments.[5] Madison's remedy was moderate. His highest estimate was that the impost would generate revenue of just under 3 million dollars, which would be enough to fund the essential functions of the federal government and make payments on the debt. It would keep the tax burden on the average American at about one-eighth the tax burden of an average Englishman.

Madison believed that taxes were an evil that should be instituted only to prevent a greater evil—such as the failure of a country to protect its citizens or honor its financial obligations. "I wish we were under less necessity than...to shackle commerce with duties, restriction, and preferences," he told Congress.[6]

On May 4 Madison had gingerly broached the topic of amendments to the Constitution. He made it known that he would be revisiting the issue on June 8, but meanwhile he wanted the House to have time to

* Meeting in the newly renamed Federal Hall, which had been built in 1700 as New York's City Hall. For a young nation with few places of historic significance, this was an exception. In 1765, the "Stamp Act Congress" had met here, and for the past four years the Congress of the Confederation; it would now serve for the two most significant sessions of Congress. The nation's capital moved to Philadelphia in 1790. Federal Hall remained standing until 1800, when it was torn down and sold as scrap for $400.

consider the subject and to finish the impost bill. By making this advance announcement, Madison could begin to satisfy the Anti-Federalists' concerns about amendments and temporarily prevent them from acting against the government or offering their own amendments. It would be Madison's amendments that were considered—ones that protected fundamental liberties but did not damage the foundation of the new government. And the Federalists would get credit for proposing these amendments on their own, in a spirit of accommodation, rather than seeming to react to the Anti-Federalists' initiative. But by delaying further discussion until June 8, he would not force the issue until the Federalists, who were more concerned with setting up the mechanics of the government, were ready.

There was much to be done. The new Congress was concerned with issues ranging from oaths of office to immigration policy to the establishment of the judiciary. Even what title the president would use had to be determined. The Senate recommended "His Highness, the President of the United States of America, and Protector of their Liberties."[7] Fortunately, the republican instincts of Madison and others prevailed—it would be simply, fittingly, "The President of the United States."

Launching the ship of state was paramount on the Federalist agenda—not messing around with a Bill of Rights. And two other issues—the president's authority to remove executive officers who had been confirmed by the Senate, and the permanent location of the nation's capital—would prove just as contentious. Both threatened the security of the new Constitutional Union; both were resolved differently because Madison, and not Monroe, won the election of 1789.

At the end of May 1789, Madison offered the House of Representatives a proposal for three departments—foreign affairs, treasury, and war—each headed by a secretary, "to be nominated by the President, and appointed by him, with the advice and consent of the Senate and removable by the President."[8]

Madison had unexpectedly touched off a constitutional crisis. To his surprise, many expressed doubts whether the president could constitutionally remove department heads. Some believed impeachment was the only proper method of removal. Others held that the president's power to remove officers, just like his authority to appoint them, required the concurrence of the Senate. And others believed that the Constitution was silent on the matter and that presidential removal power could be granted by Congress.[9]

Madison defended the removal power as essential to the balance of powers on which the new government depended. Madison, unlike Monroe, supported a strong and independent executive. He won this critical debate by joining his adversaries in striking out language making the Secretary of Foreign Affairs "removable by the President." He then narrowly won passage of an amendment creating a clerk who would become acting head of the department "whenever the principal officer shall be removed from office by the President of the United States, or in any other case of vacancy."

Thus Madison won the unequivocal vindication of the president's removal power, but in a manner no one would mistake for a grant by Congress.

The location of the national capital was another contentious issue, and it too was decided by the election of 1789. Madison and his fellow Virginians had long dreamed of winning the seat of government. But, over Madison's opposition, the House actually passed a bill to place the capital in Pennsylvania, on the Susquehanna River.[10] It would have become law had the Senate not amended it to make it more specific. This sent the bill back to the House, where Madison's quick maneuvering saved the day. Since the new Federal district would initially have no laws, Madison passed an amendment making Pennsylvania's laws the laws of the district until Congress could write its own. Thus the session ended without resolving the capital question.

In the next session, Madison emerged as the principal opponent of Hamilton's plan to assume the debts of the states. This issue, like the location of the capital, was highly contentious and dangerously sectional; Northern states badly wanted assumption, Southern states, which had largely paid off their debt, were dead set against it. Both sides threatened secession. And the compromise by Madison that resolved it was a delicate one. Over dinner at Thomas Jefferson's, Madison and Hamilton agreed to the first great compromise that preceded the Civil War. Madison "would not be strenuous" in trying to stop assumption. The Virginians would find the votes to pass Hamilton's plan for the states' debts. And Hamilton would leverage Northern support for assumption into a capital on the Potomac site. Monroe, like all Virginia leaders, opposed federal assumption of the states' debts. But Madison's position as the leader of the Federalists made him the man to be reckoned with by assumption supporters. If Monroe had been there in place of Madison, Hamilton would have won assumption outright or bargained with another delegation for the capital.[11]

James Madison was the great conciliator of the First Congress. And he would need all of his political capital to win the battle for the Bill of Rights.

Madison took the floor to introduce his draft on June 8, 1789. "This day, Mr. Speaker, is the day assigned for taking into consideration the subject of amendments to the Constitution. As I considered myself bound in honor and in duty to do what I have done on this subject, I shall proceed to bring the amendments before you as soon as possible, and advocate them until they shall be finally adopted or rejected by a constitutional majority of this House."[12]

Madison's amendments are familiar to us all, and so fundamental to our national identity that we cannot imagine America without them: the freedom of speech and of the press; the right to assemble peaceably and petition the government; the right to keep and bear arms; protection against the quartering of soldiers in private homes and against being tried twice for the same crime; the right against self-incrimination, and the protection of due process of law for life, liberty, and property; protection against cruel and unusual punishment, excessive bail, and unreasonable searches and seizures; the right to a speedy trial by a jury; and the right to be represented by an attorney. The amendments included a declaration that the enumeration of particular rights in the Constitution could not be construed to deny other rights not mentioned, as well as a reservation of power to the states and the people of all those rights not expressly given to the federal government.

Perhaps most important to Madison was the guarantee of freedom of religion. He had won his election with the support of the dissenters, and their leaders such as George Eve and John Leland. His first campaign promise had been to secure an amendment protecting the freedom of conscience. Without this promise, he would certainly have been defeated by Monroe. In its original form, the First Amendment guarantee of religious liberty read as follows:

> The civil rights of none shall be abridged on account of religious belief or worship, nor shall any national religion be established, nor shall the full and equal rights of conscience be in any manner, or under any pretext infringed.[13]

Despite Madison's enormous prestige, his proposal of the Bill of Rights met with resistance in the House. The incoming fire from Madison's fellow Federalists came fast and furious. Many believed that amending the Constitution was premature and a distraction from more important matters.[14]

James Jackson raised a number of issues. "What experience have we had of the good or bad qualities of this Constitution?" he asked. The Constitution "is like a vessel just launched, and lying at the wharf, she is untried, you can hardly discover any one of her properties; it is not known how she will answer her helm, or lay her course; whether she will bear in safety the precious freight to be deposited in her hold." Congress "may deface a beauty, or deform a well proportioned piece of workmanship." Besides, there were much more pressing issues before them. If the impost were not passed, the government would be without revenue, in which case "the wheels of government cannot move."

Jackson dismissed the claims of the Anti-Federalists. He thought their fears could be quieted by legislation without constitutional amendments: "Much has been said by the opponents to this Constitution, respecting the insecurity of jury trials, that great bulwark of personal safety; all their objections may be done away, by proper regulations on this point."[15]

Further, Jackson pointed out that his state, Georgia, had ratified the Constitution by a "unanimous vote of a numerous convention." In fact, Georgians were so enamored of the federal Constitution that they had modeled their own state constitution on it.[16] What mandate, he asked, did Madison have to make changes? Jackson suggested a postponement of debate on the amendments until March of 1790.

Madison answered that discussion of this issue had been put off long enough. At least begin the debate, he suggested, and let the people know we are listening to their concerns about the Constitution: "It would stifle the voice of complaint, and make friends of many who doubted its merits." Debate of Madison's proposed bill of rights without delay would "inspire a reasonable hope in the advocates for amendments, that full justice will be done to the important subject."[17]

Roger Sherman argued that the people had spoken and that the government should go into effect exactly as framed in the Constitution. His state, Connecticut, had ratified the Constitution and did not desire amendments. Meanwhile, "The executive part of this government wants organization; the business of the revenue is incomplete, to say nothing of the judiciary business." All these important issues, Sherman urged, should not be ignored to placate a small group of people.[18]

As a Virginia schoolboy, Madison had taken extensive notes on books about history, biography, poetry, and world affairs. One such book was the memoir of the French politician Cardinal de Retz. From de Retz, the young Madison had excerpted this passage of interest: "In some cases it is harder to please those of our own party than to act against our adversaries." One wonders whether he remembered that quotation during the debate over the Bill of Rights. Madison's own fellow Federalists were the major obstacle to its passage. And no wonder. Madison, the chief author of the Constitution, who had campaigned for his seat in Congress as a staunch Federalist, was the champion for the Anti-Federalists' major issue.

Not every Federalist joined the pile-on. John Page of Virginia was more friendly to Madison's proposal, perhaps because of the grip Anti-Federalism held on their home state. Page thought if he were an Anti-Federalist, he would suspect Congress had no intention of seriously addressing his concerns—now or in the future. If Madison's bill of rights was not passed by Congress, Page believed the Anti-Federalists would naturally turn to the other method of amendment, a new constitutional convention that would meet upon the call of two-thirds of the state legislatures. This, the Federalists all agreed, would be a disaster. Page warned that "unless you take early notice of this subject," such a convention would be the consequence.[19]

Other Federalists, such as John Vining of Delaware, did not share Page's fears. "The storm has abated," he observed, "and a calm succeeds." Good laws, not constitutional amendments, would be the best way to increase confidence in the government, Vining argued.

Madison begged the indulgence of the House and pushed ahead. He wanted the Federalists to show that they were just as devoted to liberty as their adversaries: "It will be a desirable thing to extinguish from the bosom of every member of the community any apprehensions, that there are those among his countrymen who wish to deprive them of the liberty for which they so valiantly fought and honorably bled." Madison called for his fellow representatives to "evince that spirit of deference and concession for which they have hitherto been distinguished"[20] and adopt the amendments. If they would "expressly declare the great rights of mankind secured under this Constitution" then North Carolina and Rhode Island could be brought back into the fold, and "it is a desirable thing, on our part as well as theirs, that a re-union should take place as soon as possible." With so much to gain, "and if we proceed with caution, nothing to lose," Madison urged the House forward. Everyone in the room knew that power could be abused; what would the harm be in putting their liberties on a more secure footing?

"I will own," Madison continued, "that I never considered this provision so essential to the Federal Constitution, as to make it improper to ratify it...I always conceived, that in a certain form and to a certain extent, such a provision was neither improper nor altogether useless." But many of his colleagues disagreed.

Jackson argued that Americans would become "objects of scorn" in the eyes of other nations. Amending the recently adopted Constitution would make the United States look unstable and confused. "We are not content with two revolutions in less than 14 years; we must enter upon a third, without necessity or propriety."[21] If Congress had no power to regulate free speech, he argued, no amendment was necessary to protect that right. Jackson wanted the government to have a fair trial and, if experience proved it deficient, he would be the first to step forward in favor of amendments.[22]

Even Elbridge Gerry, an Anti-Federalist who had refused to sign the Constitution in Philadelphia because it lacked a bill of rights, stood up to oppose Madison: "Whatever might have been my sentiments of the ratification of the Constitution without amendments, my sense now is, that the salvation of America depends upon the establishment of this government, whether amended or not."[23] Sherman acknowledged the imperfections in the Constitution, but said, "I do not expect any perfection on this side of the grave in the works of man."[24]

The next day, the House was again at work on the impost, which they had received back from the Senate, where it had been amended. Now they had to debate losing autumn's revenue, rather than spring's.

During this hiatus in the debate on the amendments, Madison received a letter from William Davie, a leader of the Federalists in North Carolina, which still had not ratified the Constitution. The mere fact that amendments were being considered, Davie wrote, "dispersed almost universal pleasure." Federalists in that state "hold it up as a refutation of the gloomy prophecies of the leaders of the opposition, and the honest part of our Anti-federalists have publicly expressed great satisfaction."[25] The same thing appeared to be true in Virginia.

The House did not resume debate on Madison's amendments until August 13.[26]

During the debate Madison advocated an amendment that would apply to the states as well as the federal government. It read, "No state shall infringe the equal rights of conscience, nor freedom of speech, or of the press, nor the right of trial by jury in criminal cases." But objections to this amendment were made on the grounds that the federal government already interfered too much in the rights of states. And many of the members wanted to protect the official churches of their home states. Madison argued vainly that this was the most valuable amendment on his entire list. "I think these abuses are most likely to take place under the state governments; and if they are to be restrained in any thing, this appears to me the most necessary: we shall do what will be grateful to the people by retaining the clause."[27] But this proposal was defeated. Madison's vision was not realized until the Fourteenth Amendment to the Constitution, passed in the aftermath of the Civil War, was interpreted as extending the Bill of Rights to state governments.

After more debate and revision, the amendments were agreed to on August 24.[28] Madison's steadfast advocacy and patient refusal to give way had forced their consideration. When the vote came, the members could not vote against freedom of speech and trial by jury. Madison's original bill of rights was ultimately adopted in substantially the same form in which he introduced it. According to one biographer, "Nothing short of the high standing of Mr. Madison in the public councils, and the deference accorded to his opinions and virtues, could have secured a favorable reception for propositions so counter to the prepossessions of the body to which they were addressed."[29]

For the first and not the last time in American history, a measure was adopted when the leader of the opposing party led the charge for it. The modern cliché is "Only Nixon could go to China"—only such a strong anti-communist could regularize relations with that country. The founding-era version might well have been, "Only Madison could pass the Bill of Rights."

The House sent twelve amendments to the states. The first ten, known as the Bill of Rights, were ratified by the necessary three-fourths of the state legislatures by the close of 1791.**

When Congress first sent the amendments to the states, praise for Madison came in from many quarters. Edmund Pendleton wrote him from Virginia, "I congratulate you on having got through the amendments to the Constitution, as I was very anxious that it should be done before your adjournment.... I own also that I feel some degree of pleasure, in discovering obviously from the whole progress, that the public are indebted for the measure to the friends of government, whose elections were opposed under pretense of their being adverse to amendments."[30]

** The only one of Madison's amendments never to be ratified guaranteed one representative in the House of Representatives for every thirty thousand people. If it had passed, the U.S. House would now stand at over ten thousand members, instead of its current 435.

The other of Madison's twelve proposed amendments not passed in 1791 would be ratified in 1992. It was a simple, one-sentence amendment that prevented salary increases for members of Congress from taking effect until an intervening election of the House of Representatives. There had been a great deal of concern about Congress's ability to increase its own pay, and this amendment would have put some check on that power by forcing the entire House and a third of the Senate to face the voters before receiving the salary bump. When the rest of the Bill of Rights went into effect, only six states had adopted the amendment affecting congressional pay. It was nearly forgotten until 1982, when it was championed by Gregory Watson, a twenty-year-old college student at the University of Texas at Austin who wrote a paper suggesting that ratification was still possible. For his efforts, Watson was awarded a C in a class on government, but he engaged in an aggressive campaign to win passage of the amendment, writing letters to the legislatures in every state in America. One state after another joined the bandwagon until 1992, when the amendment on congressional pay increases became the Twenty-Seventh Amendment to the Constitution, the last law written by James Madison to be passed—202 years after its introduction.

Edmund Carrington also wrote after a business trip to the most Anti-Federalist quarters of Virginia, "I can assure you that the people appear to be perfectly quiet and reconciled to the government."[31] Ironically, Carrington noted that the Anti-Federalists, who had expelled him from office simply for being Madison's friend and who had so bitterly opposed Madison's election to Congress, had a new hero. "A very considerable change has taken place amongst the Anti's as to yourself, they consider you as the patron of amendments, and it is no uncommon thing to hear confessions that they had been formerly imposed on, by representations that you were fixed against any alteration whatever."[32]

The *State Gazette* of North Carolina reported on September 24, "The amendments to the Constitution of the United States, proposed by Congress will undoubtedly satisfy the minds of all its enemies. Not a door is left open for complaint, should the amendments be ratified....Every friend to the Union may now with pleasure anticipate the adoption of the Constitution by this state, and of its again becoming one of its members." "Rank Anti's" had now become "Perfect Feds." The leader of the Anti-Federalists in North Carolina, Willie Jones, was bowing out of the state's upcoming ratification convention.[33] And Fisher Ames, congressman from Massachusetts and a frequent opponent of Madison, wrote in a letter to a friend, "He is our first man."[34]

No less an opponent of Madison than Patrick Henry would soon come around. The Bill of Rights was not remotely all that Henry wanted, to be sure. But it was sufficient that he wrote to James Monroe tendering the equivalent of his resignation as opponent-in-chief of the new government. "Although the form of government into which my countrymen determined to place themselves had my enmity, yet as we are one and all embarked, it is natural to care for the crazy machine, at least so long as we are out of sight of a port to refit."

Monroe was appointed to the United States Senate in November 1790, after the death of Senator Charles Grayson. But he spent most of the First Congress in more pedestrian pursuits. He searched for good plow horses and a new domestic servant to help his wife Elizabeth.[35] To earn extra income, Monroe had become a Deputy Attorney General for six counties of the commonwealth of Virginia.[36] He also spent long hours riding the judicial circuit from one county courthouse to the next to represent private clients. Monroe endured long separations from his young family.[37] He wrote apologetic letters to irate clients over the slow pace of litigation. Monroe wrote to his friend Madison in Congress, but cautioned, "You must not expect any communication of importance from me."[38] While James Madison was winning the adoption of the Bill of Rights to the U.S. Constitution, James Monroe had to content himself with winning an indictment against Philip Waters of Fredericksburg for stealing a dun bay mare worth six pounds from William Smock.[39]

But Monroe's challenge to Madison in the election of 1789 had set the course for the First Congress. It is otherwise unthinkable that Madison would have staked his election on a promise to seek amendments. The Bill of Rights advanced in the First Congress against the fiercest resistance imaginable, even with the dogged support of Madison. Monroe, or any Anti-Federalist—or any other Federalist, for that matter—would never have been able to get it through. Without Madison, the Bill of Rights would never have become law.

Madison had been elected to the First Congress by only 336 votes. It was in that Congress that the Bill of Rights was passed, cementing the people's confidence in the new federal government. And the Constitution was saved.

All because of one election.

Epilogue

THE FOURTH OF JULY

February, 1824
The White House
Washington, District of Columbia

As president of the United States, James Monroe was accustomed to receiving plenty of mail. But at sixty-six years old, Monroe's eyesight was not what it had been when he was a young man.

Perhaps he read the letter by candlelight with a roaring fire to keep him warm on a cold winter evening. Monroe was now in the final year of his public life, which had begun when he was in college during the Revolution. He had done what he could, always, and soon it would be the province of others to protect what he and his generation had won.

We can see his weathered hands unfolding the parchment and holding it close to his face to read its contents. The letter was from an Eleazer Early, a resident of Georgia.

"I remembered," the letter began, "indeed I could not forget it, that Joel Early and French Strother had attempted to sustain you, now just about 35 winters past, in Culpeper County, for a seat in the first Congress after the adoption of the Federal Constitution, against the same Mr. Madison who has preceded you in the presidency, and that nothing but the snow in the mountains prevented them from giving you such a vote as, in all probability, would have made you the successful candidate. My father continued to relate the circumstances of that eventual struggle to his family and friends, often after his removal to Georgia."

There is no telling what prompted this letter after the passage of so much time, or how it was received by the president.

It must have brought a smile to Monroe's face to know that the election of 1789 still had the power to excite and intrigue though so many years had passed. Perhaps he also laughed at the image of old Joel Early, and of his friends cringing as he told and retold the story of that time he helped the president on his bid for Congress.

Any regrets over the result of the election or his rivalry with his dear friend had faded with time. Monroe was an old man whose dreams had come true. Less than two years after losing to Madison, he was chosen to represent Virginia in the United States Senate. Then Monroe finally fulfilled his wish to explore Europe—in grand style, as Washington's Ambassador to France, where he and Eliza became friends with the Emperor Napoleon.

Jefferson, who had once sent his protégé on a secret mission in war, would ask Monroe to serve him in another highly sensitive matter in 1802. Monroe traveled to Paris to negotiate the Louisiana Purchase, working closely with James Madison, the Secretary of State.

In the election of 1808, the friends and allies found themselves rivals once more.

Dissatisfaction with Jefferson within his own party extended to his chosen successor, James Madison. And the disaffected Democratic-Republicans coalesced largely behind James Monroe.

Monroe was eager to run. Surely he was as qualified as anyone to serve as president, and he had developed stark differences with the administration on foreign policy.

On January 23, 1808, Democratic-Republican members of Congress met in the Senate chamber to select their nominee for president. Ninety-four representatives attended, and eighty-nine voted. Madison received eighty-three votes to three each for George Clinton and James Monroe.

In their home state of Virginia, support was more evenly split. One caucus in the Virginia legislature nominated Madison for the presidency—the other expressed a preference for Monroe.[1]

"I have ever viewed Mr. Madison and yourself as two principal pillars of my happiness. Were either to be withdrawn, I should consider it as among the greatest calamities which could assail my future peace of mind," wrote Thomas Jefferson.[2]

Still Monroe, though without actively campaigning, permitted his name to be brought forward by his supporters.

Monroe's challenge to Madison's presidential bid triggered a two-year rift, not just between Madison and Monroe, but between their respective supporters in the party. By 1811, however, Monroe had made conciliatory efforts, and Madison—reluctant not to have Monroe's considerable talents at the disposal of his administration—offered him the post of Secretary of State. Together, they would conduct the War of 1812 against the British.

In retirement, the two who had so often been separated by duty were free to indulge their friendship. "When he was with Madison," one biographer writes, "Monroe seemed to recapture something of his youth, talking and laughing without restraint."[3]

The two were active in supporting the University of Virginia. And in 1828 Monroe and Madison were chosen as Presidential Electors on the ticket for John Quincy Adams.

In the city of Richmond in the fall of 1829, Madison and Monroe gathered for their last public collaboration. The Virginia Constitutional Convention of that year sought to craft a new governing document for the Commonwealth. The western counties of Virginia were clamoring for more representation in the legislature. Counting slaves for the apportionment of representatives gave the eastern parts of Virginia a two-to-one advantage in allocating legislators. One count estimates that "Of the 450,000 slaves in the state in 1829, only 50,000 resided west of the Blue Ridge."[4]

Madison nominated Monroe for the chairmanship of the convention and he was unanimously selected.[5] Monroe was escorted to the chair by another senior delegate, his boyhood friend John Marshall. The young delegates, most of whom had spent their lives lionizing Madison and Monroe, were awestruck by the chance to serve alongside them.

Their prestige in this body, however, did not translate to anything approaching their desired results. Madison and Monroe worked tirelessly to fashion some compromise. They proposed allocating members of the House of Delegates by free population while keeping the current formula for members of the Senate. When this failed, they proposed the three-fifths compromise that had succeeded in the Constitutional Convention in Philadelphia. Their efforts only inspired anger from both sides—with both East and West threatening to secede from one another—and criticism of "putting old men in active life."[6]

But the hotheaded young politicians of Virginia, like their contemporaries throughout the country, took the union Madison and Monroe had been so critical in establishing for granted. They had never known a time when the political bonds of the United States hung in the balance. If they would but listen, the old men had some lessons to teach them yet.

Monroe, though of modest means, had refused compensation for his service in the war and the pension that would have been his as a wounded warrior. He had advanced his own funds, time and again, while serving as a diplomat and thereafter. While in office, he had delayed seeking recompense lest he seem to be using his public office for personal gain. In his six years of retirement he was plagued by oppressive debt, while politics in Washington delayed consideration and repayment of the sums he had advanced the government. Monroe was forced to sell his lands in Virginia and repair to New York to live off the generosity of his daughter.

The Monroe who wrote to Madison with this news was very different from the eager young congressman of 1784: "It is very distressing to me to sell my property in Loudon, for, besides parting with all I have in the state, I indulged a hope, if I could retain it, that I might be able occasionally to visit it, and meet my friends, or many of them, there. But ill health and advanced years prescribe a course which we must pursue."

Their friendship was stronger than ever. "I deeply regret," Monroe wrote, "that there is no prospect of our ever meeting again, since so long have we been connected, and in the most friendly intercourse, in public and private life, that a final separation is among the most distressing incidents which could occur.... I beg you to assure Mrs. Madison that I never can forget the friendly relation which has existed between her and my family. It often reminds me of incidents of the most interesting character. My daughter, Mrs. Hay, will live with me, who, with the whole family here, unite in affectionate regards to both of you." The letter was signed, "Very sincerely, your friend, James Monroe. New York. April 11, 1831."

It would be Monroe's final letter to his friend.

On April 21, Madison would write the final words of their correspondence, which was now in its fifth decade.

> I considered the advertisement of your estate in Loudoun as an omen that your friends in Virginia were to lose you.... The effect of this, in closing the prospect of our ever meeting again afflicts me deeply; certainly not less so than it can you. The pain I feel at the idea, associated as it is with a recollection of the long, close, and uninterrupted friendship which united us, amounts to a pang which I cannot well express, and which makes me seek for an alleviation in the possibility that you may be brought back to us in the wonted degree of intercourse. This is a happiness my feelings covet, notwithstanding

> the short period I could expect to enjoy it; being now, though in comfortable health, a decade beyond the canonical three-score and ten, an epoch which you have but just passed.... Whatever may be the turn of things, be assured of the unchangeable interest felt by Mrs. Madison, as well as myself, in your welfare, and in that of all who are dearest to you....[7]

The Fourth of July, 1831, was the last day in the life of James Monroe. As the country celebrated the fifty-fifth anniversary of the Independence of the United States, one of the bravest soldiers of the Revolutionary War breathed his last.

As news of Monroe's death circulated, the church bells of America rang in celebration of his life, and a procession exceeding that which had greeted Washington on his arrival for his inauguration was held in the city of New York.

Dying on the Fourth of July was a distinction Monroe would share with his friend and mentor, Thomas Jefferson, who had preceded him in death by five years. Jefferson, author of the Declaration of Independence, had died fifty years to the day from the adoption of his most famous work. His final words are believed to be, "Is this the Fourth of July?"

John Adams, fulfilling a longtime pledge to see America's fiftieth birthday, had died hours after his friend and erstwhile foe, in ignorance of Jefferson's death. His last words were, "Thomas Jefferson survives."

Tench Ringgold, who had served both Presidents Madison and Monroe and attended the latter in his final days, wrote to Madison with the news. Madison, no doubt himself in need of consolation, played the role of consoler to the young man:

> I received in due times your two favors of July 7 and 8, the first giving the earliest, the last the fullest account that reached me of the death of our excellent friend; and I cannot acknowledge these communications without adding the thanks which I owe, in common with those to whom he was most dear, for

> the devoted kindness on your part during the lingering illness which he could not survive. I need not say to you, who so well know, how highly I rated the comprehensiveness and character of his mind; the purity and nobleness of his principles; the importance of his patriotic services; and the many private virtues of which his whole life was a model; nor how deeply, therefore, I must sympathize, on his loss, with those who feel it most. A close friendship, continued through so long a period and such diversified scenes, had grown into an affection very imperfectly expressed by that term; and I value accordingly the manifestation in his last hours that the reciprocity never abated.[8]

Madison wrote also to Alexander Hamilton Jr., the son of his former friend who had been killed in a duel in 1804. The younger Hamilton had served as a captain in the War of 1812 and, like his father, was a lawyer in New York.* "We may cherish the consolation," Madison told Hamilton's son, "nevertheless, that his memory, like that of the other heroic worthies of the Revolution gone before him, will be embalmed in the grateful affections of a posterity enjoying the blessings which he contributed to procure for it."[9]

In 1858, the body of James Monroe was returned to Virginia with much fanfare, where it remains in Richmond's Hollywood Cemetery, in a simple stone coffin guarded by iron bars and displayed above the ground "[a]s an evidence of the affection of Virginia for her good and honored son."**

Madison, physically the weakest and sickliest of the Founding Fathers, outlasted them all. On June 28, 1836, at the age of eighty-five, Madison joined the others in death. He had rejected the pleas of some

* The younger Hamilton represented Eliza Jumel in her divorce suit against Aaron Burr, the man who had killed his father. Such an instance of legal representation is unique in the annals of American history.

** In the transportation of his casket from New York, an accident aboard the sloop claimed the life of Alexander Hamilton's grandson.

who wanted him to take certain medicines that might prolong his life (and his suffering) until the Fourth of July.

Madison was buried beneath the earth at Montpelier, where he had first arrived in the arms of his mother in the weeks after his baptism, and where, when not away on the business of his country, he made his home all the days of his life.

The epitaph of James Madison reads simply:

Madison
Born March 16th, 1751
Died June 28th, 1836

These unremarkable epitaphs and modest markers are all that testify, to the living, that great men lie here. For men whose monument is nothing less than the greatest, freest, and most prosperous nation in all the history of the world, perhaps nothing more is needed.

Through the choices they made, the hardships they endured, and their tireless struggles, these men won an improbable Revolution, threw off the bonds of the weak and worthless Articles of Confederation, and established the most ingenious form of government ever devised, to which they added a promise of fundamental liberties that was and is the envy of the world.

It falls to the living to protect this legacy—to strive for these principles as the first generation did. Even when circumstances appeared hopeless, when setbacks tried the fortitude of the most patient men, they saw it as their duty to persevere.

And when we confront the challenges that test every generation, when we fight to expand the blessings of liberty and fulfill the best ideals of James Madison and James Monroe, we honor their memory more than any work of marble.

Remember.

ACKNOWLEDGMENTS

My name appears alone on the cover of this book, my first, but it is the work of many hands.

I am so grateful to God, with whom all things are possible but without whom nothing is possible. "The horse is made ready for the day of battle, but victory rests with the Lord" (Proverbs 21:31 NIV).

I'm blessed with the constant support of my incredible family, my mother Anna to whom this book is dedicated and my sister Cathy, a Victorian scholar who will finally have to read something by a living author.

I have incredible friends. Your enthusiasm made it impossible for me not to finish. This work is better for your efforts.

James Slattery is simply the best friend a person can have. Nolan Davis's mentorship changed the trajectory of my life.

Some were there from the very beginning of this project, with unlimited encouragement and advice:

Chris Ashby, Jeff Choudry, Danny and Bonnie Mazza, Maggie McPherson, Erin Montgomery, Tina Ramirez, I'm talking about you.

Many others took the time to read as it grew into something resembling a book. Some took the time to offer their valuable suggestions: Danna Buchanon, Jeremy Duda, Eric Johnson, Ashley King, Rob Peck, Brooke Robinson, Jonathan Shuffield.

My agent Jason Ashlock believed instantly in this project and in me, and was soon joined by the professionals at Regnery Publishing, especially Publisher Marji Ross and Associate Publisher Alex Novak. My publicist Rebekah Meinecke helped this first-time author get in front of millions of people. Her tireless work contributed mightily to the success of this book. I'm thankful to them and to everyone on the editing and marketing teams who have worked hard to help me to tell this incredible story.

NOTES

PROLOGUE

1. Gordon R. Denboer, *The Documentary History of the First Federal Elections, 1788–1790* (Madison, WI: University of Wisconsin Press, 1990) 4:228 (hereafter cited as *First Federal Elections*).
2. Ibid.
3. *First Federal Elections*, 388.
4. Ibid., 263.
5. Ibid., 228.
6. *The Papers of James Madison* (Chicago, Charlottesville: University of Chicago Press and University of Virginia Press 1962–1991), 12:141 (hereafter cited as Madison).
7. *First Federal Elections*, 264.
8. Ibid., 210.
9. Robert Licht, *Framers and Fundamental Rights* (Washington, D.C.: AEI Press, 1992), 30.
10. Madison 12:37–38.

11. Gordon Denboer, ed., *The Documentary History of the First Federal Elections, 1788–1790* 2 (Madison: University of Wisconsin Press, 1984).

CHAPTER 1

1. Church of England 1662 *The Book of Common Prayer*, http://justus.anglican.org/resources/bcp/1662/baptism.pdf (accessed August 8, 2011).
2. George Elliot Howard, *Preliminaries of the Revolution, 1763–1775*, 19 (hereafter cited as *Preliminaries*).
3. Martha W. McCartney, *Virginia Immigrants and Adventurers, 1607–1635* (Genealogical Publishing Co., 2007), 472.
4. Ibid.
5. Samuel Blair, *An Account of the College of New Jersey* (James Parker, 1764).
6. Madison 1:66.
7. Blair, *An Account of the College of New Jersey*.
8. James Banner, Essay for Princeton University, http://etcweb.princeton.edu/CampusWWW/Companion/madison_james.html (accessed June 8, 2011).
9. Madison 1:66, editorial notes.
10. Cody Burnet, *The Continental Congress* (New York: The Macmillan Company, 1941), 17 (hereafter cited as Burnet).
11. *Preliminaries*, 274.
12. Burnet, 18.
13. Ibid.
14. Marion Mills Miller, ed., *Great Debates in American History* (New York: Current Literature Publishing Company, 1913), 1:84.
15. Burnet, 30.
16. Ibid., 47.
17. Ibid., 51.
18. Ibid.
19. *Preliminaries*, 294.
20. Burnet, 58.
21. Madison 1:147, editorial note.
22. Henry Mayer, *A Son of Thunder: Patrick Henry and the American Republic* (New York: Grove Press, 2001), 243 (hereafter cited as *Son of Thunder*).
23. Ibid., 244.
24. Ibid., 245.

25. *Preliminaries*, 305–6.
26. *Son of Thunder*, 243.
27. James Monroe, *The Autobiography of James Monroe*, edited by Stuart Gerry Brown (Syracuse University Press 1959), 21 (hereafter cited as Monroe, *Autobiography*).
28. Ibid., 22.
29. Ibid., 22–23.
30. *Preliminaries*, 287.
31. *Son of Thunder*, 62.
32. Burnet, 68.
33. Ibid., 76.
34. Ibid., 82.
35. Ibid.
36. Kenneth C. Davis, *America's Hidden History: Untold Tales of the First Pilgrims, Fighting Women, and Forgotten Founders Who Shaped a Nation* (Washington, D.C.: Smithsonian, 2008), 210.
37. Burnet, 87.
38. James Morton Smith, ed., *A Republic of Letters* (New York: W. W. Norton, 1995), 47.
39. John Fiske, *The American Revolution* (Boston and New York: Houghton Mifflin, 1897), 212.
40. Ibid.

CHAPTER 2

1. *Son of Thunder*, 292.
2. Ibid.
3. Thomas Edward Watson, *Thomas Jefferson* (Boston: Small, Maynard & Company, 1900), 46.
4. Hugh Blair Grigsby, *The Virginia Convention of 1776*, 19.
5. Virginia Constitution of 1776.
6. Letter from John Adams to Abigail Adams, found in Proceedings of the Massachusetts Historical Society, November 1884, 297.
7. Burnet, 90.
8. Ibid., 213.
9. Ibid., 219.
10. Ibid., 345.

11. Monroe, *Autobiography*, 23.
12. Ibid.
13. Ibid., 24.
14. Ibid., 25.
15. Ibid., 26.
16. Debbie Levy, *James Monroe* (Minneapolis, MN: Lerner Publications Company, 2005), 19 (hereafter cited as Levy).
17. Ibid.
18. Ibid., 26.
19. Daniel Preston, ed., *The Papers of James Monroe* (Westport, CT: Greenwood Press, 2003) 2:4 (hereafter cited as *Papers of James Monroe*).
20. Monroe, *Autobiography*, 26.
21. Journal of the Virginia House of Delegates, 77–81 (hereafter cited as JHVD).
22. Ralph Ketcham, *James Madison: A Biography*, 277 (University of Virginia Press, 1971) (hereafter cited as Ketcham).
23. *Papers of James Monroe* 2:4.
24. Monroe, *Autobiography*, 6.
25. Ibid., 29.
26. *Papers of James Monroe* 5:2.
27. Harry Ammon, *James Monroe: The Quest for National Identity* (Charlottesville and London: University of Virginia Press, 1990), 19 (hereafter cited as Ammon).
28. Robert Middlekauf, *The Glorious Cause* (New York: Oxford University Press, 1982), 387 (hereafter cited as *Glorious Cause*).
29. *Glorious Cause*, 396.
30. Ibid.
31. Ibid., 397.
32. Ibid.
33. Ammon, 19.
34. *Glorious Cause*, 391.
35. Burnet, 249–50.
36. Ibid., 250–51
37. Ibid., 255.
38. Ibid.
39. Ibid.
40. Madison 1:216.
41. Ibid., 223.

42. President's House, Colonial Williamsburg, http://www.history.org/almanack/places/hb/hbpres.cfm (accessed June 8, 2011).
43. *Glorious Cause*, 411.
44. *Papers of James Monroe* 2:7.
45. *Glorious Cause*, 412.
46. *Papers of James Monroe* 2:8.
47. Madison 1:241.
48. Ibid., 240.
49. Ibid.
50. Ibid., editorial notes.
51. Ibid., 300, editorial notes.
52. Ibid.
53. *Papers of James Monroe* 2:10.
54. Ibid., 11–12.
55. Madison 1:318.
56. *Papers of James Monroe* 2:14.
57. Ibid., 16.
58. Madison 1:319.

CHAPTER 3

1. Madison 2:3.
2. Ketcham, 88.
3. Madison 2:3.
4. Ibid., 6.
5. *Papers of James Monroe* 2:17.
6. Ibid., 19.
7. Madison 2:5.
8. Ibid.
9. Ibid., 8–9.
10. Ibid., 13, 15.
11. Ibid., 14.
12. Ibid., 16.
13. *Papers of James Monroe* 2:18, footnotes.
14. Ibid.
15. Ibid., 22–23.
16. Ibid., 30.

17. Ibid., 26.
18. Ibid.
19. Madison 2:92, and editorial notes.
20. Ibid., 127.
21. Ibid., 158.
22. Ibid., 161.
23. Ibid., 175.
24. Burnet, 478.
25. Madison 2:202–4.
26. Ibid., 219.
27. Ibid., 265.
28. Ibid., 289.
29. Ibid., 293.
30. Ibid. 3:26.
31. Ibid. 2:273.
32. Ibid., 302.
33. Ibid., 303.
34. Ibid. 3:17–18.
35. Ibid., 71.
36. Ibid., 29.
37. Ibid., 17–18.
38. Ibid., 78.
39. Ibid., 90.
40. *Papers of James Monroe*, 2:118.
41. Ibid.
42. Ibid., 120, footnotes.
43. Ibid., 121
44. Ibid., 40.
45. Ibid., 31.
46. Ibid.
47. Ibid.
48. Madison 3:292.
49. Monroe, *Autobiography*, 40.
50. Joy Hakim, *Freedom: A History of Us* (New York: Oxford University Press, 2003).

CHAPTER 4

1. Madison 4:151.
2. *Papers of James Monroe* 2:44.
3. Ibid., 46.
4. Madison 4:169.
5. Ibid., 189.
6. Ibid., 188.
7. Ibid., 254–55 and editorial notes.
8. Ibid., 288.
9. Ibid., 275.
10. Ibid., 255–56.
11. *Papers of James Monroe* 2:37.
12. Ibid.
13. Thomas Nelson's successor, Speaker of the House of Delegates, and a signer of the Declaration of Independence.
14. *Papers of James Monroe* 2:40.
15. Ibid., 43.
16. Ibid., 45.
17. Len Barcousky, "Eyewitness 1782: While Fort Pitt is spared, Hanna's Town burns," *Pittsburgh Post-Gazette*, http://www.post-gazette.com/pg/08013/848634-426.stm (accessed December 24, 2010).
18. Ibid.
19. *Papers of James Monroe* 2:48.
20. Ibid., 51.
21. Ibid., 43.
22. Ibid., 56.
23. Madison 4:344.
24. Ibid. 5:127.
25. Ibid., 44.
26. Charles Grove Haines, *The American Doctrine of Judicial Supremacy* (New York: MacMillan, 1914), 84–85.
27. Madison 5:415.
28. Evarts Greene, *American Population Before the Census of 1790* (New York: Columbia University 1932), 7.

29. William R. Staples, *Rhode Island in the Continental Congress* (Providence, RI: Providence Press Company, 1870), 412.
30. Madison 5:441.
31. Ibid. 5:449.
32. Ibid. 6:32.
33. Ibid., 121.
34. Ibid., 123, and editorial notes.
35. Ibid., 156.
36. Ibid., 161.
37. Ibid., 163.
38. Ibid., 223.
39. Ibid.
40. Records of the Columbia Historical Society 14:108.
41. Ibid., 109.
42. Madison 6:333–36.
43. Ibid., 348.
44. *Papers of James Monroe* 2:57.
45. Gaillard Hunt, *The Life of James Madison* (New York: Doubleday Page and Company, 1902), 68.
46. Madison 6:459.
47. Sydney Howard Gay, *James Madison* (Boston: Houghton-Mifflin, 1884), 43.
48. Madison 7:25.
49. Ibid. 6:459.
50. Ibid., 486.
51. Ibid., 491.
52. Ibid., 498.
53. Ibid. 7:18.
54. Ibid.
55. Virginia Magazine of History and Biography 9:72.
56. Madison 7:108.
57. Selections for Congress were often made well in advance, travel time was significant, and a congressman would normally have many affairs to put in order before commencing service.
58. Madison 7:119.
59. Ibid., 165.
60. Ibid., 177.

61. Ibid., 202.
62. Ibid. 6:447.
63. Ibid. 7:151.
64. Ibid., 216.
65. Ibid., 315.
66. Ibid., 255.

CHAPTER 5

1. Sydney Howard Gay, *James Madison*, 45.
2. Ibid.
3. Madison 7:268.
4. Ibid., 298–99.
5. *Papers of James Monroe* 2:61.
6. Ibid., 64.
7. Madison 7:304.
8. Ibid., 314.
9. Ibid., 379.
10. *Papers of James Monroe* 7:304.
11. Madison 7:411.
12. Ibid., 402.
13. Ibid., 404, and editorial notes.
14. Ibid., 401.
15. Harlow G. Ungar, *The Last Founding Father: James Monroe and a Nation's Call to Greatness* (Da Capo Press, 2009), 49.
16. Madison 7:406.
17. The Maryland State House is in use to the present day, the oldest such state capitol.
18. W. Hickey, *The Constitution of the United States of America* (Philadelphia: T. K. & P. G. Collins, 1847), 208.
19. Ibid., 209
20. Monroe, *Autobiography*, 34.
21. *Papers of James Monroe* 2:76.
22. Don Higginbotham, ed., *George Washington Reconsidered* (Charlottesville, VA: University Press of Virginia, 2001), 316.

23. Madison, 418, 421.
24. Ibid. 7:422.
25. Ibid., 423.
26. Monroe, *Autobiography*, 34.
27. Madison 7:426.
28. Monroe, *Autobiography*, 35.
29. Ibid., 37.
30. *Papers of James Monroe* 2:98.
31. Madison 7:427.
32. Ibid. 8:18.
33. Johann David Schoepf, "Travels in the Confederation," http://www.archive.org/stream/travelsinconfede02schp/travelsinconfede02schp_djvu.txt (accessed November 25, 2010).
34. Ibid., 49.
35. Ibid.
36. Ibid., 56–57.
37. Madison 8:38.
38. Ibid., 48.
39. Ibid., 81.
40. Ibid., 93–94.
41. Ibid., 32.
42. *Annual Report of the American Historical Association* 1:153.
43. Madison 8:157.
44. *Papers of James Monroe* 2:117.
45. Ibid., 118
46. Ibid., 120, editorial notes.
47. Ibid., 121.
48. Ibid., 40.
49. Monroe, *Autobiography*, 40.
50. Ibid.
51. Ibid.
52. Ibid.
53. Ibid.
54. Madison 8:115.
55. Ibid., 117–18.
56. Ibid., 134.
57. *Papers of James Monroe* 2:126.
58. Ibid., 146.

59. Madison 8:134.
60. Ibid., 135.
61. Ibid., 114.
62. Ibid., 124–25.
63. Ibid., 142–43.
64. For one example, see James Madison's letter to Thomas Jefferson, January 9, 1785 (Papers of James Madison, Library of Congress).

CHAPTER 6

1. *Papers of James Monroe* 2:108–10.
2. Madison 8:125.
3. Ibid., 140–42.
4. *Papers of James Monroe* 2:159.
5. Madison 8:136–37.
6. Ibid., 156.
7. Ibid., 157.
8. George Ticknor Curtis, *The History of the Origin, Formation, and Adoption of the Constitution* (New York: Harper and Brothers, 1854) 1:334.
9. Ibid., 336.
10. Madison 8:152.
11. Ibid. 9:116.
12. Ibid. 8:185–86.
13. *Papers of James Monroe* 2:156–57.
14. Madison 8:220–21.
15. Ibid., 176.
16. *Papers of James Monroe* 2:210–12.
17. Ibid., 197.
18. Madison 8:238.
19. Ibid., 245–46.
20. *Papers of James Monroe* 2:193.
21. Ibid.
22. Ibid., 175.
23. Madison 8:206.
24. Ibid., 261.

25. *Son of Thunder*, 33.
26. Ibid., 34.
27. Ibid., 34–35.
28. Robert Semple, *A History of the Rise and Progress of the Baptists of Virginia* (Published by the author, 1810), 14.
29. Ibid., 18.
30. Ibid., 23.
31. Madison 8:195–99.
32. Ibid., 289–90, 300, and editorial notes.
33. Ibid., 301.
34. Ibid., 302.
35. William Cabell Rives, *History of the Life and Times of James Madison* (Freeport, NY: Books for Libraries Press, 1970) 1:606 (hereafter cited as Rives).
36. Ibid., 608.
37. Madison 8:268.
38. Ibid., 272–73.
39. Ibid., 278–81.
40. *Papers of James Monroe* 2:163.
41. Ibid., 207–8.
42. Ibid., 215.
43. Ibid.
44. Madison 8:317–19.
45. Monroe, *Autobiography*, 46.
46. Ibid., 43.
47. Madison 8:374.

CHAPTER 7

1. Madison 8:474.
2. Ibid.
3. Ibid., 429.
4. Ibid., 439.
5. Ibid., 446.
6. Ibid., 448.

7. Ibid., 465–66.
8. Ibid.
9. Gaillard Hunt, *The Life of James Madison*, 92.
10. Madison 8:471.
11. Ibid., 483.
12. Monroe, *Autobiography* 2:271.
13. Ibid., 49.
14. Madison 8:492.
15. Ibid., 493.
16. *Papers of James Monroe* 8:493.
17. Madison 8:504–5.
18. Monroe, *Autobiography* 2:270
19. *Papers of James Monroe* 2:278.
20. Madison 8:493.
21. Ibid., 497–98.
22. Ibid., 504–5.
23. Ibid. 9:59.
24. Ibid. 9:105–7.
25. Ibid. 9:25–26.
26. *Papers of James Monroe* 2:291.
27. Madison 9:55.
28. *Papers of James Monroe* 2:293.
29. Madison 9:88.
30. *Papers of James Monroe* 2:324.
31. Ibid., 333.
32. Walter Stahr, *John Jay: Founding Father* (New York: Hambledon & Continuum, 2006), 215.
33. Ibid.
34. Ibid.
35. *Papers of James Monroe* 2:333.
36. Walter Stahr, *John Jay*, 216.
37. Madison 9:104.
38. Ibid., 108.
39. *Papers of James Monroe* 2:340.
40. Ibid., 343.
41. Ammon, 58.
42. Ibid.

CHAPTER 8

1. Madison 8:497–98.
2. Ibid. 9:3.
3. For all references from "Notes on Ancient and Modern Confederacies," see Madison 9:3–24.
4. *Papers of James Monroe* 2:338.
5. Monroe would go on to clobber Rufus King for the Presidency in 1816, cruising to re-election with 183 electoral votes to King's 34, and nearly 70 percent of the popular vote.
6. Madison 9:113.
7. Ibid., 120.
8. Ibid., 121.
9. Jonathan Elliot, ed., *Debates on the Adoption of the Federal Constitution, in the Convention Held at Philadelphia, in 1787; with a Diary of the Debates of the Congress of the Confedration as Reported by James Madison, a Member, and Deputy from Virginia* 5 (Washington, 1845).
10. Madison 9:146.
11. *Papers of James Monroe* 2:364.
12. Madison 9:155.
13. Ibid., 162.
14. Ibid., 163–64.
15. Ibid., 164.
16. Ibid., 166.
17. Ibid., 170.
18. Ibid., 199.
19. *Journal of the Virginia House of Delegates*, October 1786, 85–86.
20. Madison 9:224.
21. Ibid., 218.
22. Ibid., 256.
23. Ibid., 260.
24. Ibid., 298.
25. Ibid.
26. Ibid., 284.

27. Ibid., 299.
28. Ibid., 304, editorial notes.
29. Ibid., 359.
30. Ibid., 315–16.
31. Ibid., 364.
32. Ibid., 369.
33. Ibid., 370.
34. Ibid., 345.
35. Ibid., 380.
36. Walter Stahr, *John Jay: Founding Father*, 217.
37. Ibid.
38. *Papers of James Monroe* 2:378.
39. Madison 9:391.

CHAPTER 9

1. James Monroe in Stanislaus Murray Hamilton, ed., *The Writings of James Monroe* (New York: G. P. Putnam's Sons, 1898), 171.
2. Madison 10:10.
3. Ibid., 12.
4. Ibid., 31.
5. He also took copious and detailed notes on the debates. (James Madison, "Notes on the Debates in the Federal Convention.") Unless otherwise noted, all information about the proceedings of the Philadelphia Constitutional Convention is drawn from Madison's notes.
6. Alfred B. Street, *The Council of Revision of the State of New York* (Albany: William Gould, 1859), 5–6.
7. Robert J. Spitzer, *The Presidential Veto: Touchstone of the American Presidency* (State University of New York Press, 1988), 8–9.
8. James Madison, *Notes of Debates in the Federal Convention of 1787* (New York: W. W. Norton 1966).
9. *Papers of James Monroe* 2:386.
10. 1790 Federal Census, http://www2.census.gov/prod2/decennial/documents/1790m-02.pdf (accessed December 30, 2010).

11. J. G. Adel, *Official Report of the Proceedings and Debates of the Third Constitutional Convention of Ohio, Assembled in the City of Cincinnati* 2, Part 2 (Cleveland, 1874).
12. *Papers of James Monroe* 2:378.
13. Ibid.
14. Legislative override might be a solution to out-of-control judicial review. Judicial review was well understood by the delegates at Philadelphia. Starting with *Commonwealth v. Caton* in 1782, state courts had already exercised this power. In the first Congress under the Constitution, Madison specifically noted that judges would exercise judicial review at the national level. But in the years that followed, this judicial review would have increasingly wider scope. The ability to interpret the Constitution in a particular manner became the de facto power to amend the Constitution. Increasingly, matters of great national importance are removed from the consideration of the representative branches of government, and therefore from the influence of the people—locked away by the smallest, least accountable, least representative branch of government. The only real check on judicial review is a constitutional amendment, and that option has been exercised only once, when the Eleventh Amendment overruled *Chisholm v. Georgia.*

CHAPTER 10

1. William George Carr, *The Oldest Delegate: Franklin in the Constitutional Convention* (DE: University of Delaware, 1990), 74.
2. Jonathan Elliott, ed., *The Debates in the Several State Conventions on the Adoption of the Federal Constitution Held at Philadelphia, in 1787; with a Diary of the Debates of the Congress of the Confederation; as Reported by James Madison, a Member, and Deputy from Virginia* 5 (Philadelphia: J. B. Lippincott, 1876).
3. *Papers of James Monroe* 2:396.
4. Richard H. Lee (grandson), *Memoir of the Life of Richard Henry Lee, and His Correspondence with the Most Distinguished Men in America and Europe, Illustrative of Their Characters, and of the Events of the American Revolution* (Philadelphia: William Brown, 1825) 2:78.
5. Rives 2:478.
6. Ibid., 479.

7. Madison 10:173.
8. *Papers of James Monroe* 2:398.
9. Ibid., 401.
10. Ibid., 403.
11. *Son of Thunder*, 12.
12. Ibid.
13. Ibid., 13.
14. Ibid.
15. Ibid., 14.
16. Ibid.
17. Madison 11:4.
18. *The Documentary History of the Ratification of the Constitution*, ed. Merrill Jensen (Madison: State Historical Society of Wisconsin) 8:601–2.
19. Madison 11:5.
20. Ibid., 12.
21. Ibid., 13.
22. Ibid., 15.
23. *Papers of James Monroe* 11:16.
24. Madison 11:20.
25. Ibid.
26. Ibid.
27. Ibid., 31.
28. *Papers of James Monroe* 2:405.
29. Madison 11:28.
30. Ibid., 36.
31. Ibid., 54.
32. *Papers of James Monroe* 2:405.
33. Ibid., 408–27.

CHAPTER 11

1. Kevin R. C. Gutzman, *James Madison and the Making of America* (New York: St. Martin's Press, 2012).
2. Madison 11:76–77
3. Herbert Baxter Adams, *Thomas Jefferson and the University of Virginia* (Washington, D.C.: Government Printing Office, 1888), 21.

4. Ibid., 29.
5. Unless otherwise noted, all information in this chapter appears in the transcript of the ratification convention found in *Documentary History of the Ratification of the Constitution* vol. 8, as cited above.
6. *Documentary History of the Ratification of the Constitution*, 8:917.
7. John R. Vile, *The Constitutional Convention of 1787: A Comprehensive Encyclopedia of America's Founding* (Santa Barbara: ABC-CLIO, 2005).
8. *Documentary History of the Ratification of the Constitution*, 8:929–30.
9. Ibid., 932–36
10. Ibid., 946.
11. Ibid., 951.
12. Ibid., debates of June 5.
13. Madison 11:99–100.
14. Records of the Columbia Historical Society, 1052.
15. Madison 11:101, and editorial notes.
16. Jonathan Elliott, ed., *The Debates in the Several State Conventions on the Adoption of the Federal Constitution, in the Convention Held at Philadelphia, in 1787; with a Diary of the Debates of the Congress of the Confederation; as Reported by James Madison, a Member, and Deputy from Virginia* 3 (Philadelphia: J. B. Lippincott, 1876).
17. Ibid.
18. Ibid.
19. Ibid.
20. *Papers of James Monroe* 2:333.
21. Monroe, *Autobiography*, 50.
22. Ibid.

CHAPTER 12

1. Unless otherwise noted, all information in this chapter appears in the transcript of the ratification convention found in *Documentary History of the Ratification of the Constitution* vol. 8, as cited above.
2. Jonathan Elliott, ed., *The Debates in the Several State Conventions on the Adoption of the Federal Constitution, in the Convention Held at Philadelphia, in 1787; with a Diary of the Debates of the Congress of the Confederation; as Reported by James Madison, a Member, and Deputy from Virginia* 5 (Philadelphia: J. B. Lippincott, 1876).

3. Madison 11:133.
4. Elliott, ed., *The Debates in the Several State Conventions on the Adoption of the Federal Constitution.*
5. Ibid.
6. Madison 11:179.
7. *The Southern Literary Messenger* (Richmond: T. W. White 1834–1835), 332.
8. Ron Chernow, *Alexander Hamilton* (New York: Penguin 2004), 327.
9. Ibid., 268.
10. Rives 2:610.

CHAPTER 13

1. Madison 11:227–28.
2. Ibid., 237.
3. Rives 2:629.
4. Ibid., 630.
5. Madison 11:249.
6. Monroe to Madison, September 24, 1788.
7. Madison 11:246.
8. Ibid., 267.
9. Ibid., 297.
10. *Journal of the Virginia House of Delegates*, 1786–1790, 3.
11. *Son of Thunder*, 443.
12. *Journal of the Virginia House of Delegates*, 5.
13. Ibid., 7.
14. *Papers of James Monroe* 2:457.
15. *Journal of the Virginia House of Delegates*, 42.
16. Alexander White to Mary Wood, November 5, 1788.
17. *Virginia Centinel*, Winchester, VA, November 19, 1788.
18. Henry Lee to James Madison, November 19, 1788.
19. Edward Carrington to James Madison, November 9, 1788.
20. Pennsylvania, New Jersey, New Hampshire, and Connecticut elected their first congressmen on a statewide ticket.
21. Moses Coit Tyler, *Patrick Henry* (Boston and New York: Houghton Mifflin, 1894), 313.

22. The U.S. Marshal for the District of Virginia in 1790 was none other than Edward Carrington.
23. Tyler, *Patrick Henry*, 190.
24. Madison 8:268.
25. Madison 8:435.
26. Ibid.
27. Robert Allen Rutland, *James Madison: The Founding Father* (Columbia: University of Missouri Press 1997), 46.
28. Ibid.
29. Mark S. Scarberry, "John Leland and James Madison: Religious Influence on the Ratification of the Constitution and on the Proposal of the Bill of Rights," *Penn State Law Review* 113, no. 3 (2008–2009).

CHAPTER 14

1. Excerpt of George Lee Turberville to James Madison, 12 December, in *First Federal Elections*, 327.
2. Mathew Carey, ed., *The American Museum: or Repository of Ancient and Modern Fugitive Pieces, &c., Prose and Poetical* 6 (Philadelphia, 1789).
3. Gordon DenBoer, ed., *The Documentary History of the First Federal Elections, 1788–1790* 2 (Madison: University of Wisconsin Press, 1984).
4. Excerpt of George Lee Turberville to James Madison, 12 December, in *First Federal Elections*, 327.
5. One theory is that Madison had already met with Leland while seeking a place as a convention delegate for Orange, and that the latter had been instrumental to his election.
6. *First Federal Elections*, 329.
7. Electoral College results appear in Ibid., 308.
8. James Barnett Taylor, *Virginia Baptist Ministers* (New York: Sheldon & Company, 1860).
9. Robert Semple, *Baptists of Virginia*, 180.
10. Letter of George Eve, in *First Federal Elections*, 331–33.
11. Barry Adamson, *Freedom of Religion, The First Amendment, and the Supreme Court: How the Court Flunked History* (Gretna: Pelican Publishing, 2008).
12. Letter of Thomas Mann Randolph, Ibid., 338–40.

13. Ibid., 342.
14. Gaillard Hunt, *The Life of James Madison*, 165.
15. Ibid.
16. Remarks by Monroe before the Virginia Ratification Convention, in Jensen, ed., *The Documentary History of the Ratification of the Constitution*, vol. 8.
17. Ibid.
18. Letter of George Thompson, *First Federal Elections*, 341.
19. *The Albany Law Journal: A Weekly Record of the Law and the Lawyers* 51–52 (Albany: Albany Law Journal, 1895).
20. Ibid.
21. Ibid.
22. Ketcham, 277.
23. Gaillard Hunt, *The Life of James Madison*, 165.
24. Ibid.
25. Ibid.

CHAPTER 15

1. *First Federal Elections*, 341.
2. *The American Lawyer* 2:524.
3. George Cary Eggleston, *Westover of Wanalah* (Boston: Lothrop, Lee & Shepard, 1910), 254.
4. John Fiske, *Civil Government in the United States* (Boston, New York, and Chicago: Houghton Mifflin, 1890).
5. Eggleston, *Westover of Wanalah*, 254.
6. Ibid.
7. Francis Taylor Diary, Virginia Historical Society.
8. Gordon DenBoer, ed., *The Documentary History of the First Federal Elections, 1788–1790* 2 (Madison: University of Wisconsin Press, 1984).
9. Ketcham, 183.
10. *First Federal Elections*, 344.
11. Statistics related to turnout appear in Richard Labunski, *James Madison and the Struggle for the Bill of Rights* (New York: Oxford University Press, 2006). The original hardcover edition of *Founding Rivals* mistakenly does not attribute a source for these statistics. The author regrets the error.

12. *Papers of James Monroe* 2:461.
13. Ibid.
14. Gordon DenBoer, ed., *The Documentary History of the First Federal Elections, 1788–1790* 2 (Madison: University of Wisconsin Press, 1984).
15. Burnet, 726.
16. Ibid.

CHAPTER 16

1. Rives 2:612.
2. Today, the Speaker of the House leads his party. But in the First Congress the Speaker, while prestigious and certainly important, was not necessarily the party leader. And the powers of the Speaker's office were also less than the powers of the Speaker today. Duties of the Speaker of the House in the first Congress—Frederick Augustus Conrad Muhlenberg of Pennsylvania—included calling the House to order, presiding over the debates, preserving order and decorum, and conducting votes. The Speaker could choose assignments for committees only of three or less; otherwise, they were decided by a vote of the full House. (*The Documentary History of the First Federal Congress* 3:11.) Muhlenberg was a respected and powerful member, but Madison was the real leader of the House.
3. *First Federal Elections* 3:9.
4. Rives 3:14.
5. Ketcham, 307.
6. *First Federal Elections* 10:223.
7. Rives 3:10.
8. *First Federal Elections* 10:727.
9. Ibid.
10. Madison 12:419.
11. Jefferson's written account, reprinted in Joseph Ellis, *Founding Brothers: The Revolutionary Generation* (New York: Vintage), 49.
12. *First Federal Elections* 11:811.
13. Paul Finkelman, ed., *Encyclopedia of American Civil Liberties* 1 (New York: Taylor & Francis Group, 2006).
14. *First Federal Elections* 11:812.
15. Ibid., 812–13.
16. Ibid. 10:813.

17. Ibid., 814.
18. Ibid., 815.
19. Ibid., 816.
20. Ibid., 819.
21. *First Federal Elections*, 829.
22. Ibid., 830.
23. Ibid., 831.
24. Ibid., 834.
25. Madison 12:211.
26. Rives 3:41.
27. 1284
28. Rives 3:41.
29. Ibid., 40.
30. Madison 12:369.
31. Ibid., 392.
32. Ibid., 393.
33. *First Federal Elections* 4:321.
34. John Thornton Kirkland, *Works of Fisher Ames* (Boston: Little Brown and Company, 1854), 36.
35. *Papers of James Monroe* 2:463.
36. Ibid.
37. Ibid. 2:467.
38. Ibid. 2:468.
39. Ibid.

EPILOGUE

1. Edward Stanwood, *A History of Presidential Elections* (Boston: James R. Osgood and Company, 1884), 52–54.
2. Ammon, 273.
3. Ibid., 551.
4. Ibid., 563.
5. Ibid., 564.
6. Ketcham, 638.
7. Daniel C. Gilman, *American Statesmen: James Monroe; in His Relations to the Public Service during Half a Century; 1776 to 1826* (Boston: Houghton Mifflin, 1883).

8. *Letters and Other Writings of James Madison; Fourth President of the United States* 4 (Philadelphia: J. B. Lippincott, 1865).
9. James Madison, *Letters and Other Writings of James Madison*, 189.

INDEX

N

O

P

R

S